ROMAN BRITAIN

AND WHERE TO FIND IT

ROMAN BRITAIN
BRITAIN
AND WHERE TO FIND IT

DENISE ALLEN AND MIKE BRYAN

AMBERLEY

About the Authors

Dr Denise Allen began in archaeology as a digger, working on excavations throughout the 1970s. She completed her PhD at Cardiff University on Roman glass, and published *Roman Glass in Britain*, a popular introduction. For nearly 20 years she was a director of Andante Travels, Britain's leading archaeological tour company, designing and leading many tours and writing fieldnotes for them – useful training for this book!

Mike Bryan has been visiting Romano-British sites since he was a small boy when he caught 'Roman Legionnaire's disease'. Following a long and distinguished career in publishing with Penguin Books where he was CEO of a number of Penguin's international publishing companies, he is at present studying Roman Archaeology and evangelising to one and all on his favourite subject. Mike is also the author of a book on the history of early English fountain pens.

Front cover: The Old Work at Wroxeter. Photo: English Heritage Trust.

Back cover: Cockerel-headed man mosaic from Brading Roman Villa, IOW.

Page 1: The late third-century curtain wall of Portchester Castle, the best-surviving Roman fort in northern Europe.

Page 2: Three mother goddesses, much-worshipped in Roman Britain, found at Ashcroft, Cirencester. *Photo: Dot Smith.*

First published 2020

Amberley Publishing
The Hill, Stroud
Gloucestershire, GL5 4EP

www.amberley-books.com

British Library Cataloguing in Publication Data.
A catalogue record for this book is available from the British Library.

ISBN 978 1 4456 9014 8 (paperback)
ISBN 978 1 3981 0703 8 (hardback)
ISBN 978 1 4456 9015 5 (ebook)

1 2 3 4 5 6 7 8 9 10

Typesetting by Aura Technology and Software Services, India.
Printed in the UK.

Contents

Foreword

Three and a half centuries of occupation does not vanish into thin air. The footprint left on Britain by Rome lingers to this day. A large percentage of the population will know of a Roman ruin or museum near where they live. The majority will have heard of Hadrian's Wall and the Roman baths at Bath, and almost as many will be aware of the Vindolanda tablets and the Ribchester helmet. People know that Julius Caesar invaded, that Boudica rebelled against the Roman yoke and burned Colchester to the ground.

Given the vast array of archaeological sites and museums throughout this green and pleasant land, it is strange that guidebooks to Roman sites in the UK are hard to come by. To my knowledge, *Roman Britain and Where to Find It* is the first published in many years. The paucity of reading material means that this most excellent volume is to be welcomed with open arms not just by Romanophiles, but readers with an interest in history, and those wanting to know more about the area in which they live.

As these pages reveal, there is scarcely a corner in England, Scotland and Wales that the Romans did not explore and build upon. From Chysauster in Cornwall to Ardoch in Scotland, from Caernarfon in Wales to Dover in Kent, there are villages and towns, forts, camps and even a lighthouse to be visited. Museums abound, each with its own unique artefacts, and reasons to go. Many Roman artefacts have only been found in a handful of locations, you see, sometimes only one. It is a most frustrating aspect to Roman archaeology! This book is of enormous help in that regard, thanks to its generous descriptions of sites and museums. If you want to see a soldier's mail shirt in the UK, head to Arbeia in South Shields. Curses inscribed on lead sheets? The Roman baths at Bath. A rare personal grinding stone for making flour? Chesters fort on Hadrian's Wall. The extraordinary Vindolanda tablets? The British Museum.

Ancient Rome has shaped my world for nigh on twenty years. As well as my novels, there have been visits to scores of sites in the UK, Europe and the Middle East, many repeated. I have walked Hadrian's Wall twice in full Roman legionary kit (the third time will be in May 2020) – for charity, I hasten to add, although it is great fun too! I've guided members of my family and friends to the Roman baths in Bath, given talks at Chedworth Villa and Fishbourne Palace, and taken part in Roman festivals in York and Chester. I have marched at Saturnalia in the latter town and continue to raise funds for Park in the Past, an ambitious project building a Roman fort near Chester (see parkinthepast.org.uk). Writing a foreword to this book then, has been not only an honour but a pleasure.

It has also been revelatory. While far from encyclopaedic, my knowledge of Roman Britain is passing decent, yet there are countless sites and treasures in the UK that I had never heard of, and others whose quality I had not appreciated. Useful nuggets of information also abound in *Roman Britain and Where to Find It*. Little did I know that two Roman sites were found thanks to men hunting with ferrets (Rockbourne in Hampshire and a personal favourite, Chedworth Villa in Gloucestershire), or that there is an excellent pub in the top half of the Balkerne Gate in Colchester. Rather than drive past Reading unthinkingly, I will now find a suitable time to visit its museum. In there lies the Silchester Eagle, the object which gave rise to Rosemary Sutcliff's marvellous novel, *The Eagle of the Ninth*. I knew of the Roman mineworking in Dolaucothi in Wales, but am newly inspired to seek them out.

You have in your hands a superb resource to add value to trips or holidays around Britain. When planning a visit to the capital, book tickets for the incredible London Mithraeum. Stuck for something to do with the children in Devon or Cornwall? Take them to a Roman site, and spark an interest in history. Visiting Cumbria? Do not miss Hardknott fort – even if it's just for the hair-raising drive up there.

The choice is all yours!

Ben Kane, 2020

London's Wall, a palimpsest of building periods, starting with the Romans. *Photo: Dot Smith.*

Introduction

The Romans ruled Britannia for more than 350 years, leaving an indelible mark on our landscape as they drew us firmly into the Mediterranean world. Town and country were transformed by innovations in comfort and taste, albeit shot through with a uniquely British twist. Many glimpses of this can still be seen at numerous splendid sites and museums in England, Wales and Scotland.

History tells us that Roman Britain lasted from the AD 43 invasion under the Emperor Claudius to AD 410 when, traditionally, the Britons were told that Rome could no longer help repel invaders. This was a long time, which saw huge change. Late Romans lived as long after the first colonists as we in the twenty-first century do after Samuel Pepys and the Great Plague and Great Fire of London.

Archaeology has supplied evidence of everyday life to augment the grand events described by historians, and this has shown that neither the beginning nor the end of Roman Britain was clear-cut. It began with increasing contact between British and Roman aristocracy and traders, and ended with a gradual withdrawal due to pressure from barbarian forces and conflict within the administration itself.

The armies of dedicated diggers who have brought the discarded or forgotten items of Roman Britain to light have helped to tell the story of a vastly changing world.

The pagan legionary and auxiliary troops who arrived in the south-east in AD 43 were ruled by an Emperor with total power over an expanding empire. They were met by tribal Britons who lived in settlements of simple roundhouses. Many embraced the idea of being Roman, with client kings appointed from amongst the British aristocracy. Some rebelled and resisted, and their stories are told below. In AD 212 the Emperor Caracalla had issued an edict stating that all free males in the Empire were Roman citizens, possibly in order to raise tax revenue, and that free women had the same rights as Roman women. This didn't prevent the third century from being a time of chaos, with galloping inflation, frequent changes of Emperor and conflict with 'barbarians'.

Perhaps because of its position at the edge of the Empire, the fourth century was the most prosperous time for Roman Britain, and many people lived in walled towns, or on sophisticated villa estates. It continued to be a maelstrom of 'nationalities', with soldiers, administrators, traders, slaves and their families moving in and out of the province. Finally, however, from the later fourth century the troops, now officially Christian and organised into frontier and field armies,

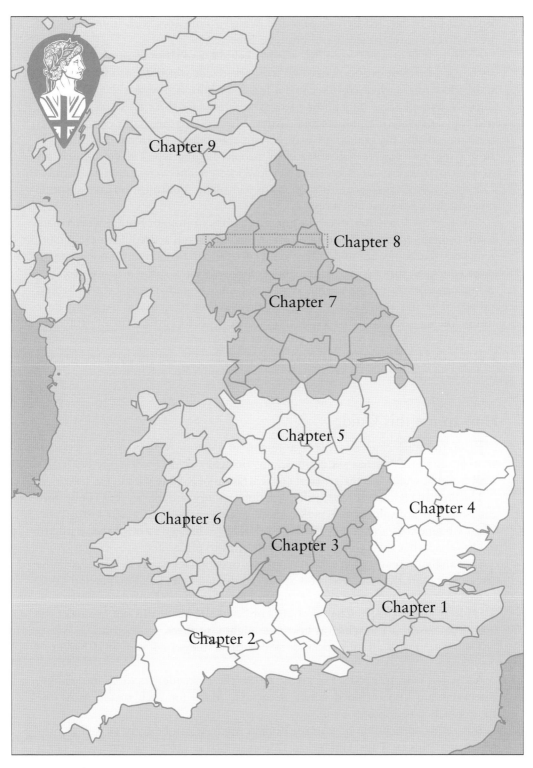

Key to Chapters.

departed bit by bit, led by usurpers and Western Emperors with limited control over a divided, overstretched and besieged Empire.

An incredible array of buildings was left behind, and these continued to have a life beyond the Empire. Forts became strongholds for warlords; people 'squatted' in deserted villas, which also became a focus for burials; towns either thrived or failed; and in all cases the building stones were plundered for reuse for churches, field walls, new town buildings and castles. Much disappeared above ground, but some remarkably big chunks of wall remain standing to this very day. Many of those lying buried were rediscovered by people digging holes in the ground for all sorts of reasons – it is remarkable how many villas were found by farmers with ferrets. Archaeological excavations of increasing sophistication and scientific expertise have revealed lots more.

This book will tell you where to find all the bits of Roman Britain where there is still something to see. Where sites are made visible and accessible to the public, it means that someone, and often many people, cared enough about them to make sure they survived in plain sight. Some have state-of-the-art interpretative technology. Others are somewhat sterile and unimaginative 'small walls' behind railings. The star ratings we have given them reflect this. Many museums have mind-blowing collections of artefacts showing the sophistication of Romano-British culture, with a particular character of its own, unlike that of any other province. All have a part in the story of Roman Britain, and we have tried to tell that tale, bringing this remarkable episode in Britain's history to life.

How to use this Guide

Each of the nine chapters covers a region of Britain. Wales is one, Scotland another, and England has six regions, plus one chapter devoted to the Hadrian's Wall frontier, which has the greatest concentration of Roman sites in the province.

The English regions are mostly divided along county boundaries, but Hampshire and Somerset are split as this makes more sense geographically and historically. County boundaries and names all over the UK have changed so often that it is hard to keep track, but their common usage still helps to place sites.

Sites and museums within each region are listed alphabetically by place, so some places have more than one site. This applies to Roman cities like London and York, as well as non-Roman cities like Bristol and Peterborough.

Hadrian's Wall sites in Chapter 8 are not listed alphabetically, but in clusters of sites, from east to west, which is how one might visit them.

The Antonine Wall in Scotland is described the same way in Chapter 9 (Scotland).

Addresses with postcodes are given, unless the postcode would be misleading. Directions are also included where necessary. Maps for each region show the approximate position of the site.

Star ratings depend on how much Roman material can be seen, as well as how spectacular this is. Thus Tintagel in Devon, which is spectacular but only has a little visible of Roman date, gets one star.

EH is English Heritage; NT is National Trust; HS is Historic Scotland (Cadw sites are also marked). Seasonal Opening means that you should check before visiting as the site is only open at limited times of year, sometimes only a couple of days a week. This information can usually be found online. Open Site means that access is not restricted or charged (at the time of writing!). All the sites in the book allow public access.

We have thoroughly enjoyed seeking out all these sites again, in order to describe them for you. We do hope you get as much fun out of following this guide and that you enjoy finding Roman Britain.

The Balkerne Gate, Colchester, earliest and largest surviving Roman gate in Britain.

1

The South East – The Solent to the Kent Coast
Berkshire, Hampshire east of the Solent, Kent, London, Surrey, Sussex

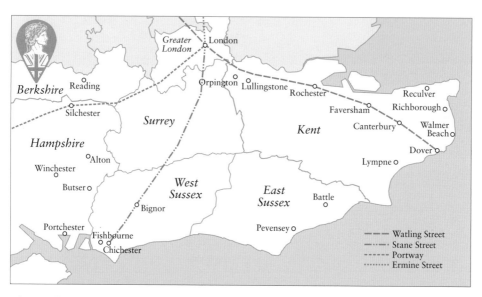

The South-East, the Solent to the Kent Coast.

The South East is where the story of Roman Britain starts, and where the beginning of the end can be most clearly seen today. This is hardly surprising, since it is here that our islands lie closest to the European mainland, whence for millennia the spark of innovation and change had arrived, fusing with and fertilising home-grown ingenuity.

Julius Caesar's campaigns in Gaul from 58 BC had brought Rome's army to the doorstep. The first force in 55 BC aimed for **Dover**, where a landing was thwarted by the fearsome Britons (who must have seen them coming) massed along the cliffs. The fleet diverted, and was traditionally believed to have landed at **Walmer Beach**, Deal, where a modern concrete memorial marks a likely spot. However, recent archaeological work and a close study of the topographical clues provided by Caesar's own account have diverted attention to Pegwell Bay, on the Isle of Thanet, a few miles to the north. There is nothing of this fleeting first invasion to be seen now, as the troops were soon defeated by weather and topography, and the fleet departed before winter closed their escape channel.

They returned the next year to the same beachhead, with a larger force, and again there are few physical traces of this more intense but still very short campaign. Ultimately, having gained much intelligence about Britain and her resources, Caesar once more departed to deal with Gallic insurrection, leaving Britain unconquered but within the sphere of Roman political influence.

It was another ninety-seven years before the real invasion force arrived, a period during which Rome evolved in bloody fashion from a Republic to an Empire with an Emperor in supreme command. By AD 43 the circumstances were right: British chiefs had been appealing to Rome for support in their territorial squabbles amongst themselves for some time; Claudius needed a victory to consolidate his position as Emperor and the scene had been set by Caligula's eccentric abortive invasion in AD 40.

About 20,000 legionaries from four legions and 20,000 auxiliaries sailed across the channel – probably departing from Boulogne, and perhaps arriving at **Richborough** (Rutupiae), Kent. Alternative suggestions for the first landing sites are Walmer, Lympne and Dover, and some scholars are persuaded that Roman military features found beneath the grand first-century palace at **Fishbourne**, Sussex, mark a first landing site. Ancient sources suggest that the force was divided, so maybe a south coast arrival and one or more Kentish footholds are all feasible.

From this corner, the troops advanced through southern Britain, meeting fierce resistance in some tribal areas, a warm welcome and ready alliance in others. According to ancient sources, Claudius spent just sixteen days in Britain, during which he accepted the submission of eleven kings, and made a triumphal entrance into Colchester (Camulodunum). Whether he was riding an elephant at the time is a matter for debate, as the only evidence is a mention by a later historian of elephants being part of the invasion preparations.

The subsequent construction of forts, fortresses, roads, villas, towns and all the public and private buildings therein transformed the landscape of Britain. Colchester was the first capital of the province, but by the late first century a completely new city had been built at a crossing point of the Thames – **London** (Londinium). Much has been revealed of this metropolis beneath the streets of the modern City of London over the years, and there is a surprising amount still to be seen today.

Other towns in this region have Roman remains beneath, between and within their streets, including **Canterbury** (Durovernum Cantiacorum) and **Dover** (Portus Dubris) in Kent. Dover was the base for the *Classis Britannica* naval fleet and has the only remains of a Roman lighthouse in Britain, as well as the largest area of wall-painting visible *in situ* in the country, in the Painted House. In Hampshire, Roman **Winchester** (Venta Belgarum) has been overshadowed by its later buildings, but **Silchester** (Calleva Atrebatum) was abandoned not long after the Roman period and lies under green fields.

The principal Roman roads crossing the region were Watling Street, which ran from Richborough and later also from Dover, via Canterbury to London and then Wroxeter; Stane Street, running from Chichester to London; and the Portway, running from Old Sarum to Silchester, then on to London. We can blame the Romans for our London-centric road system!

The extensive fertile farmland in the South East, with easy access to trade routes to the continent, encouraged the development of wealthy villas controlling huge agricultural estates. A uniquely early palace is the magnificent establishment at **Fishbourne**. Most palatial villas were much later in date, and there are several fine examples still to be seen in the South East, including **Bignor**, Sussex and **Lullingstone**, Kent. Crofton villa in **Orpington** is the only villa now visible within the M25 ring, showing that more must have once stood where London's suburbs now sprawl. In East Hampshire you can see a reconstruction of the villa found at Sparsholt (near Winchester) at **Butser Ancient Farm**.

The Weald in Sussex was exploited for its iron, and many smelting sites have been identified from this period. One of the largest in Europe has been partially excavated at Beauport Park, near Hastings. It lies on private land, but information and finds can be seen in **Battle Museum**.

The general mayhem of the third century is marked in Britain with the construction of town walls, the move from town to country estates for the wealthy, and the construction of forts. Against expectations, the fourth century was the time when Britain's wealth reached its peak, perhaps because it was a relatively safe haven at the edge of the Empire, away from much of the disruptive action.

During the third century a chain of coastal defences was constructed from north Norfolk (Brancaster) to south Hampshire (Portchester). These may have been to protect the 'Saxon Shore' itself from seaborne attackers or, perhaps more likely, to safeguard the trade to and from the continent. The initial impetus for many may have come from Carausius, who was briefly in charge of the Roman fleet stationed in the Channel in AD 286. Later, accused of corruption and outlawed, he declared himself Emperor of Britain and Gaul. The *Notitia Dignitatum* of the fourth century listed nine forts, of which three were built in the late second or early third century, the rest in the late third century. In this region **Reculver** (Regulbium), Kent, was early and **Portchester** (Portus Adurni), Hampshire, **Pevensey**, East Sussex, and **Lympne** (Portus Lemanis), **Dover** (Portus Dubris), **Richborough** (Rutupiae), all in Kent, were late. Their locations are often spectacular.

We have listed the museums with important Roman displays, but you will also find local artefacts in museums at Andover, Basingstoke, Fareham and Southampton in Hampshire, and Arundel, Brighton, Lewes, Hastings, Littlehampton and Worthing in Sussex. Guildford and Leatherhead museums have finds from the villa and tileworks at Ashstead, Surrey, now reburied.

Alton, Hampshire **

Curtis Museum with Roman displays

Founded by Dr William Curtis in 1865 to house his own wide-ranging collections, the Curtis Museum is now part of the Hampshire Cultural Trust (1A High Street, GU34 1BA). It has a good display of Roman artefacts, including many finds from excavations at the nearby small Roman town of Neatham. The greatest treasure is the second-century intricately enamelled Selborne Cup, found inside a large earthenware jar at Blackmoor House in the 1860s, together with a coin of Lucius Verus (AD 161–9). Although not our period, the fabulous jewelled Anglo-Saxon Alton buckle should not be missed.

Battle, East Sussex *

Museum with Roman displays. Seasonal opening.

There is a surprising amount of Roman material on display at the small but packed Battle Museum (The Almonry, High Street, TN33 0EA). Most of this comes from a bath-house excavated at Beauport Park near Hastings, now on private land and inaccessible.

The presence of a huge slag heap of iron on the site was first noted in the nineteenth century, and archaeologist Gerald Brodribb used divining rods, displayed here, to investigate, leading to the excavation of the bath-house in the 1970s. It is thought that this was one of the largest centres of iron production in the Empire, and the baths were provided for those involved in the iron works. Many tiles stamped with the letters CL BR were found, some of them displayed here, standing for *Classis Britannica*, the British fleet. They indicate that the navy was involved somehow in working, protecting and/or transporting the iron. Operations lasted from about AD 80 to 250, when the site was abandoned.

Given the location of the museum, it is not surprising to find the Battle of Hastings featuring strongly, with the only battleaxe ever found at the site on show.

Bignor, West Sussex *****

Roman villa with mosaics; museum. Seasonal opening.

The villa at Bignor (RH20 1PH) provides the perfect counterpoint to Fishbourne (below), the most famous Roman palatial residence in Sussex. Since they are only 17 miles (27 km) apart, both can be visited on a perfect Roman day out. Bignor reached its heyday in the early fourth century, contrasting with the early splendour of Fishbourne, and the covering nineteenth-century thatched structures are very different from the modern covering at Fishbourne. At Bignor, the small buildings standing over some of the rooms of the villa are rare survivors of traditional Sussex agricultural architecture and are of great historic value in themselves. They break up the unity of the Roman architecture but are gorgeous to look at and fun to explore. The setting is very lovely, on the edge of the Sussex Downs.

Mosaic at Bignor Villa showing gladiatorial combat.

The sequence at Bignor is of gradual enhancement from a simple enclosed farmstead in the late first century to a timber-framed house at the end of the second century. This in turn was rebuilt in stone, with just four rooms, during the mid-third century, later extended to include more rooms, a corridor and baths. This then formed the west wing of the large three-phased courtyard villa of the early fourth century, with a long corridor linking the north and south wings. The entrance in the eastern façade faced Stane Street, the main road between Chichester and London, lying just a few hundred yards to the east. Farm buildings have also been found to the east, and the complex was surrounded by an enclosing wall.

Begin with the excellent, old-fashioned site museum, which displays many finds and tells the story of the excavations since the villa's discovery by farmer George Tupper whilst ploughing in 1811. The Tupper family still owns and manages the site. The cover buildings were erected not long after this to protect and display the mosaics to the visitors who flocked to see the sensational discovery. More recent digs have clarified the complex chronology.

The glory of the late villa is its fine mosaics, many of which are figurative, including scenes of cupids engaged in gladiatorial combat, overlooked by a slightly disapproving-looking Venus. A sombre-faced Winter survives from a four-seasons mosaic and Zeus appears as an eagle abducting Ganymede. All are familiar Roman characters, but whether the owner at this date was of British, Roman or other heritage is not known. At the western end of the long corridor is a well-preserved mosaic dolphin which, unusually, may have been signed by the maker with the letters TER, perhaps Terentius.

The south-east corner of the south wing is also exposed and protected. This is a second bath suite with another Medusa mosaic. The full size of the complex can be appreciated by looking from this corner back to the thatched buildings.

Butser, Hampshire ***

Ancient farm with reconstructed Roman villa. Seasonal opening.

There are no authentic Roman remains at Butser, but this is currently the only place in Britain where you can see a reconstructed villa (Chalton Lane, Chalton, Waterlooville PO8 0BG). It has been based on a villa excavated in the late 1960s at Sparsholt, near Winchester, nearly 25 miles (40 km) to the north-west. An almost complete mosaic and other finds from the site are displayed in Winchester Museum. The reconstruction is well worth a visit, and might be recognisable to some as a film location for *Horrible Histories: The Rotten Romans*.

The villa project at Butser began in 2000 as an extension of many years' experimental work building Iron Age round-houses, and in 2019 a copy of the mosaic displayed in Winchester Museum was triumphantly completed.

The villa at Sparsholt developed and changed over many years, so a single period had to be chosen for the reconstruction: the aisled hall of the second century AD.

Reconstruction of Sparsholt Villa at Butser Ancient Farm.

The walls of the original only survived to a height of 50 cm, so the superstructure is conjectural, based on evidence from a variety of sources. In addition, compromises with available building materials had to be made.

This mix of scholarly conjecture, experimentation and trial and error provides a valuable insight into how it might have felt to visit a villa, the wall-paintings, floors and furniture bringing the building vividly to life. One nice touch is that two small windows have panes of glass made by different methods known to have been employed by the Romans. One is glazed with the cast, thicker variety used during the earlier Roman period, the other is thinner, cylinder-blown, of a type in use from about AD 300. The fireplace in the room to the left of the entrance, which seems odd in a Roman house, is based on excavated evidence of a hearth with a canopy – but whether it vented into a chimney, as reconstructed, is a matter of debate.

The rest of the farm, including a Neolithic longhouse, Iron Age round-houses and a Saxon hall, along with ancient breeds of animals, plant species and crop storage facilities, allows you to indulge in time travel of some longevity.

Canterbury (Durovernum Cantiacorum), Kent ****

Civitas capital, Roman museum; Roman sections of city walls.

Before the arrival of the Romans, the local Cantiaci tribe had chosen a crossing point of the River Stour for their main settlement, with territory that included Bigbury Camp hillfort, to the north-west. The Romans followed their lead, establishing their civitas capital on more or less the same site not long after AD 43. It may not have been ideal, since the name is thought to mean 'the settlement of the Cantiaci by the alder swamp', but it was strategically good. It stood on Watling Street, linking Dover and Richborough with London, St Albans and Wroxeter. The River Stour, once vital for transporting goods, still runs through and around the north-west part of the town. Excavations have revealed many glimpses of Roman buildings over the years, a few of which can still be seen.

A visit to the excellent **Roman Museum** (Butchery Lane CT1 2JR) is the only way to understand the layout of the town 2,000 years ago. The imposing pillared entrance makes it easy to recognise, with a modern copy of an 'unswept floor' mosaic to greet you.

Two excellent reconstruction drawings on the wall inside show the town in *c.* AD 150, with forum, theatre, baths, several temples and houses, and in *c.* AD 300, when the walls had been constructed and the theatre much enlarged. The keys relate these to the modern street layout, which is invaluable. Many finds from the town and the surrounding area are displayed.

The site of the museum was determined by the discovery of a large, wealthy Roman town house, revealed after Second World War bombing. Mosaic floors with hypocaust are displayed *in situ*, and fragments of painted wall plaster and other finds show its high status. Built *c.* AD 70, it was enlarged and enhanced until it was abandoned *c.* AD 350.

Displays include remarkable bits of plumbing and engineering from the town bath-house, exquisite complete vessels of pottery and glass from the cemeteries, and a range of figurines from shrines and temples. The many excavations of the Canterbury Archaeological Trust are well explained.

The end of the town is graphically illustrated by a fabulous collection of silver treasure found near the London Gate during roadworks in 1962. Many of the objects, including spoons and jewellery, have Christian symbols, and were presumably buried soon after AD 410 when danger was approaching, never to be retrieved by their owner.

The city walls follow the 1.7 mile (2.7 km) Roman circuit, built in the late third century. The Roman wall was originally topped with crenellations and had a substantial bank with a walkway behind it. The surviving city wall has been rebuilt many times; Roman patches can be identified by the facing of water-rounded boulders and flint pebbles from the coast as well as earlier reused Roman stones. A good place to see this, where the largest stretch of Roman work survives, is in St Radigund's Street, where it meets The Borough, near to where the North Gate once stood. The nave of St Mary Northgate Church stands in a small garden, its north wall consisting of the remains of the city wall standing to full height, with water-rounded boulders of Greensand and large rounded flints marking the Roman face. Information boards here provide more information.

Follow the walls around the eastern side of the town to Queningate, the only surviving Roman gate in the circuit, with other fragments of Roman wall adjoining the car park here. There is a bit more surviving to a surprising height near Burgate.

Carry on the wall walk, and opposite the bus station, inside the walls, the last shop in the row is called 'Roman Tower'. Through the windows part of the wall of the tower can be seen, with information about various excavations. This was one of two interval towers (observation towers?), built within the bank approximately 60 metres apart, mid-way between Ridingate and Burgate, perhaps to carry a *ballista*. In the Dane John Gardens is a mound, originally a late Iron Age or early Roman burial mound which was incorporated into the Roman defences and later used by William the Conqueror in October 1066 for a motte and bailey castle.

Continue along the wall to Canterbury Castle, where the southern Worthgate once stood. Opposite the remains of the castle keep is a further section of Roman wall in coursed flints. This is the inside face of the wall and would have originally been buried by the earthen bank.

One more remnant of Roman Canterbury survives in the basement of the shop at 20–21 St Margarets Street. It used to be Waterstones, but is currently a haberdashers', and a member of staff will escort you down to look at a display with part of a second-century hypocaust from one of the town baths. A section of curving wall, part of the *cavea* of the **Roman theatre**, is accessible to view further along the street in the basement of the Hilton hotel.

The town was more or less abandoned in the early fifth century, but people were soon building houses over the ruins, and by the seventh century the first cathedral had been built, ensuring its prosperity to this day.

Chichester (Noviomagus Reginorum), West Sussex ***

Novium Museum and Bath-house; Chichester Cathedral Mosaic; Togidubnus Inscription; Town Defences; Amphitheatre.

Roman activity here may have begun with a fort for the Second Legion Augusta shortly after its arrival in Britain in AD 43, during the push west towards Exeter. This was the territory of the Regni, whose chief Togidubnus / Cogidubnus was an ally of Rome, and was set up by them as a client king. The nearby palace at Fishbourne is believed by many to have belonged to him. Remarkably, an inscription naming him was found long ago in the town (below). The name Noviomagus Reginorum means 'new place / market of the Regni', and by about AD 75 a new street layout and all public amenities seem to have been lavished on the town. It is tempting to see this as resulting either from Roman favour towards a client king or after the absorption of the kingdom into the Roman province following Togidubnus' death. A major Roman road, later known as Stane Street, led the way 56 miles (90 km) to London.

The new **Novium Museum** (Tower Street PO19 1QH) stands next to the Cathedral, over part of a Roman bath-house which is preserved *in situ*. This was built in about AD 75 and continued to be used, with alterations, until the early fifth century. A splendid projected film above the remains shows how the baths would have been used and explains the later uses of the site, including a period as a bell foundry for the cathedral bells. The site was then buried under a car park, before being revealed again as a focus for this museum.

There are also artefacts from other parts of the town, including some fine mosaics and the remarkable inscribed and decorated 'Jupiter Stone' found in West Street, probably a statue base. A very worn imperial stone head, either Vespasian or Trajan, was retrieved from the vicarage garden at Bosham. It may originally have stood, with its body, at the entrance of the nearby harbour.

In nearby **Chichester Cathedral** a piece of *in situ* black and white mosaic of second-century date can be seen in an illuminated case beneath the floor, towards the east end of the south aisle.

The **Togidubnus Inscription** outside the Assembly Rooms, North Street, was found in Chichester in 1723 and can be seen behind glass within the porticoed frontage. Critically missing the first two letters of the name, it recognises the authority of a great king, and is evidence of an early temple in the town, not yet located: 'To Neptune and Minerva, for the welfare of the Divine Temple, by the authority of Tiberius Claudius [To]gidubnus, great king of the Britons, the guild of smiths and those in it gave this temple at their own expense [...]ens, son of Pudentinus, presented the forecourt.'

The **town defences** initially comprised an earthen bank with palisade erected in the second century, replaced by a stone wall in the late third century, with at least nineteen D-shaped bastions added in the fourth century. There is a 1.5-mile (1 km) wall walk, with two bastions visible in the Bishop's Palace Garden in the south-west quadrant of the town; the lower parts probably have a Roman core. Another can be seen facing Orchard Street on the north-west side of the city, with a fourth on the south-east side which carries a later brick gazebo.

The **amphitheatre**, partially excavated in 1934-5, is now barely visible as a hollow surrounded by a low elliptical bank in a small park outside the walls to the south-east.

Dover (Portus Dubris), Kent ✳✳✳✳

Roman lighthouse; The 'Painted House'; Dover Museum.

Dover has always been defined by its closeness to France and has been a fortified military port since the Roman period, linked to London and beyond by Watling Street. It lies at the mouth of the River Dour, but the appearance of the coastline and river today is well-nigh impossible to relate to that of Roman times. Until excavations took place in the 1970s nothing was known of what lay under the streets, but now it is better understood.

The fleet defending the trade route across the Channel, the *Classis Britannica*, was stationed both here and in Boulogne. Excavations in the town centre have revealed remains of two successive stone forts for the navy, the first begun *c*. AD 115, the second abandoned in the early third century when the fleet was withdrawn. A new fort was built around AD 270 as part of the Saxon Shore fort system, overlapping the old fort site in the north-east corner. This seems to have been used until the sixth century, beyond the end of Roman Britain. Dover Museum lies on the site of this sequence of military buildings; begin your visit here to stand a chance of understanding the layout. This is also where the Roman harbour is believed to have been situated, at the mouth of the river, which now flows partly beneath the streets of the town, much further inland than the current port.

The **Dover Museum** (Market Square CT16 1PH) is part of a large modern complex that includes the Discovery Centre and the library. It stands on top of the Classis Britannicus fort, which was overlain by the Saxon Shore fort. A tiny glimpse of masonry from both of these, consisting of the base of the east gateway of the former, next to a rounded bastion of the latter, can be seen by peeping over

Roman lighthouse re-used as church bell-tower at Dover.

a high wall by the Discovery Centre on the east side of York Street, or by looking through the arch of windows in the library. Further north a few more bits of wall can be seen, and further north again the Roman Painted House exhibition (below) preserves part of the western wall of the Saxon Shore fort. Do look at the useful plans in the museum to understand how it all relates to the modern streets.

The Roman section of the museum is otherwise fairly limited, as pride of place is given, justifiably, to the incredible Bronze Age Boat Gallery upstairs. Dramatic tableaux with models include Claudius' triumphant arrival with elephants, a life-sized Celt and Roman and a model of the lighthouse in its heyday. There are three cases of Roman artefacts. A statue of Venus found in the Market Place in the nineteenth century looks rather gruesome as her face has been completely sliced off at some time.

A remarkable set of circumstances led to the excellent preservation of the **Painted House** (25 New Street, Dover CT17 9AJ; seasonal opening). This was probably a *mansio* or coaching inn for official travellers, standing right in the way of the builders of the third-century Saxon Shore fort. The great western wall of the fort was therefore built right across the west end of the house whilst the painted walls were still quite fresh and serviceable. The construction of a rampart of clay and rubble against the fort wall buried the remains of the house, thus preserving the largest area of painted wall plaster found *in situ* in Britain.

The *mansio* had been constructed about seventy years earlier, around AD 200, and had brightly painted walls and underfloor heating in the larger rooms. Parts of five rooms and a passageway have been excavated, with some walls surviving to a height of 4–6 feet (1.2–1.8 metres). The trompe l'oeil architectural scheme, of fluted columns on bases above a stage, frames coloured panels within which are figures or motifs relating to Bacchus, the Roman god of wine.

The remains are preserved within a flat-roofed building that opened to the public in 1977 as a result of fund-raising efforts and voluntary work by the Dover Roman Painted House Trust, directed by Brian Philp, the excavator. The layout and information are splendid, but it is now looking a little dated. However, the remains are exceptional and is the main Roman attraction in the town centre.

The **Roman lighthouse** or Pharos is located above the town in the grounds of Dover Castle (EH), beyond the ticket office and therefore subject to the entry fee.

Two Roman lighthouses once stood atop the Western and Eastern Heights, both built in the early second century. The eastern one still stands, built on the headland over the site of Iron Age defences. The only surviving Roman lighthouse in Britain, and one of only three surviving in the world, its preservation is due to the fact that the well-built octagonal structure was utilised as a free-standing bell tower for the Saxon church of St-Mary-in-Castro, perhaps in the seventh century. Its original height was probably 80 feet (24 metres), consisting of eight storeys, each getting slightly smaller towards the top. Contemporary depictions of lighthouses show just such features with a fire burning, often in a cylindrical structure on the top, apparently without any sort of protection around the flames. The fuel would have been either wood or oil.

Just four storeys of the eastern lighthouse are Roman; the top part was added in the fifteenth century. Three original arched doorways survive, leading into the rectangular interior. Nothing can be seen of the western lighthouse, once known as the Bredenstone, which was destroyed during the construction of new defensive works in the early nineteenth century.

The setting is dramatic, with views out to sea, where you have to imagine Roman merchant vessels in place of the frequent cross-Channel ferries.

Faversham, Kent **

Temple beneath Christian Chapel.

Beside the busy A2 London Road, a short distance west of Faversham, lies a ruined chapel. Look for a footpath signposted to 'stone chapel', just north of the A2, shortly before the turning into Four Oaks Road. The ruins of the chapel can be seen from the road in front of a small clump of trees, with a mown area around it. It's best to park in the quiet Four Oaks Road.

Once you have taken the footpath and left the traffic behind you, this is a peaceful haven in the middle of a field. The A2 is the modern successor to Watling Street, the main Roman road from Richborough to London, so the busy passing traffic is not just a modern phenomenon, though the speed has increased.

The on-site information explains that the walls of the square Roman structure can be easily identified by the courses of red brick running through them.

Ruined chapel with remnants of Roman temple at Faversham.

This simple structure was used to form the chancel of a church, perhaps as early as the seventh century. By the eleventh century the church had been expanded, and a late Saxon nave was added. Further extensions to the west and east were added in the thirteenth century, and it was finally abandoned in the sixteenth century.

Recent archaeological investigation by the Kent Archaeological Field School has offered a more complex interpretation. The foundation of a pentagonal perimeter wall around the whole complex was identified, along with two Roman buildings of some longevity, in use from the early second century to the end of the Roman period. This is now thought to have been a Romano-Celtic temple complex, part of which was rebuilt in the post-Roman period, and this was incorporated into the Christian church, a sequence hitherto unknown in Britain.

A lot of Roman activity has been found nearby, and many believe that Faversham may have been the town of Durolevum, mentioned in the *Antonine Itinerary*. Some of the finds are in the Maison Dieu Museum, Ospringe Road, in Faversham, along with other Roman artefacts from the area.

Fishbourne Roman Palace, Sussex *****

Roman palace with mosaics; site museum.

The massive Roman residence at Fishbourne is exceptional for the early date at which it achieved a standard of magnificence unique in Britain at that time. The many black and white geometric mosaics displayed *in situ* are some of the first to have graced British floors. It was a palace rather than a mere villa.

The site lies about 2 miles (just over 3 km) west of the Roman town of Chichester (Roman Way, Chichester PO19 3QR). Now landlocked, it once stood near an inlet from the sea, and ships would have brought both building materials and supplies for maintaining a lavish lifestyle. Excavations have revealed a sequence of buildings from an early military harbourside depot, which was replaced first by a well-constructed timber-framed house, then a more substantial stone 'proto-palace', then the vast palace. This would have been larger than Buckingham Palace, covering 500 square feet (150 square metres). The meteoric increase in wealth all happened during the first century, perhaps *c.* AD 75–80, though some think the date was closer to AD 92.

The most likely owner of the substantial first-century house was long ago identified as the client king Tiberius Claudius Togidubnus (or perhaps Cogidubnus), known from the inscription found in Chichester and from the writing of Tacitus, the first-century Roman historian. We know of no-one else who might have achieved such high status at this date in this part of the country. Doubt may be thrown on this ownership if the date of the huge palace was very late in the first century, although we don't know when Togidubnus died.

There is a useful model inside the entrance of the covered area showing the appearance of the palace at this time. It had four large wings set in a square with a large central garden, and two smaller courtyard gardens within both the North and the East Wings.

The West Wing included a substantial audience chamber where formal receptions would have been held. The South Wing, which lies mainly beneath the A27,

Early geometric mosaics at Fishbourne Palace.

is believed to have contained the private quarters of the owner. There was another formal entrance in the East Wing, leading to rooms for lower-ranking guests. The North Wing contained rooms for high status guests, and it is this area that is roofed, preserved and displayed today, with walkways allowing you to look down on the wall foundations and amazing array of mosaic floors, made with local stones.

Alterations continued to be made into the second century, with early geometric mosaics being replaced by later figurative ones, occasionally visible one above the other in the excavations. New bath suites were also added. Alterations were still being made in AD 270, when the palace was destroyed by fire and abandoned, valuable building materials being salvaged for use elsewhere.

Outside, the formal gardens have been reinstated and the wall-lines of other wings laid out in concrete. Don't miss these parts, as they give an invaluable impression of the huge size of the whole palace, and include the audience chamber with statue base, perhaps once supporting an imperial statue.

The complex was first uncovered when a water pipe was laid across the site, and systematic excavations began under the direction of Barry Cunliffe in 1961. A huge screen with photos and audio commentary tells the exciting story of these pre-health-and-safety excavations, as well as more recent discoveries. There is a really excellent on-site museum and a finds depot, or Discovery Centre, which is open to the public.

It is less than an hour's drive from here to Bignor Roman villa (above), so you should try to see both in one day.

London (Londinium) *****

City walls; Cripplegate Fort West Gate; Museum of London; amphitheatre; Bank of England mosaic; Mithraeum; Billingsgate Bath-house; British Museum.

Extraordinary though it seems, the town that became the capital of Britannia did not develop out of a pre-existing settlement like all the others of the province. It emerged on a green-field site at a crossing point of the River Thames, where navigation to the sea for supplies and communications was still easy. Before Londinium, the Thames was a barrier and a boundary between tribes; the Romans used the river as a thoroughfare.

The very name of the city may derive from ancient British words related to ships and river: plowo and nida, emphasising the navigational advantages for which the site was chosen. For the first time Britain was becoming united under a single regime, rather than being contested territory for many tribes vying for supremacy. The new site fulfilled all the needs for communication by sea with Europe and, ultimately, Rome and the rest of the Mediterranean world, and Britons were now part of a much larger network.

The crossing point lay very slightly downstream (east) of the modern London Bridge. Roman engineers were able to conquer the physical difficulties of bridging a wide, shallow tidal river, with extensive mudflats to the south, as no-one had been able to do before. A rope ferry might have been employed for the first few years

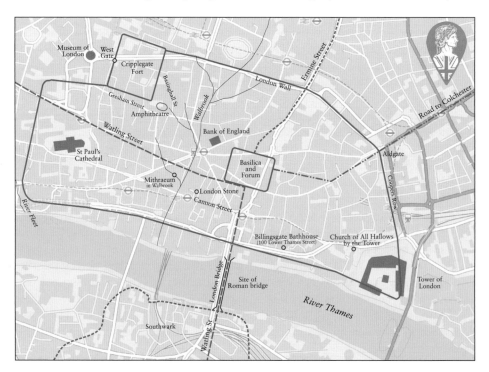

The remains of Roman London within the modern street plan.

after AD 43, but sometime between AD 50 and AD 60 a wooden bridge with piles and decking was constructed.

To the north of the river a settlement of wooden houses, shops and administrative buildings developed around two low hills, first at Cornhill and then at Ludgate Hill, where St Paul's now stands, with the Walbrook Stream between them. The development extended almost as far as the River Fleet in the west. Major roads led east to Colchester (Camulodunum) and west to St Albans (Verulamium) and Silchester (Calleva Atrebatum).

South of the river the road to the bridgehead ran from the junction of Watling Street, the main road from the Kent coast, and Stane Street, the main road from Chichester and the south coast. Settlement developed on each side of this axis road, with streets being carried on wooden piles across the marshy islands of Southwark. Wharfs with warehouses and quays soon developed along both sides of the river, which was much wider than it is today.

The thriving settlement and trading hub suffered a major setback in AD 60/61 when Boudica's revolutionaries burnt many of the wooden buildings. A tell-tale layer of red burnt earth and black charcoal has been revealed during excavations all over the inhabited area, though no bodies have been found, suggesting that most of the inhabitants had time to get away. In any case, Londinium immediately rose from the ashes, gradually rebuilt in stone: remains of an amphitheatre, temples, town houses, and a forum and basilica have all been revealed at various times. By the second century it had replaced Camulodunum as the capital of Britannia, and was the largest city in the province at 300 acres (134 hectares), stretching along the river from the Tower of London in the east almost to Blackfriars in the west, and as far north as the street known as London Wall. The forum and basilica, excavated on Cornhill, straddling Gracechurch Street, was one of the largest buildings north of the Alps.

In the second century, perhaps *c.* AD 120, Cripplegate Fort was built in the north-west of the city, possibly housing the governor's bodyguards and staff. The Emperor Hadrian visited the city in AD 122; soon afterwards another huge fire, cause unknown, resulted in much destruction.

Around the beginning of the third century, stone city walls were erected on the three landward sides north of the river, encapsulating the remains of the fort, which may have gone out of use within a few decades of its construction. During the turbulent third century another wall was added along the north bank of the Thames to make a complete circuit.

There is evidence of a decline in population size, perhaps also of prosperity, during the second half of this century, and soon after AD 410 the city was more or less abandoned, its fortunes closely linked to that of the wider Roman administration. It did not really begin to thrive again until the end of the ninth century, when Alfred moved the centre of population back inside the city walls.

Masses of excavation work has been carried out all over the Roman city, whenever redevelopment has taken place amongst the roads, shops and office blocks. Substantial remains also came to light during clearance after the Blitz bombing in the Second World War. Many publications describe the discoveries, but visible and restored bits of Roman Londinium can also be seen at a number of points around the city, some of them spectacularly well-displayed. The Museum of London sells an excellent map with descriptions of most of the sites, both visible and now reburied, and this is highly recommended.

The city walls *** can be traced for much of their circuit, but in bits and pieces rather than a continuous curtain. The surviving stretches are a glorious palimpsest of periods, following the route and built on the foundations of the Roman circuit, and occasionally surviving as Roman stonework above ground level. There are Wall Walk information boards along the way. One of the best places to start walking is outside the current Museum of London in the Barbican, where a good stretch of wall can be seen on the west side of Noble Street, south of the museum. The foundations of the **West Gate of Cripplegate Fort** survive in an underground car park below London Wall road – access by arrangement with the Museum of London. This is the only gate in the London walls that was not rebuilt in later times, so it retains its Roman form.

The Wall Walk is signposted from this point; you can either follow this or divert to visit the sites described below which will take you diagonally across the city, ending near the Tower of London.

If you follow the Wall Walk, your next short stretch of Roman wall will be in St Alphage Garden, EC2Y 5DE, just outside the Salters' Company building. This has recently been landscaped and is a popular spot to escape bustling city life.

The final, rather spectacular, stretch is just north of the Tower of London, in Coopers Row behind the façade of the Grange City Hotel. There is public access through the open forecourt of the hotel to look at the 35 foot (10.6 metre) high surviving wall and read the information boards. The Roman remains survive to the height of the sentry walk at 14.5 feet (4.4 metres) and can be distinguished by the narrow Roman red brick courses separating the ragstone facing stones on a rubble and cement core. Everything above that is medieval or later.

From here, you can follow the wall south through Tower Hill Garden, where it is fronted by a modern bronze statue of Trajan. In the modern wall to the north of the garden there is a copy of a tombstone fragment commemorating Gaius Julius Alpinus Classicianus, *procurator* of Britannia in AD 61, just after the Boudican rebellion, who advocated reconciling with the Britons rather than continued punishment. He died in London in AD 65, and the tombstone fragment was found reused in a fourth-century Roman bastion. The original is in the British Museum.

If you cross Tower Hill road you are at the Tower of London – inside the grounds (and subject to the substantial fee) the foundations of a bastion of the eastern wall can be seen, as well as a short stretch of the riverside wall added to the defences in the third century. They cannot be glimpsed from the outside, but they are marked on the free map of the Tower in the visitor centre.

The Museum of London ***** (150 London Wall, EC2Y 5HN) tells the story of London and is currently part of the Barbican Centre, built during the 1960s and 70s as a major redevelopment of a bomb-damaged area of the city.

The Roman galleries contain important finds from all over the city, including sculptures from the Temple of Mithras, a beautifully ornate geometric mosaic from Bucklersbury, near Queen Street, and the wonderful fourth-century burial of a young woman, in her twenties, found in a cemetery at Spitalfield. Analysis of her teeth showed that she may have come originally from Spain or Italy and she was buried in a lead coffin, accompanied by unique and elaborate glass vessels, jet jewellery and bay leaves, with some rich fabrics leaving traces in the coffin of gold thread, silk and fine wool. Her reconstructed face gazes back at visitors. There are several reconstructions to help you visualise the Roman city, and illuminating models of the waterfront and bridge, and the forum and surrounding civic buildings.

All these treasures will at some stage, perhaps in 2021, move to a new museum housed in Smithfield market, less than half a mile to the west, as part of a major reorganisation of both the Barbican and the historic market area.

The amphitheatre **** that provided entertainment for the inhabitants of Londinium was only discovered in 1988. It lies partly beneath the Guildhall Art Gallery (EC2V 5AE) and partly to the south of it, where the line of the elliptical walls is laid out in black paving in Guildhall Yard. Go downstairs to the basement of the Art Gallery to view parts of the foundations, with illuminated reconstructions of spectators in their seats watching the performing gladiators. It is a splendidly minimalistic way of evoking the atmosphere of the games.

It stood on the margins of the city, though firmly within the wall circuit. Excavations to the north-east have revealed a large area of industrial activity, with glass furnaces, pottery kilns and evidence for leather-working. This was clearly not prime real estate, probably because of the sogginess of the Upper Walbrook Valley.

The capacity of the amphitheatre was about 6,000 spectators, quite modest compared with the Colosseum at 50,000. The structure was first built of wood in about AD 70, then replaced in stone in the early second century, with tiled entrances and ragstone walls. Some of the timber-lined drains have been preserved in the waterlogged conditions beneath the Guildhall.

The remains of the Roman amphitheatre beneath the London Guildhall. *Photo: Dot Smith.*

The amphitheatre was abandoned in about AD 360, after which the stone was robbed for other buildings, then the site was left as a ruin. The road system which was established in the eleventh century, especially Aldermanbury and Basinghall Street, swerves around the amphitheatre walls, probably just a bank by that time. Once archaeologists knew that the amphitheatre was there, the reason for the routes of these roads became obvious. The first Guildhall was erected here in the twelfth century when the fortunes of the city began to revive, and the site of the bloody games was forgotten.

The Bank of England Museum * (Bartholomew Lane, EC2R 8AH) tells you all you might want to know about money and banking, but it also has something for the very keen Roman enthusiast. On a wall beyond the entrance hall, through security, is a very nice fourth-century geometric mosaic, restored to completeness. It was found below the bank during rebuilding work in the early twentieth century. Another is laid at the bottom of a staircase within the bank itself and cannot generally be visited. The elaborate mosaics on the floor of the entrance hall are of twentieth-century date, by Boris Anrep, who also made the floors of the National Gallery.

The London Mithraeum ***** (12 Walbrook, EC4N 8AA) lies a 5–10-minute walk south, underneath the ultra-modern office block of Bloomberg. Entry is free but pre-booking is required via a website (www.londonmithraeum.com).

Mithras, a god of light and creation, was chief deity of a mystery religion which may have originated, in part, in Persia. It spread rapidly through the Roman world from the first century AD. It was popular with soldiers, merchants and civil servants, which meant that, by default, it was men only. We know of seven stages of elaborate initiation rites and a strict hierarchy of priests. The temples were always enclosed spaces, at least partly underground, involving a banquet area. The most important cult icon was a painting or a sculpture of the Tauroctony – Mithras stabbing his short sword into the shoulder of a bull, from whose blood sprang all life.

It was first discovered in 1954, when bomb-damaged buildings from the Second World War were being cleared. The discovery of the head of Mithras on the last day of formal excavations caused a public sensation, with an estimated 40,000 people queuing to see what came out of the ground. Many other sculptures were discovered, including Serapis and Minerva, which can be seen along with Mithras in the Museum of London.

Built in the mid-third century, it may have been financed by Ulpius Silvanis, veteran of the Second Legion Augusta, as an inscription testifies to his generosity. In the mid-fourth century there were large-scale renovations, and it may have been rededicated to Bacchus. It continued to be used until the end of the Roman period but was then abandoned.

In 1962 the remains of the temple were lifted and reconstructed nearby, since the site itself was required for office buildings. The resulting inauspicious lump of concrete in Queen Victoria Street must have been passed by millions of people without being noticed, in spite of the information boards.

All has been changed by a new phase in the temple's history: the purchase of the site by US media company Bloomberg, the construction of a new office block

designed by Sir Norman Foster, and the archaeological excavations in advance of
this work in 2010–4. The temple was moved again, not quite to its original position
but very close, just slightly to the west. The excavations had unexpectedly turned
up parts of the temple still *in situ*, and it was decided to leave these for posterity
rather than building over them.

Finds are displayed from excavations carried out before the new offices were
built, including spectacular objects of wood, leather and other organic substances
preserved by the waterlogged ground of the Walbrook Valley. One of the
405 wooden writing tablets discovered bears the earliest mention, from AD 65,
of the name of the city as part of an address: 'To Mongontius in Londinium'.
Particularly apt is another tablet which represents the earliest recorded financial
transaction in Roman Britain. Dated 8 January AD 57, it records a debt of
150 denarii which was due to be paid by one freed slave to another. After weaving
your way through formally dressed financiers in the streets outside, it provides the
perfect reminder that many aspects of life never change. This has been emphasised
by recent conservation work on an iron stylus revealing an inscription reading:
'I have come from the City. I bring you a welcome gift with a sharp point that you
may remember me...' In other words: 'I visited the city and bought you a pen'.

A descent through time, with informative presentations, takes you to the temple
platform, displayed in its earliest phases from *c.* AD 240, as revealed by the
excavations of 1954. Only a few people are allowed in at a time, which contributes
to the haunting atmosphere of the short show, using light, sound and haze. To say
more would spoil the experience – book a visit and see for yourself!

Exit the Mithraeum and turn right, and at the junction of Walbrook and Cannon
Street there is a bronze cascade entitled *Forgotten Streams* with branches and twigs
lying each side of the flowing stream. This is a beautiful memorial to the Walbrook
itself, which was such an important feature of Roman London, now running
invisibly underground.

Further down Cannon Street, at No. 111, lies the **London Stone** *, recently
rehoused in a glass-fronted marble canopy beside the pavement opposite Cannon
Street station. A notice explains some of the movements and history of this rather
unprepossessing-looking oolitic limestone block. The first reference dates back to
about 1100, and it appeared on the first map of the city in 1550, standing opposite
St Swithin's church. It has moved several times since, shrinking in the process,
arriving in its current spot in 1962, first sitting forlornly behind a metal grille,
now looking much more regal. The stone is not native to London, but just when
it arrived has long been a puzzle, and many legends have grown up around it, not
least, 'So long as the stone of Brutus is safe, So long will London flourish' ... Is it
Roman? Who knows? As the author of a learned paper on the stone has put it, 'the
London Stone is simply famous for being famous'.

The Church of All Hallows by the Tower (Byward Street, EC3R 5BJ) proclaims
itself the oldest church in London. Down in the **Crypt Museum** ** a small area
of plain red tessellated floor can be seen *in situ* where a late second-century house
once stood. There is a model of Roman London and cases of Roman finds from
the vicinity, including pots, tombstones, a roof tile with a dog's paw print, lamps
and stamped *mortaria* fragments. This little gem of a display results from the

enthusiasm of the Revd 'Tubby' Clayton, vicar from 1922 to 1962. From here you can easily walk to the sections of city wall north of the Tower of London.

Billingsgate Bath-house ** is preserved in an office basement in 100 Lower Thames Street (EC3R 6DL). Access can be booked on-line. The remains of a Roman house of the late second century were discovered in 1848, and these still lie preserved beneath the various structures built above. A bath-house added in the third century was the most impressive of the remains, and these can be seen, with a particularly well-preserved semi-circular *caldarium* with hypocaust. The baths remained in use until the early fifth century, thus showing that some parts of Londinium continued to function after the end of Roman rule.

The British Museum ***** (WC1B 3DG) lies to the west of Londinium in Bloomsbury and is the home of many of the greatest treasures of Roman Britain. It has long had the pick of the finds from all over the province, but the advantages of seeing so many mind-blowing objects in one Roman Britain Gallery must make up for any sense of unfairness about this. Some would have been considered treasure in the Roman period, others are the everyday items that make us realise that people 2,000 years ago were really just like us.

Start your visit in the adjacent Iron Age Gallery where you can come face to (somewhat distorted) face – skin, whiskers, hair and all – with someone who lived in Roman Britain. This is Lindow Man, also known as Pete Marsh, who was found unusually well-preserved by the peat bog conditions at Lindow Moss, near Manchester, by peat cutters in 1984. He had suffered a violent death – strangled, throat cut and hit on the head – probably in the early 60s AD. Was he sacrificed to the gods or the victim of crime? Was Lindow in Cheshire a part of the province when he died or still beyond the Roman advance? We may never know.

Near him is a formal burial with rich grave goods from Welwyn Garden City dating to the end of the first century BC, midway between the invasions of Caesar and Claudius. This was a very different death from that of Lindow Man, and the amphorae of Italian wine, a silver cup from Italy and fine tableware from Gaul show how connected Britain was to the Mediterranean world at this time.

And then into the incomparable Roman Gallery with thematic displays. The Vindolanda writing tablets dominate that on literacy. These fragile thin wooden tablets, about the size of a postcard, with handwritten messages in ink, were preserved by the damp, anaerobic conditions at the Northumberland fort. They date to between AD 92 and103, and years of careful conservation, infrared photography and research have revealed the wonderfully mundane messages which speak across the millennia: 'please send more beer'; 'I could do with some warm socks' and 'do come to my birthday party', the latter signed by the wife of a nearby fort commander, and therefore the earliest surviving example of a woman's handwriting.

Amongst votive offerings from temples are lead curse tablets, which also provide insights into preoccupations of ordinary people. One from Uley in Gloucestershire asks Mercury to wreak vengeance by taking 'blood and health' from a glove thief.

Highlight of the Roman military display is the Ribchester cavalry helmet, complete with fear-inducing face, part of a hoard of military equipment found as a heap of corroded metal by a clog-maker's son in 1796. Another lucky child was nine-year-old Isabel Cutler, who found the magnificent silver tray known as the Corbridge Lanx in the bank of the River Tyne in 1735. The engraved scene is thought to depict the shrine of the sacred island of Delos, with the goddess Leto seated between her twin offspring Apollo and Artemis.

More shining wonders make up the Thetford Treasure of late Roman jewellery, the Hoxne Hoard of coins, jewellery and tableware, hidden at the very end of the Roman period, and the amazing Mildenhall Treasure of fourth-century silver vessels.

Some exceptional architectural pieces are displayed, including a whole fourth-century façade with an arched window aperture from Meonstoke in Hampshire which fell flat and survived horizontally. A fourth-century mosaic from Thruxton in Hampshire has Bacchus as the centrepiece and a number of personal names around the outside. From the villa at Lullingstone in Kent comes a painted wall panel showing fourth-century Christians with arms outstretched in prayer.

There are cases devoted to medicine, industries such as glass, pottery and metal, including the Snettisham jeweller's kit of the second century, and much, much more. Visit as often as you can to see the best of what has come from all the sites you will be exploring. Don't forget to continue into the Saxon Gallery to see objects from the very end of Roman Britain too.

Nearly everything in the gallery has been woven into a historic narrative, with excellent photographs, in a book called *Roman Britain* by BM curators Richard Hobbs and Ralph Jackson.

Lullingstone, Kent *****

Roman villa; museum. EH. Seasonal opening.

This is an exceptionally well-displayed villa with a complex history and fascinating finds. (Lullingstone Lane, Eynsford DA4 0JA). It lies in a river valley beside the Darent, and the setting is still peaceful and bucolic. Watling Street crossed the valley 5 miles to the north, and flat-bottomed boats could have taken goods along the river to the Thames estuary, so it was well-connected to markets.

The site was first discovered in the mid-eighteenth century, when fence posts were driven through mosaics. Excavation took place largely throughout the 1950s.

Its development followed the usual pattern of increasing wealth through the centuries, starting as a fairly simple house in the early second century, with three major phases of enhancement until by c. AD 360 it was a lavish mansion. The wall paintings and mosaics are exceptional, some of them here, others displayed in the British Museum. The site seems to have been abandoned after a fire in the early fifth century.

The latest phase unsurprisingly survives the best, and the rooms included a large central apsed dining room and audience chamber, with a mosaic depicting Europa being abducted by Jupiter, in the form of a bull. An inscription in the mosaic alludes to a fairly obscure passage from the *Aeneid*, perhaps the villa owner showing off his learning. All sorts of hypotheses, including a hidden Christian meaning, have been suggested.

Elsewhere, there is more overt Christian imagery, and indeed one of the rooms in the north-west corner of the villa has been interpreted as a house-church. A complex evolution from a second-century water cult, to third-century ancestor

Mosaic of Europa and the bull at Lullingstone Villa.

worship, to fourth-century Christian worship has been identified. Wall paintings in an upper room added in this late phase show six figures with arms raised in an attitude of prayer, as well as at least two Christian *chi-rho* symbols. This room ultimately collapsed into the cult room below, and these paintings were found in thousands of pieces, restored, and are now in the British Museum.

Two marble busts found in this part of the villa have been tentatively identified as portraits of Publius Helvius Pertinax and his father. Pertinax was governor of Britain in AD 175–6 and became Emperor for three months in AD 193, until he was murdered by the Praetorian Guard. This identification has led to the bold suggestion that the villa might have been owned by the family for a while, or at least rented by them.

Outside, behind the house, evidence for a mausoleum and a Roman-Celtic temple has been found. The former contained the body of a young man in a very fine lead coffin, with rich grave goods, all of which are displayed in the museum. A granary was identified to the east.

Lympne (Portus Lemanis), Kent *

Saxon Shore fort. Open site to view.

There have been tremendous changes to the coastline in this part of the world. You now park on the Royal Military Road where it meets West Hythe Road, Hythe (CT21 4NT), just north of the Royal Military Canal. The sea would once have been lapping at your feet on this spot, and Portus Lemanis would indeed have been on the shore, first as a base for the *Classis Britannica* in the early second century, then as a stone Saxon Shore fort in the third-century system protecting the south and east coasts. The maps displayed in the car park explain all.

The natural growth of shingle banks at the tip of Dungeness began the silting process, and the area became Romney Marsh, isolating the site from the sea. This spot remained on the frontline of defence against cross-channel invaders, and during the Napoleonic Wars, between 1804 and 1809, the Royal Military Canal was constructed, running for 28 miles (45 km) behind the marsh.

Walk about half a mile west along the accompanying Royal Military Road beside the canal and you will see the tumbled walls of the fort on a hill slope below the thirteenth-century Lympne Castle. The fort, sometimes known as Stutfall Castle, no doubt provided a lot of stones for this later replacement. You can walk up a footpath to the west of the fort to get a closer look at the big chunks of masonry, but it stands on private land which is inaccessible. The shape of the fort is hard to make out, as there has been a lot of slippage down the hill. It seems to have had a rather irregular outline with semi-circular bastions, suggesting that it was built in the late third century. It is far from being the most spectacular of the Shore Forts, but a visit helps to understand the late Roman defensive system.

Orpington, Kent ***

Crofton Roman Villa. Seasonal opening.

The remains of the villa, under its covering building, lie right next to the railway station in Orpington (Crofton Road, Orpington BR6 8AF). Indeed, the cutting for the railway destroyed part of it in the nineteenth century, but this went either unnoticed or unrecorded. In 1926 building work on driveways for the new council offices also cut through several rooms, leading to limited excavation. More was revealed in the 1950s, and in 1988 the surviving section was saved from being turned into a car park, excavated and preserved under the present building.

The original siting is difficult to imagine now, but it stood in open countryside, on a hill overlooking the River Cray, about 11 miles (17.5 km) from London. There was a simple farm here from the mid-first century, rebuilt in flint on chalk foundations in the mid-second century. It grew in size and grandeur, gaining heated rooms and a bath-suite, but suffered a decline in fortune during the third century, when the northern half of the complex was abandoned. The rest was left to fall apart after AD 400.

The foundations of parts of nine of the fifteen rooms can be seen, with a partially reconstructed hypocaust and flue. The plan of the whole rectangular house is prominently displayed, but the surrounding farm outbuildings have never been found. The site is well set up for children, with handling collections. It is the only villa to be seen inside the M25, though others have been found, and is an important part of the story of the Romans in this region.

Pevensey Castle (Anderida), East Sussex ****

Saxon Shore fort. EH.

Pevensey, like Portchester, is a massive Roman fort masquerading as a medieval castle (Castle Rd, Westham BN24 5LE). The fort was chosen by William the Conqueror as his base after his landing here in 1066. He created defences and a temporary castle within the surviving Roman circuit walls, and later entrusted his half-brother with converting it into a Norman stronghold. The inner bailey walls, towers, gatehouse and keep have various phases of work from the twelfth to fourteenth centuries.

The outer bailey walls are Roman, standing to virtually their original height, with a flint rubble core faced with small blocks of dressed greensand and having brick bonding courses. The circuit is remarkably complete apart from the south wall and a small section of the north wall, which have fallen.

The plan of the fort is unusually oval and asymmetrical, rejecting the standard playing card shape of earlier forts for one dictated by the lie of the land. Three of the Roman gates survive: the West Gate with monumental outer D-shaped towers, the smaller East Gate with a perfect Roman arch, and a small postern gate along the North Wall. In addition, eight projecting D-shaped bastions also survive in good order. It is thought that these would have been mounted with heavy artillery, probably *ballistae*.

The Roman curtain wall at Pevensey Castle.

Archaeological evidence suggests that the fort was built around AD 290, making it one of the six later forts listed in the *Notitia Dignitatum*, many of them with rather irregular outlines and with large rounded bastions.

Later generations adopted their own defensive systems against invaders to this 'Hell Fire Corner' of England, including the medieval Cinque Ports, the Tudor forts of Henry VIII and the Napoleonic Martello Towers. Second World War pill boxes and machine gun emplacements dotted amongst the walls graphically demonstrate the recent military importance of the site.

Portchester (Portus Adurni), Hampshire ****

Walls of a Saxon Shore fort. EH.

A walk around the curtain walls of Portchester gives you the most authentic view of a Roman fort available in northern Europe, justifying its claim to fame as the best-preserved fort in the region. (Seasonal opening, free access to walk around outside of walls.) The paths on the east and south sides take you close under the

Portchester Castle, Roman curtain wall with rounded bastions, Norman keep within.

walls, allowing you to admire their awe-inspiring height as well as the splendid view across Portsmouth harbour to the Solent beyond (Church Road, Portchester PO16 9QW).

This commanding position at the head of a large natural harbour made it an obvious choice for a stronghold, and it is the most westerly of the nine forts listed in the *Notitia Dignitatum* as being under the command of the Count of the Saxon Shore, built in the late third century.

The use of the fort at Portchester extended far beyond the Roman period. Life within the walls continued with the Saxons, and after the Norman Conquest the twelfth-century keep in the north-west corner was constructed. It remained a royal castle until the seventeenth century, was then a prisoner of war camp until the early nineteenth century, and a privately owned tourist attraction until 1984, when it came under the care of English Heritage. The church of St Mary in the south-east corner was founded in the twelfth century as part of a priory.

So what is genuinely Roman? Much of the outer face of the magnificent 20 foot (6 metre) high walls is third or fourth-century in date, particularly along the waterfront. These enclose an area of 9 acres (3.6 hectares) and were originally strengthened with twenty rounded bastions, one at each corner and four along each side, of which fourteen survive. There may originally have been a large earthen bank behind the walls, as in other Shore Forts, but now the back of the wall is exposed. One of two external ditches is still discernible as a moat on the north and west side. There are two surviving gates which have Roman origins: the Watergate in the east wall and the Landgate in the west, both of which were altered and narrowed.

Excavations between 1961 and 1979 found evidence of all aspects of Roman life within the walls, not just military, but everything you now see in the interior is an impressive mix of post-Roman features. The museum in the Norman keep tells the long history of the site. Recent work suggests there was a jetty to the north of the castle, where ships offloaded cargo.

The free walk around the outside of the castle allows you to wonder at the walls, smell the salty tang and imagine the turmoil of the third and fourth centuries. A climb to the top of the Norman keep gives the best view of the whole wall circuit with the harbour beyond.

Reading, Berkshire ***

Museum with Roman finds from Silchester, including bronze eagle and Ogham Stone, and other sites.

Reading Museum began as a wing of the imposing red and grey brick town hall in the centre of the town, opening in 1883 (Blagrave Street, RG1 1QH). It has a wonderful archaeology gallery, with finds from the Victorian excavations at Silchester (below) providing the stars of the collection. Two huge mosaics are displayed in the atrium, including one with a geometric design from the fourth-century church on the site.

Look out for the Silchester Eagle, made famous by its starring role in Rosemary Sutcliff's 1954 children's novel *The Eagle of the Ninth*. It is a second-century cast bronze statue 6 inches (15 cm) high, with wings missing. Once thought to be from a legionary standard, it is now considered to have been part of a larger statue group, possibly imperial, damaged and awaiting recycling as scrap.

Another object of great importance is the Ogham Stone, actually a 'dwarf' Roman column made of greensand, with a Latin inscription transcribed in Ogham script, consisting of groups of horizontal strokes on a vertical axis. This is better known in Wales and Ireland than in England, and it was used between the late fourth and sixth centuries. Found in 1893 in a blocked well in Insula IX, it was one of the reasons the Reading University team decided to explore this part of the site so thoroughly, since it was considered a potential clue in understanding the end of Roman Silchester.

Reculver (Regulbium), Kent **

Saxon Shore fort platform. EH. Open site.

About half the area of the Roman fort at Reculver has disappeared into the sea. All you see as you approach the site is the twin-towered west façade of St Mary's Church, now standing just above the water's edge, but actually close to the centre of the original fort platform. This was the parish church until 1805, when it was demolished, leaving the towers as aids to navigation. More of its foundations can be seen behind these (Reculver Road, Herne Bay CT6 6SS).

The coastline has changed in other ways too. The fort was constructed *c.* AD 200 on the northern edge of the Wantsum Channel, which separated the Isle of Thanet from the mainland. Roman ships could have travelled from here to Richborough, once on a promontory at the eastern end of this channel. By the twelfth century silting had left only a tiny river, which eventually closed completely, and after 1600 the land was drained and reclaimed as farmland. There is no sign of the channel now.

This was one of the three early Saxon Shore forts, along with Brancaster and Caister-on-Sea in Norfolk, which had a conventional square plan with rounded corners and a gate in the centre of each side. The core of the lower walls of the east side can still be seen quite clearly beside the track leading to the sea; the modern path leads the way through the East Gate. The north wall foundations, alongside the caravan park, survive and parts of the west wall can also be seen. The on-site information provides reconstruction drawings, and the site of the *principia* is also indicated. A fragmentary inscription was found here recording the construction of a regimental shrine and hall under the supervision of Fortunatus, probably the commander, between AD 210 and 240. Excavations in the 1960s also revealed two barracks blocks, each of which would have housed thirty-two men.

After the abandonment of the fort in the early fifth century, a monastic church was built out of the tumbled stones and tile in the seventh century, and this was then replaced in the Norman period by the church still visible in ruins today.

Richborough (Rutupiae), Kent ****

Site of early fortifications, settlement, Saxon Shore fort, museum and amphitheatre. EH. Seasonal opening.

Richborough is another east coast site where the topography has completely changed since Roman times (Richborough Road, Sandwich CT13 9JW). Today it stands in an isolated position surrounded by flat countryside, but 2,000 years ago it was a promontory joined by a causeway to the mainland, jutting out into the Wantsum Channel. The shingle banks at each end of the channel had already started to form during the Roman period, and by the sixteenth century the Isle of Thanet was absorbed into the mainland. The third-century fort here, together with Reculver (above), would have guarded the shipping lanes through the channel and received goods and supplies. Before that, though, it was important right at the very beginning of the Claudian invasion of AD 43 as a favourite candidate for the landing site, and it continued as the gateway into the province from the Continent. Watling Street led from here to London.

The site now is dominated by the standing walls of the later third-century Saxon Shore fort, with two ditches outside these. The walls survive in places to a height of 26 feet (8 metres), where the sentry walk would have been; the crenellated parapet would have stood above this. In most sections the rectangular facing stones have been robbed, but they do survive in some lower patches. Hollows in the walls were made by the medieval stone robbers, taking the conveniently cut stone

Remains of 1st-century arch, 3rd-century ditches and Shore Fort wall at Richborough.

for reuse, probably at nearby Sandwich. The east side of the fort disappeared off the cliff edge at some time before the fifteenth century, but the west side is complete, along with parts of the north and south. Foundations of hollow rectangular interval towers can be seen between the gates and corners, as can those of two of the solid rounded corner towers.

Within this curtain wall a complex series of features can be seen, representing more than 200 years of Roman history before the large stone fort was built. In the north-west corner are two parallel ditches, dug at the time of the Claudian invasion in AD 43. These originally ran for about a third of a mile (650 metres), extending beyond the fort walls in both directions, defending the invaders and their ships whilst a beachhead was established.

These defences were replaced later in the first century by twelve large rectangular granaries, two of which are marked out by concrete strips. Shops and living quarters soon followed, also marked out on the ground, as a thriving community grew up at this point of entrance for goods into and out of Britain. A large house, which became a *mansio* or inn with a bath-house, was built for official travellers.

Most spectacularly, a huge monumental arch was constructed in *c*. AD 85, now represented by its cruciform foundation in the centre of the fort. This was one of the largest arches in the Empire, probably visible from half-way across the English Channel. Fragments of its decorative cladding of white Carrera marble from Italy have been found, with scraps of bronze from statues that may have included a bronze *quadriga*, or four-horse chariot, right on the top. It would have provided a spectacular entry into the province.

In the mid-third century a set of triple ditches was dug around the arch, turning it into a military installation, probably a lookout tower to warn of raiders. Many of the buildings of the town were demolished at this time. About twenty-five to thirty years later the arch itself was demolished and the Shore Fort was built. One large piece of marble, displayed in the site museum, was reused as a gaming board; the rest was burnt in lime kilns to use in the concrete of the fort walls. A bath-house for this fort stood in the north-east corner.

The latest Roman building on the site is a baptismal font of a late Roman church in the north-west corner of the fort. To the east is the platform of a medieval chapel dedicated to St Augustine.

The **site museum** has some wonderful objects, a model of the arch, and explanations of the complex history of the site. As you arrive or leave, look out for the amphitheatre which survives as a low, unploughed earthwork to the south-west of the fort.

Rochester (Durobrivae), Kent *

Site of Roman bridge over the Medway; Guildhall Museum.

The Roman town of Durobrivae is pretty much invisible now, but it stood where Watling Street crossed the River Medway, at the lowest point where a fixed crossing was possible. When the Victorian 'old' Rochester Bridge was constructed workmen reported finding the piers of the Roman bridge, which would probably have supported a wooden superstructure. This crossing point, now carrying the A2 to London, was strategically important and may have featured in the early events of the conquest of AD 43. Some believe that one of the first battles between Britons and Romans took place here, often called the Battle of the Medway. The bridge is marked with an information panel, but you need to visit the **Guildhall Museum** (17 High Street) to see Roman remains.

Silchester (Calleva Atrebatum), Hampshire ***

Entire Roman town buried beneath fields of grassland; footpath around circuit of standing walls; amphitheatre. EH. Open site.

Calleva Atrebatum is that relative rarity in Britain, an entire Roman town with no subsequent building over it. The only structures now standing within its walls are Manor Farm and the twelfth-century St Mary's Church. Follow signs to Silchester Roman Town car park in Wall Lane (RG7 2HP).

The layout of the grid of streets beneath the grass, with thirty-seven blocks or *insulae*, appears as parch marks during dry summers, and has been captured by aerial photography. Surveys have produced more detailed data, and parts of the town have been excavated, but it all lies buried again now. A visit is, nonetheless, highly recommended to admire the sheer size of the town, and to explore the walls and amphitheatre, which are amongst the best-preserved in Britain. It is a lovely walk of 1.5 miles (2.4 km) around the walls, which still stand to a height of 13 feet (4 metres) in places. The amphitheatre lies beyond these on the north-east side. If you visit in the spring, you may see hares jumping around and during the summer months you might encounter an excavation team from Reading University, who have worked there since the 1970s.

The site once formed part of the Duke of Wellington's estate, and it was the rector of the 2nd duke who began excavations in 1864. His most famous find was the Silchester Eagle. Large areas continued to be opened and superficially explored, particularly between 1890 and 1909, by the Society of Antiquaries of London. Finds from these excavations are exhibited in Reading Museum.

Excavation sites through the twentieth century included the North Gate, amphitheatre, forum and basilica, but the big Reading University project was the complete investigation of Insula IX, over a period of eighteen years starting in 1997. Since 2014 the University has been examining a temple and bath-house in other parts of the town, in the hope that evidence of imperial favour for the town from Nero might be found. The results of all these excavations, directed by Prof. Mike Fulford and Amanda Clarke, form an impressive series of monographs.

Scant traces of the banks and ditches of an **Iron Age town** or *oppidum*, Calleva, established *c.* 25 BC, can be seen in the trees to the south-west outside the Roman walls. This covered an area of over 100 acres (40 hectares); the walled Roman civitas capital lies over much of this but does not match it exactly. The original occupants may have been Gaulish settlers who came to Britain with Commius,

Entrance to the amphitheatre at Silchester.

leader of the Atrebates, from Arras in France. By the first century AD the town is thought to have been the centre of the kingdom of the client king Togidubnus (or Cogidubnus), who may have had his palace at Fishbourne in Sussex (above).

The sequence of building revealed by the excavations in **Insula IX** started in the late first century BC with the largest Iron Age rectangular hall found in Britain. Finds included the earliest olive stone discovered on these shores, a clear sign of contact with the Mediterranean world.

The buildings were replaced by Roman military-style structures, which were burnt down after about twenty years, perhaps during the Boudican revolt. In the late first century AD a large town house was set diagonally to the town grid, and a complex series of buildings including shops and workshops followed on from this.

The defences consisted first of an earthen bank and ditch with stone gateways, constructed in about AD 200. The stone wall was constructed in AD 270, originally with an outer facing of flint and stone blocks. These were later removed for use as building stone elsewhere, and only the rubble and mortar core survives, nearly 10 feet (3 metres) thick at the base.

The amphitheatre was first built between AD 55 and AD 75, with the earth excavated from a circular arena forming the bank of seating, contained by a timber wall. This was rebuilt in stone in the third century, when the plan became more traditionally elliptical. It is now a peaceful site just outside the town walls, not far from the twelfth-century Church of St Michael.

Walmer Beach, Deal *

Modern plaque commemorating the site of Caesar's landing.

This is no more than a passing nod to the certainty of twentieth-century worthies who raised a monument to mark the spot where Caesar's forces landed in 55 BC (The Beach, Walmer CT14 7HE). The first marker was erected in 1946, 2,000 years after the event, and this was replaced more recently by a concrete plinth. There is no real evidence that this is the right place.

Winchester (Venta Belgarum), Hampshire **

City Museum; tiny bit of city wall; mosaic in Deanery entrance.

Venta Belgarum, the civitas capital of the Belgari, is thought to have been the sixth largest town in Roman Britain, covering 144 acres (58 hectares). However, its success as a Saxon and medieval city, the capital of Alfred the Great, has rather overwhelmed its Roman structures.

Just one tiny and rather sad fragment of the third-century Roman stone wall of the city survives on the east side near the City Bridge, behind an iron grille in a niche within the later city wall which follows the same course. The East Gate into the city was once nearby, but this was demolished in 1763. The medieval Westgate stands on the site of the Roman one.

One other glimpse of Roman Winchester can be seen in a small geometric mosaic in black, white and red, re-laid in the floor at the entrance of the Deanery, to the south of the cathedral.

The story of Roman Venta Bulgarum can be found in **Winchester City Museum** (The Square, Winchester SO23 9ES), where the settlement sequence beside the River Itchen is well explained. The Roman town was founded *c*. AD 70 on the floodplain of the river, which had been diverted by canalisation to run further to the east. In the third century the earthen boundary was replaced by a stone wall.

The museum displays some fine mosaics, from the city itself and also from Sparsholt Roman Villa, excavated in the late 1960s and reconstructed at Butser Ancient Farm (above). An almost-perfect geometric mosaic from this site is the centre-piece of the Roman gallery.

There are some exceptionally fine grave goods from a late Roman cemetery at Lankhills, just outside the city to the north, alongside the road to Cirencester. One skeleton is displayed, a young man who died in his twenties between AD 330 and 350. He had coins in his mouth to pay Charon, the ferryman over the River Styx, and hobnails beneath his feet, showing that he was buried with his boots on.

On the ground floor is a large model of the nineteenth-century city, which is very useful for seeing the lie of the land.

2

The South West – The Solent to the Lizard
Cornwall, Devon, Dorset, Hampshire west of the Solent, Isle of Wight, South Somerset, Wiltshire

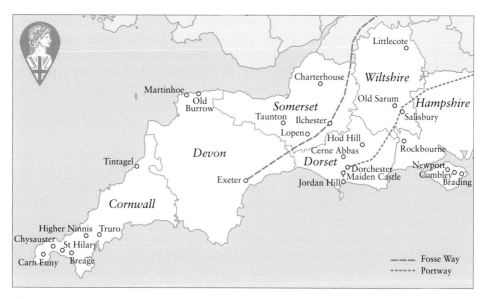

The South-West, the Solent to the Lizard.

The fertile rolling countryside of Wiltshire and Dorset and the mineral wealth of the south-western peninsula quickly drew the Romans into this region.

This branch of the three-pronged advance from the South East into the rest of Britain was led by the Second Legion Augusta commanded by Vespasian, which by AD 44 was moving through Dorset and south Somerset, establishing its fortress at Exeter by AD 55. There was opposition from local tribes, including the Durotriges of Dorset and south Somerset and the Dumnonii of Devon and Cornwall. The Roman historian Suetonius tells us that thirty battles were fought, and twenty settlements, two powerful tribes and the Isle of Wight (Vectis) reduced to submission.

Excavations and surveys have revealed a number of forts from this early phase of occupation, and just a few have visible remains for visitors today. The best place to see an early Roman military site is at **Hod Hill** in Dorset, where a fort built in AD 44–45 can be traced as an earthwork within the Iron Age defences. Fortlets or possible signal stations can be seen as earthworks at **Old Burrow** and **Martinhoe Beacon** overlooking the north Devon coast, and there may have been another at **Tintagel**.

Towns developed out of the civilian settlements (*vici*) that had developed around the forts, thriving on the trading opportunities, and when the soldiers moved on these continued to grow. Civitas capitals were also established as successors for nearby native settlements, with largely British populations. The best example in this region is **Dorchester** (Durnovaria), where impressive Roman structures are still visible within the modern town. **Exeter** (Isca Dumnoniorum) became a thriving town once the legion had moved on, and still retains much of its splendid circuit of walls. Roman **Ilchester** (Lindinis) and **Old Sarum** (Sorviodunum) are now pretty much invisible except for finds in museums, but the latter, in particular, is worth visiting for its nodal position on the road network.

Large numbers of villas have been found in the eastern part of this region, reflecting the wealth available through agriculture, and a few can be seen *in situ*. There are two very fine examples on the Isle of Wight (**Brading** and **Newport**), and a third marked by an interpretation centre (**Combley**). Wiltshire has **Littlecote**, with its wonderful Orpheus mosaic, and south-west Hampshire has **Rockbourne**. A beautiful narrative mosaic from a villa at Low Ham, Somerset, can be seen in **Taunton Museum**. An ambitious reconstruction of a wealthy villa at Castle Cary in Somerset is incomplete at the time of writing.

Traditional Roman villas do not seem to have been built in the far South West. Only one outlier has been found west of Exeter, at Magor Farm, Illogan, near Redruth in Cornwall (nothing visible; finds in **Truro Museum**). The settlements at **Chysauster** and **Carn Euny** at the tip of Cornwall show that people adopted a more hybrid form of Roman life in this corner of the Empire. Cornish tin was certainly being exploited, particularly in the third and fourth centuries and a road network was needed to support this trade. Lead was also mined in the Mendips, as can be seen at **Charterhouse**. It is well worth seeking out Cornwall's five inscribed granite pillars, often described as milestones, at **Breage**, **Higher Ninnis**, **St Hilary**, **Tintagel** and **Trethevy**.

You will also find artefacts from local excavations in museums at Topsham and Seaton in Devon, and Devizes in Wiltshire.

Brading, Isle of Wight *****

Roman villa and museum.

Brading is the most lavishly displayed Roman villa in this region and is one of the best in Britain (Morton Old Rd, Brading, PO36 0PH). A state-of-the-art cedar-clad structure covers the West Range, the most spectacular part of the large house, with raised walkways to allow a good view of the impressive mosaics. Significant finds from each room are displayed nearby. As you approach the modern entrance, look at the circular tower to the right, in the centre of the facing wall of the building which covers the villa – this indicates where the original entrance was, probably flanked by pillars, of which one is partly preserved.

Outside this building the positions of the North and South Ranges are marked. Before or after visiting the main structure, don't forget to look at the hypocaust of the North Range, which is protected within a small wooden structure. Recent excavations have explored further areas to the east, which are described within the West Range. The site thus provides not only a vivid glimpse of the luxurious lifestyle of the late Roman inhabitants, but also explains how the whole estate worked, beyond the main living quarters, and how it developed over time.

The situation chosen for the villa is a commanding one, looking out over a stretch of water between the main island of Vectis (Isle of Wight) and what was then a smaller uninhabited island to the east – now Bembridge and no longer an island. It is thought that the owner traded extensively with northern Gaul and beyond, as well as farming locally. The house began as a simple structure, built during the first century AD. This was gradually enhanced, enlarged and upgraded until its most magnificent phase in the fourth century. We don't know whether the same family owned it throughout.

The North Range, to the right of the path approaching the entrance, was where the early house once stood. It began as a simple aisled hall which was enlarged during the second century. A hypocaust for underfloor heating is still visible at its west end.

By the late third or early fourth century it had expanded to a large winged corridor villa with a central formal garden. The West Range, now under cover, was the main residential area. Elaborate figurative mosaics include a unique curious figure in room III with the head of a cockerel, dressed as a trainer either of gladiators or of wild beasts for the arena. The bones of a large cockerel were found nearby, and the central panel of the mosaic depicts the head of Bacchus. Was this a cult figure in a room used for offerings? More easily identified are busts of the four seasons, and characters from mythology including Orpheus, Medusa, Lycurgus and a philosopher. They make one of best assemblages of mosaics to be seen *in situ* anywhere in Britain.

Evidence suggests that this wealthy home was destroyed by fire, though whether this was accidental or caused by attacking raiders is not known. The buildings were still used after this, but the peak of luxurious living was over. By the late fourth century there were workshops in the main villa building, with corn-drying ovens dug through the mosaic floors. A family was living in the old aisled house in the North Range. Finally, even these were abandoned; human bones found in the rubble may suggest violence, or that the ruins provided a focus for a burial site.

The villa was rediscovered in the late nineteenth century, when children showed pottery they had found to a retired army captain, John Thorpe. He and a local farmer investigated further, finding the mosaic with the cock-headed man. A model of Captain Thorpe kneels near this mosaic in the covered display. The land was purchased by the Oglander family, who provided funds for covering and displaying the mosaics, modernised in 2004.

One more Roman villa of the eight known on the Isle of Wight can still be seen today, at Newport (below). There is an interpretation centre at the site of another at Combley (below).

Breage, Cornwall *

Inscribed stone.

This inscribed stone standing in St Breaca's Church (Helston, TR13 9PD) is one of five of late Roman date found in Cornwall. They all bear dedications to Emperors, but no mention of distance or destination. Although they are sometimes described as milestones, they may instead be a sign of imperial monopoly over the road exporting tin from the peninsula, or just a sign of loyalty to a reigning emperor.

The inscription, part of which is missing, reads:

IMP [...] DO NO MARC CASSIANO
For the Emperor [Caesar], our lord, Marcus Cassianus [Latinus Postumus]

It dates to the reign of the Emperor usually known as Postumus, AD 260–269, who seized power from Gallienus to rule the Gallic Empire for ten years. He was ultimately murdered by his own troops. This is the only stone from Britain found with an inscription to Postumus.

The granite pillar was first noticed in 1920, reused as a gate-post. It was brought into the church for safe-keeping, and now leans in the corner of the tower.

The church also has remarkable medieval wall-paintings, previously hidden for 300 years beneath whitewash. Two giant figures, of St Christopher and the Sabbath Christ surrounded by work tools, are particularly powerful.

Carn Euny, Cornwall ***

Settlement of Romano-British houses. EH. Open site.

This site, about 5 miles (8km) from Land's End as the crow flies, provides a wonderful insight into life in rural communities in the furthest corner of Roman Britain (Sancreed, Penzance, TR20 8RB). Don't expect columns, arches or mosaics; instead you can see the very diffuse version of the material culture of Rome that made its way to the tip of the South West peninsula. Chysauster (below) is another great example.

The remains of this remote walled settlement of stone-built houses lie on a hill slope beneath the Iron Age hillfort of Caer Bran. There is good on-site information. Excavations between 1964 and 1972 revealed activity from as early as the fifth century BC, and there was at least one Iron Age timber roundhouse beneath perhaps ten stone houses of the second to fourth centuries AD. Three of the houses were oval in shape, with a central courtyard, while the rest are simpler in plan.

Both Carn Euny and Chysauster have a *fogou*. These granite-lined underground tunnels, unique to Cornwall, may have been used as storage for food or other valuables, as a refuge in time of trouble, or even for some religious function. The Carn Euny *fogou* is one of the best-preserved anywhere and was found in the 1840s by prospecting tin miners, then excavated by local antiquarian William Copeland Borlase. The passage has a sinuous plan with a round central chamber of a beehive construction, walled with granite blocks and a corbelled roof with central opening. It is still possible to enter the structure, probably erected in the fifth century BC, with alterations made until the first century AD. The care taken with its elaborate construction makes a religious interpretation of some sort very tempting, although no evidence survives to confirm this.

Much later the ruins were utilised for pigsties and gardens, and the remains of a mid-eighteenth-century cottage can still be seen. To the west are two ancient wells believed to have healing powers, with trees adorned with modern offerings.

Cerne Abbas, Dorset *

Chalk-cut naked giant on a hillside.

The giant chalk-cut hill figure, 180 feet (55 metres) high, can be seen from a viewing area beside the A352 (Dorchester DT2 7AL), though there is no access onto the figure itself. It gets one star here, not because of any doubt about its spectacular nature, but because of uncertainty surrounding its date. There is no mention of it in the landscape before 1684, even though land surveys had taken place before then, whereas the Uffington White Horse is first mentioned in 1190 and 'White Horse Hill' even earlier.

Detailed surveys show that the giant has changed a little over the past 300 years. He carries a club in his right hand, but traces of a cloak which once hung over his left arm have only recently been noted, and this has strengthened the case of those who see him as a depiction of Hercules, and therefore of Roman date. Even if he does indeed depict the popular and well-known hero Hercules, he could, of course, have been created much later. The debate continues... In the meantime, he is well worth a look!

North-east of the giant's head is a series of earthworks called The Trendle, the date of which is also uncertain.

Charterhouse, Somerset *

Lead-mining site; earthworks of Roman fort and town; small amphitheatre. Open site.

This is a beautiful walk through an extraordinary landscape in the Mendip Hills, enhanced by the fun of trying to make sense of the many humps and bumps in the ground. It lies near Charterhouse Outdoor Activity Centre (BS40 7XR). Take the easterly road from the crossroads to a car park at Velvet Bottom.

Lead pig from Chewton Mendip with stamp of the Emperor Vespasian, in Taunton Museum. *Photo: Somerset County Council and South West Heritage Trust, 2019.*

Deposits of lead lay close to the surface here and were therefore relatively easily accessible. There is evidence that these were mined, not necessarily continuously, over more than 2,000 years, from before the Romans arrived until the Victorian period. Much of what is visible on the surface is from late periods of activity, but the Roman presence was identified from surface finds as long ago as 1819 by the Rector of Camerton, John Skinner, and surveys and excavations since have confirmed this.

Earthworks to the left of the path north from the car park have been identified as a Roman fort, although it is hard now to make out the rectangular shape. Excavations in the 1990s suggested that it was occupied during the first century AD, between the 50s and the 70s, and then activity shifted to a site further west in the Charterhouse Valley.

The processing and storage of metal is thought to have taken place here, guarded by the military. The lead was needed for water pipes, cisterns and lead coffins, and was also used to make pewter, and in the process of cupellation, extracting silver, so it was a valuable commodity.

Further along the northern footpath is a pool of water, and mounds of iridescent glassy waste, presumably from the nineteenth century.

Back at the crossroads near the activity centre, turn right to take the northern road. In the field to the left you will see further earthwork enclosures, identified as the site of a Roman town. Excavations here, in what is known as Town Field, took place in 2005 as part of the *Time Team's Big Roman Dig*. Although features were found in their trenches, these could not be excavated due to levels of contamination by lead, cadmium and arsenic! The town appears to have been abandoned at the end of the Roman period, although mining activity returned at various later times.

Turn first left into Rains Batch, and about halfway along the road on the left, viewable only from the road, is an oval earthwork with opposing entrances, clearly recognisable (with the eye of faith) as a small, neat amphitheatre. Since there has been very little exploration of this site, however, it is always possible that it has prehistoric origins.

The conclusive evidence of Roman activity here thus reveals itself on site only as rather muddled earthworks. Various lead ingots, crucibles and stamped lead weights of Roman date found in the region can be seen in Taunton Museum.

Chysauster, Cornwall ***

Settlement of Romano-British houses. EH. Seasonal opening.

This walled settlement is similar to Carn Euny (above), but the house remains are even more impressive, and Chysauster's particular claim to fame is the 'earliest identifiable village street in England'. It is well signposted, lying 4 km (2.5 miles) north-west of Gulval (TR20 8XA) and there is excellent on-site information and an interpretation centre.

The site lies on a slope below the Iron Age hillfort of Castle-an-Dinas and above the valley of Rosemorran Stream, surrounded by ancient field systems and with views to the sea. Occupation began in the late Iron Age, from perhaps 100 BC, but the ten large stone-built houses which can be seen today date from the second century AD, firmly within the Roman period. Some were abandoned by the late second century, but others continued into the third century, surviving for perhaps 100 years all told. Dwellings of this type and date have only been found on the Land's End peninsula and the Scilly Isles. The reason for abandonment is not known – perhaps some change in the local infrastructure and economy.

The houses have an oval courtyard plan, with rooms originally roofed with thatch or turf, surrounding a central open space. Stone-lined drains can still be seen in places, as can the paved surface of the street. Terraced plots outside some of the houses were perhaps vegetable gardens. Excavations between 1873 and 1939 produced spindle whorls, quernstones, whetstones, and Romano-British pottery, showing that

Romano-British walled settlement at Chysauster.

the economy relied on both sheep and grain. Imported pottery show that the inhabitants had Roman tastes. Finds can be seen in Truro Museum (below). A large block of granite found in one house has been interpreted as a weight to measure tin, which might have been panned from the neighbouring stream.

Near the site entrance a metal grill covers the entrance to a *fogou*. It may have originally been about 53 feet (16 metres) in length. There is a better-preserved *fogou* at Carn Euny (above), and between fifteen and twenty-five examples elsewhere in Cornwall.

In the nineteenth century a platform was built in House 7 for use by Methodist ministers, who were not allowed to preach in churches.

Combley, Isle of Wight (Vectis) *

Interpretation centre in a converted barn c. 1.5 km (1 mile) from the site of the villa. Seasonal opening.

Combley Roman Villa was officially discovered in 1910, and there were further excavations between 1968 and 1979, but the site was then covered over and there is nothing to be seen of it now. It showed the usual development from simple structure in the first century AD to larger farmhouse by *c.* AD 300. Several third-century pottery kilns may have played an important role in the production of 'Vectis ware'. A bath-house and a mosaic floor with a dolphin date to the fourth century.

The interpretation centre (Robin Hill Country Park, Downend Rd, Newport PO30 2NU) is mainly aimed at schools and visiting families but is worth including on a tour of the villas of Vectis – there are substantial visible remains at Brading and Newport, and this is en route between the two.

Dorchester (Durnovaria), Dorset ****

Roman town house; Maumbury Rings amphitheatre; Dorset County Museum; town wall; course of aqueduct; inscription in church.

Thomas Hardy based his fictional town of Casterbridge on Dorchester, saying of it 'Casterbridge announced old Rome on every street, alley and precinct. It looked Roman, bespoke the art of Rome, concealed dead men of Rome...'

Today's Dorchester cannot make the same claim, but the form and extent of the Roman settlement are unusually well-preserved because the walls were replaced by tree-lined walkways in the eighteenth century. You can therefore still discern the Roman boundaries on a walk through the town, and sometimes you will be proceeding along the ditch of the early defences. Within the compass of the walls lie the most complete remains of a Roman town house in Britain, and beyond them you can still see an entire amphitheatre and an aqueduct channel. Be warned, though, that these last two are earthworks rather than stone monuments, so don't expect the Colosseum or the Pont du Gard.

The Town House at Colliton Park, Dorchester.

The Roman name of the town, founded *c.* AD 70, has long been believed to be Durnovaria, although this is only based on a single mention in the *Antonine Itinerary*. The name does not include that of the local tribe, the Durotriges, but it is assumed that this was their tribal capital. There is likely to have been a conquest period fort here, to guard the strategic crossing of the River Frome.

Defences – An earthen bank was thrown up inside a wide ditch to enclose the 80-acre (32-hectare) settlement in the second century AD. The northern boundary was defined by the River Frome; the other three sides can be traced within the modern road system. Stone walls replaced the earthen banks around AD 300, but only one short stretch of the rubble and cement core is visible today on the east side of Albert Street, close to Thomas Hardy's statue. It survived by being incorporated into a garden wall, and an inscription records that it was given to the town by the aptly named Lucia Stone, in 1886.

The Roman town house – 'the most complete in Britain' – lies not far from the visible chunk of wall and is well signposted. It was excavated in 1937–8 prior to County Hall being built in the grounds of Colliton Park, in the north-west corner of the Roman town. Many of the structures now lie beneath the council offices, but the high-class fourth-century town house has been redisplayed beneath tile roofs and behind glass walls and can be freely visited at any time. Information boards describe the development from three individual units to an extensive single dwelling abandoned in the fifth century. There are fine geometric mosaics, rooms with hypocausts, and a kitchen. A number of infant burials were found (babies were commonly interred indoors), and the locations are marked.

The aqueduct was constructed not long after the town was established, to carry water from a source near Notton, following a meandering 12-mile (19-km) course along the river valley. The channel, originally *c.* 3 feet (1 metre) deep, can still be seen as an earthwork from the ramparts of Poundbury hillfort, on the western edge of the town. Occasional glimpses have been made of its course through the town including a site in Princes Street, behind the High Street, where a modern fountain with inscription now marks 'the spot where a Roman aqueduct delivered water into Durnovaria.'

The amphitheatre was constructed in the late first or second century. This was ingeniously created from a Neolithic henge, known now as Maumbury Rings. This would have been a part of the landscape south of the town for between 2,000 and 3,000 years, and it was a pragmatic way of providing a high-status monument for the new town. Excavations in the early twentieth century revealed that the Romans enhanced the circular bank, increasing the height from around 11 to 30 feet (*c.* 3.5 to 9 metres). They also lowered the floor level to make the arena, and constructed a timber walkway around it. The main entrance was to the north, with a smaller one to the south. It was later a Civil War fort, a place of execution, a gathering point (the Queen addressed the people of Dorset here in 1952), and is now an attractive grassy park, in which the banks are still very prominent, beside the road to Weymouth.

The Dorset County Museum in the High Street, Gothic-inspired and purpose-built, contains Roman artefacts from Colliton Park, and from other excavated villas in Dorset which are no longer visible, such as Dewlish, Bucknowle and Halstock. The prosperity of Roman Dorchester in the late Roman period is illustrated by fine mosaics uncovered at various points around the town, which were lifted and set into the floor of the museum after it was opened in 1885.

The displays include a model of the fourth-century Romano-British temple built inside Maiden Castle hillfort (below) and a display of skeletons from archaeologist Mortimer Wheeler's 'war cemetery' at this site, which he believed contained victims of the Roman siege on the Durotrigan stronghold. This idea has now been discredited, since the burials were made over a period of time, with proper local rites. One of the dead met his end by being shot through with a weapon often identified as a Roman ballista bolt, though doubt has now been cast on this too. The museum is due to re-open after refurbishment in 2020.

A burial inscription in St George's Church, Fordington, can be sought out for those who are keen. The dedication is 'Carinus, Roman citizen, aged 50, Rufinus and Carina and Avita his children, and Romana, his wife'. It has been dated to the mid-second century and was found in 1908 and reused as a foundation stone in the church porch. Since then it has been moved into the church and it can be found to the right of the door to the tower. A replica resides in Dorchester museum.

A possible Roman milestone was noted in the nineteenth century about 1 Roman mile from the east gate of the town, on the south side of the A35 near a roundabout giving access to Hollow Hill, Stinsford. The roughly cylindrical stone, 5 feet (1.5 metres) high, has no visible inscription, but the identification is based on its shape and size. It has been moved a couple of times since it was noted, and is supposed to still be visible, but proved impossible to find in 2019 amongst overgrown embankments and busy traffic.

Exeter (Isca Dumnoniorum), Devon **

City walls on Roman circuit with many later additions; Roman Gallery in the Royal Albert Memorial Museum, including the Seaton Down coin hoard.

The Second Legion Augusta established its fortress at Exeter by AD 55, at a strategic crossing point on the River Exe. An extensive infrastructure of supply and communications was necessary, and a fort discovered at Topsham, further along the estuary, with a larger supply base in between (beneath Exeter and Devon Crematorium on Topsham Road) were important elements of this. All these were revealed by excavation, but there is nothing to be seen on the ground now except occasional information boards.

The military had moved on by AD 75, and the area of the fortress was doubled in size to become a town. The site of the huge fortress bath-house, one of the most important in Europe, excavated in the 1970s just in front of the cathedral, became the town's forum basilica. This all lies carefully reburied for the time being under the cathedral green.

The town walls first consisted of an earthen bank and ditch constructed in the late second century, strengthened by adding a stone wall in about AD 200. It is still

The much-repaired and modified site of the West Gate of the walls of Exeter. Roman stretches can be seen nearer the Quay.

possible to walk around the entire circuit of 1.5 miles (2.3 km), nearly three-quarters of which can still be seen, with some of the missing parts laid out on the paving of the shopping centre, all well signposted. Part of the wall near the North Gate is accessible via a door and walkway from the Royal Albert Memorial Museum.

There has been much rebuilding and strengthening over the centuries, and you have to look for uninterrupted areas of rectangular blocks of grey/purple volcanic lava or trap for Roman facing work. One of the best stretches is towards the south-eastern corner of the walls, leading to the quay. Look out for a herring-bone pattern in the rubble and cement core for Roman internal structure. There were once gates at the cardinal points, but all were destroyed to improve access to the city between 1769 and 1866. The positions are marked by sign-boards or, in the case of the South Gate, by coloured stones in the modern pavement.

The Royal Albert Memorial Museum displays objects in its Roman Gallery from Exeter and Topsham, and also from villas at Seaton and Holcombe. The original of a beautiful first-century mirror from the latter is in the British Museum, but there is a replica here. Other finds range from a wooden tent peg, which would have been part of a legionary's equipment, found in the city, to a bronze furniture fitting with Achilles riding the centaur Chiron, found on Sidmouth beach. Another rare find is a little ceramic mother goddess suckling twins, also found in the city. A recent acquisition is the enormous Seaton Down hoard, the third largest in Britain (after Cunetio, near Mildenhall, and Frome, Somerset). Found by a metal detectorist, it comprises 22,888 bronze coins spanning the years AD 260–348, most of them from the reign of Constantine the Great.

Higher Ninnis, Cornwall *

Inscribed stone.

This is one of the late Roman inscribed stones found in Cornwall (see Breage above), this one standing in a private garden, so please contact the owners before visiting (Mynheer Farm, Higher Ninnis, Redruth, TR16 5HD; info@mynheerfarm.co.uk).

It was dedicated to the young Emperor Gordian III, thrust to power in AD 238 at the age of thirteen due to the political ambitions of his family. He died just six years later whilst campaigning in Mesopotamia, probably murdered by the army on the orders of his guardian. The inscription reads: IMP CAES ANT GORDIANO PIO FEL – for the Emperor Caesar Antonius Gordianus Pius Felix ('pious and fortunate').

The granite pillar was found in 1942 during ploughing, apparently almost vertical and therefore perhaps in its original position close to an old hollow way. It was moved to its current situation in 1946, set into a modern granite base in the private garden of Mynheer Farm, then the home of the finder, William Born. The best time to view it, by appointment only, with oblique sunlight across the inscription, is around 1 p.m.

Two minutes along the road is the rather spectacular site of the open-air preaching theatre of Gwennap Pit used by John Wesley in the eighteenth century, looking very much like a Greek bouleterion or council chamber.

Hod Hill, Dorset **

Roman fort visible as earthwork within an Iron Age hillfort. NT, open site.

The Iron Age hillfort at Hod Hill is one of the finest in Wessex, with well-defined ramparts and spectacular views over the valley of the River Stour and the rolling Dorset countryside. It is also, so far, unique in having an early Roman fort in one corner, the banks and ditches of which are still clearly visible at ground level. There is a small car park to the north of the hill, beside a minor road (Duck Street / Hanford Lane) off the A350 1 mile (1.6 km) north of Stourpaine, near Blandford Forum.

The best views of the juxtaposition between Iron Age and Roman forts are to be had from the air, early or late on a winter's day when the grass is short and the sunlight is low. However, the full scale of the earthworks and the fine situation are best appreciated by walking over them, with the added bonus of the views, the flowers and the butterflies. As you tackle the steepish climb from the car park, remind yourself that you will be soon be standing on the one of the best-preserved Claudian forts in Britain. It is not until you reach the ramparts on the north-west corner that there is any identification of the National Trust site.

Whether you follow the ramparts to the left or to the right you will soon see the earthworks of the rectangular Roman fort in this corner heading off into the interior – two, sometimes three, parallel ditches are clearly visible. It is easier to understand if you take a plan with you (the small National Trust notice does not include one, or indeed any information).

The defended settlement was first established *c.* 500 BC, with occupation intensifying after *c.* 50 BC. There seems to have been an attempt to strengthen the defences in AD 43 as news of the invasion reached the area, but work was not finished. The site is often identified as Dunium from a mention in Ptolemy's *Geography* of 'the Durotriges whose town is Dunium'.

Excavations by Sir Ian Richmond in the 1950s in the south-eastern corner of the hillfort revealed a marked concentration of Roman *ballista* bolts found in the area of an unusually large roundhouse. This was interpreted as focussed fire on the Durotrigan chief's dwelling during the Roman assault of AD 44. The lack of evidence for a prolonged attack led to the conclusion that Roman victory was swift, and an iron spearhead found within the large roundhouse sparked the suggestion that the chief did not even have time to grab his spear during the sudden and fearsome hail of superior weapons. Like the similarly dramatic interpretation of the 'war cemetery' at Maiden Castle this has now been challenged, and the bolts may be evidence of ballista practice, having been fired from the Roman fort at a later date.

Richmond also excavated part of the Roman fort, and identified the entire plan of the interior, including the *principia*, the *praetorium* and infantry and cavalry barracks blocks, the latter with stables attached. All were timber-framed buildings, identified by foundation slots cut into the chalk bedrock. The garrison is calculated as having been 600 legionaries and a 250-strong cavalry auxiliary unit. The Roman rampart was made of packed chalk, originally 10 feet (3 metres) high, enclosing 6.5 acres (2.6 hectares) within the 52-acre (21-hectare) Iron Age fort. The northern and western sides utilised the Iron Age ramparts. Outside the newer rampart on the southern and eastern sides were three ditches, the inner two with ankle-twisting slots in the bottom, with a wider platform between these and the third, all designed to hamper approach and departure except by the well-defended east and south gates.

Some habitation of the Iron Age hillfort continued after the fort was built, perhaps the local Durotrigan population taking advantage of the markets provided by the Roman garrison. The Roman fort was abandoned after just a few years, by *c*. AD 51, as the troops were required further north, and the rest of the settlement seems to have moved on too.

Ilchester (Lendiniae or Lindinis), Somerset *

Ilchester Museum; finds in Taunton Museum.

Ilchester was the most important Roman administrative centre in present-day Somerset, and the town signs proudly proclaim this as the 'Ancient Roman town of Lendiniae'. Excavations, chance finds and surveys have produced evidence for its status and development from native *oppidum* to fort, to port town, but nothing of its monuments can be seen today. You have to visit the town museum or go to Taunton Museum to see anything of its Roman past.

Its position on the important Fosseway meant that it became prosperous, with its peak in the fourth century after *c*. AD 320. Much reused Roman stone has been identified in the tower of St Mary's Church, and so many fine mosaics have been found locally that it is thought there may have been a Lindinis school of mosaicists, similar to those at Cirencester and Dorchester.

Ilchester Museum (High Street, BA22 8NQ) occupies just one room, arranged chronologically, so the Roman section is small. However, it tells the story well, and includes a complete female skeleton in a lead coffin from the very end of the Roman period, as well as a hamstone statue of Mercury found in the garden of Kingsham Farm House and used as a doorstop for many years.

Jordan Hill, Dorset **

Romano-Celtic temple (wall foundations). EH. Open site.

The remains of the fourth-century Romano-Celtic temple at Jordan Hill lie on a hill in the eastern suburbs of Weymouth, between a holiday park and nature reserve (Bowleaze Coveway, Weymouth DT3 6PL). There are still fine views out over Weymouth Bay, and also inland towards the South Dorset Downs. The vista includes large caravan parks and the 1808 chalk-cut figure of George III, a regular visitor to Weymouth but controversially shown here riding his horse away from the town, which was seen as a bit of a snub. Still, the rolling downs and the sea look good from up here, perhaps contributing to the choice of site.

The remains now appear very sterile and uncompromising, with the stone and concrete square of the wall foundations displayed within a fenced enclosure. However, excavations have shown that the rituals held here were complex and fascinating, attracting many devotees to the as yet unnamed deity. The notice board shows a reconstruction similar to the temple of the same date and plan in the hillfort of Maiden Castle, just 7 miles (11 km) to the north-west as the crow flies. The temple lies within a larger enclosure, about 100 feet (30 metres) square, but this can no longer be seen.

The first discovery was in 1812 when workmen found a pot containing silver coins. The dry summer of 1842 and resultant cropmarks then drew a local amateur archaeologist, James Medhurst, to the site, and he found the massive wall foundations. A flight of steps on the south side marked an entrance, and four Purbeck marble columns suggested there had been a portico. Fragments of these are now in Dorchester Museum. Four sacks of bulls' bones, including many horns, were found in the portico, presumably from sacrifices. Beneath the south-east corner of the temple a deep pit was discovered, lined with roof tiles and with sixteen layers of offerings separated by ash and roof tiles, each including the bones of birds (buzzards, ravens, crows and starlings) and a coin. Beneath these was a cist containing two urns, a sword and a spearhead. Many of the finds from Medhurst's excavations were acquired by Pitt Rivers, and are in the Pitt Rivers Museum in Oxford. At least two (a silver spoon and a bronze armlet) are on display in the second-floor gallery, at the far end from the entrance – you have to look hard amongst the thousands of objects.

In 1928, another hoard of more than 4,000 bronze coins was found nearby, most of them dating to the reign of Theodosius I (AD 379–395). Excavations in the 1930s north of the site revealed a cemetery of at least eighty bodies.

Littlecote, Wiltshire ***

Roman villa; Fourth-century Orpheus mosaic and Orphic hall.

The villa at Littlecote has a remarkable backstory of 'lost and found'. It was first discovered in 1727 by the steward of Sir Francis Popham, who owned the magnificent Littlecote estate with its wonderful Jacobean mansion. The eminent court artist George Virtue was commissioned to make an engraving of the Orpheus mosaic which was described as 'The finest pavement that the sun ever shone upon in England'.

For reasons unknown Sir Francis soon had the villa reburied and it was declared 'lost'. Thankfully it was rediscovered in 1976 and the then owner of Littlecote, Sir Seaton Wills of the tobacco dynasty, helped to fund comprehensive excavations and redisplay. Littlecote Estate today is owned by Mark Warner Holidays and the villa can be visited during hotel opening times. It lies to the west of the main house (Littlecote Park, Ramsbury RG17 0SU).

Roman activity at the site began shortly after the invasion of AD 43, probably safeguarding a crossing of the River Kennet. Occupation soon reverted from military to agricultural with a villa being established in the late first century. The estate evolved over the next two centuries, developing from simple timber buildings to sophisticated flint-built structures including a bakery, brewery, kitchens, stables, a smoke house and a two-storey house with an internal bath suite.

The Orpheus mosaic in the apsed room at Littlecote Villa.

Extensive modifications made in the fourth century included the construction of a huge twin-towered three-storey gatehouse and, *c.* AD 360, an elaborate three-apsed chamber with towers which housed the huge and magnificent mosaic depicting Orpheus. This building is unique in Britain and the earliest of its type in the Roman Empire. The excavator, Bryn Walters, interpreted it as a cult hall in what had become a pagan monastery.

The central panel of the mosaic shows Orpheus with his lyre, a popular mythological subject in Britain. Around him gallop Persephone, Venus, Leda and Demeter, riding a goat, a hind, a panther and a horse respectively, representing the four seasons. It has been dated to the period of the Emperor Julian the Apostate (AD 360–363), who attempted to revive traditional religious cults at the expense of Christianity, and it is therefore usually interpreted as showing the reach of the Emperor's pagan reforms. Much of the villa fell into decay around AD 400, shortly after the Emperor Theodosius outlawed pagan cults. Some activity continued, but the glory days were over.

The villa now, it has to be said, is in need of some conservation. The buildings and spaces are not as tidy as they once were, judging by the images in the excellent guidebook which is available at the hotel gift shop.

The mosaic is protected from the worst of the elements by a substantial roof but, alas, the tesserae were last seen covered in green mould and guano. Despite this the mosaic is spectacular and shouldn't be missed.

Lopen, Somerset *

Reconstructed mosaic panel in church.

The mosaic panel in All Saints' Church (Church St, Lopen, South Petherton TA13 5JX) is included here because it is a good illustration of how the Roman past can be commemorated, even when the structural remains have to be reburied. The church is tucked away in a peaceful location in Church Street, and the panel is set in the floor of an aisle between the pews.

In 2001 a digger driver working on a private access road noticed some tesserae in his spoil. The site was then partially excavated, revealing eight rooms of a villa dated *c.* AD 360. In one of these was one of the largest mosaics ever found in Britain, measuring 30 feet x 18 feet (9 x 5.5 metres), with decorative panels including a dolphin, a *cantharus*, flowers, leaves, saltires and guilloche. The site has now been carefully covered over again to protect the remains.

Some of the loose tesserae were given to the village and used to reproduce the panel with a *cantharus*, a device often used as an early Christian symbol. Although the panel is modern, the tesserae and the design are both Roman.

Maiden Castle, Dorset *

Romano-British temple wall foundations within an Iron Age hillfort. EH. Open site.

The glorious hillfort of Maiden Castle is the largest in Europe, gaining more fame when it starred in an encounter between Julie Christie and Terence Stamp in the 1970s film of *Far from the Madding Crowd*. It lies 1.5 miles (2.5 km) south-west of Dorchester near Winterborne Monkton (DT2 9EY).

It was once believed that the Durotrigan inhabitants had come into conflict with advancing Roman forces in the mid-first century AD (see Dorchester Museum above). However, recent investigations suggest that the glory days of the hillfort were over by *c.* 100 BC, and very few people were still living within the ramparts. There is no evidence of a Roman garrison inhabiting the site, but in the late Roman period, probably the fourth century, a temple of Romano-Celtic type was constructed inside the remains of the ramparts, suggesting that it still had some significance. The stone foundations can still be clearly seen, with a central square room within an outer square, likely to have been a passage.

A model in Dorchester Museum gives a clear idea of its appearance, and there is a reconstruction illustrated on site. The foundations of a two-roomed building nearby may have been the priest's house, and an oval hut, which was found to overlie an earlier Iron Age hut, may have been the shrine itself. Many offerings were found in both the temple and the shrine, including coins and statuettes. The deity is not known for sure, but it may have been a local god or goddess, perhaps conflated with a Roman one. A bronze plaque depicting Minerva found here may give a clue, but an alternate theory sees the cult as that of Mithras, a mystery religion popular with soldiers.

Martinhoe Beacon, Devon *

Fortlet, possible signal station (earthwork). Open site.

There is a spectacular walk to the fortlet at Martinhoe Beacon from the NT car park at Hunter's Inn (Barnstable EX31 4PX), along the coast path, with wonderful views out to sea towards the Welsh coast.

The earthworks here are less well-preserved than the one at Old Burrow (below), but the form, with a double-banked round-corned rectangular enclosure within a single-banked, roughly circular one, is very similar. This style of defensive earthwork may well have been the result of local Dumnonian influence. The outer bank on the northern side has suffered some erosion. Excavations in the 1960s revealed evidence for two timber barrack blocks within the inner enclosure as well as ovens. It probably housed a century of men, eighty in total. Evidence for fires that had been burned in the outer enclosure have been interpreted as the remains of signalling beacons. However, it remains a puzzle as to who would see the signals, as there is no line of sight to Old Burrow 8 miles (13 km) to the east, nor have any other beacon sites been found inland.

The excavators dated its occupation to *c.* AD 55–75, and thought that it was the successor to Old Burrow, but many now think that the two may have been contemporary. It could have been part of a defence system to monitor the movements of the Silures tribe from South Wales across the Bristol Channel or, more likely, general maritime approaches to Exmoor. Martinhoe has a view over the approach to Lynmouth, a likely landing ground, and Old Burrow (below) overlooks Porlock Bay, another good landing point.

Newport, Isle of Wight ****

Roman villa with bath-house and mosaics (seasonal opening); Newport museum.

The villa at Newport (Cypress Road, PO30 1HA) does not have the grand aspect of the better-known Isle of Wight villa at Brading, but the substantial remains of the bath-house and living rooms are well displayed, bringing the site to life.

Contained within an inconspicuous covering building, the site is set back from a residential street on the outskirts of Newport, with parking in the street. Outside the museum is a late Roman corn-drier oven, moved and reassembled from nearby Parsonage Farm, Newchurch, where it was found during ploughing. It might have been used for malting barley to make beer rather than drying grain prior to threshing for flour.

Inside, the displays are well set up for schools and families, with life-sized models of people in the bath-house and kitchen, reconstructions of furniture and food and good explanations of the various local building materials used for the construction.

The discovery was made when the foundations for a garage extension were dug in the 1920s. An excavation supervised by antiquarian Percy Stone revealed the tessellated floor with guilloche border and the hypocaust of a bath-house, both still visible. The dig was extended, revealing the full extent of the plan of the winged corridor villa.

The bath-house of Newport Villa on Vectis (IOW).

The bath-house is very well preserved, as is the chequered tessellated floor of a living room nearby. The wall-paintings are modern, devised from elements of designs from other sites on the Isle of Wight and elsewhere. Only residual traces of red paint were actually found on plaster at this site. The fire-place in this living room is based on excavated evidence, and it seems to have been a late addition to the room. Some of the living rooms had underfloor heating provided by the hypocaust system, which may have stopped working in the last years of the life of the house.

Beside the bookshop there are displays of finds from this site and others in the area, including the skull of a woman in her early thirties, found buried in the ruins of the villa.

A fifteen-minute walk from the Roman villa takes you to the **Guildhall museum** (High St, PO30 1TY), which tells the story of the Isle of Wight. A good range of Roman artefacts is spread through the various themed cases, including a little bronze dog found in 2005 which is similar to the one found at Lydney, Glos., and a coarse pottery sherd scratched with the name Alatucca – the only name of an inhabitant of Roman Vectis which is known to us.

Old Burrow, Devon **

Fortlet, possible signal station.

Spectacularly situated on high ground overlooking the Bristol Channel, this earthwork can be reached either by following a signpost and climbing from the South West Coast Path, or by parking at County Gates (Countisbury, Lynton, EX35 6NQ) and walking alongside the A39.

This is one of the best-preserved turf-built fortlets in Britain, and the earthworks are easily visible, comprising two concentric enclosures, the inner being a round-cornered rectangle formed from two banks, 87 x 93 feet (27 x 28 metres), with an entrance on the northern side. The outer bank is more rounded, formed from a single bank, 295 feet (90 metres) in diameter, with an entrance, which excavations showed to have been metalled, on its south-west side.

Excavations in 1911 and the 1960s dated the occupation to a short period in the mid-first century, probably by auxiliaries supporting the Second Legion Augusta at Exeter. Post-holes within the interior suggested that accommodation was in tents, and the remains of a large clay field oven behind the southern rampart is presumably evidence of catering arrangements. This had been repaired at least once, indicating there was a garrison for more than one season. It may have predated Martinhoe Beacon, but is more likely to have been contemporary, both monitoring the access points to Exmoor from the Bristol Channel, in this case Porlock Bay.

Rockbourne, Hampshire **

Roman villa foundations including bath-house and mosaics. Seasonal opening.

Only a small part of the spacious villa at Rockbourne can be seen today, but a good impression of the original layout is provided by the wall lines of many of the house's forty rooms, marked out in gravel on a flat lawn. It is the only one of the forty or so villas known in Hampshire which can be viewed *in situ*, so this, its lovely aspect, and the array of finds make it worth a visit (Rockbourne Rd, Fordingbridge, SP6 3PG).

Discovered in 1942 by a farmer digging out a ferret, the site was purchased by local estate agent and antiquarian Morley Hewitt, who devoted much of his life to uncovering it. Most of the site was later backfilled, preserving it for posterity. Hewitt personally funded a site museum to display the artefacts found at the site, later modernised to tell the story of the villa and its excavations, and how it fits into the broader picture of Roman Hampshire. Episodes such as the discovery of a hoard of 7,717 bronze coins in a New Forest pottery jar, buried in about AD 305, and the excavation of deep wells, helped by the British Sub-Aqua Club, are well told. There are also tableaux explaining different aspects of villa life, such as bathing, dining and trading.

Out on the site the wall foundations and floor of the hypocaust, the *frigidarium* with mosaic and a late octagonal plunge bath of the East Baths can be seen. Next to it is the mosaic of the dining room in the North Range with a labyrinthine meander design. The villa's development from circular Iron Age hut to modest rectangular farmhouse to full courtyard plan by *c*. AD 250 is explained on site. There is also a well-kept Roman garden, with plants known to have been cultivated at this date.

The villa was abandoned *c*. AD 420, but two intriguing skeletons of later date were found during the excavations, both males of about forty. One may have been

Mosaics in the North Range of Rockbourne Villa.

killed by a falling roof when the ruins were no longer sound; the other, who had survived a hole being cut in his skull (trepanation), perhaps to relieve the pain of a deformed jaw, was buried face down in a shallow grave, presumably also at a time when the site was a remote ruin.

Salisbury, Wiltshire ***

Salisbury and South Wilts Museum; Old Sarum settlement and probable fort.

The Salisbury and South Wilts Museum (The King's House, 65 The Close, SP1 2EN) lies in a prime position next to Salisbury Cathedral, the spectacularly spired successor to the Norman cathedral at Old Sarum, below. Head to the Wessex Gallery for the archaeology, where it is admittedly hard not to be distracted by the incredible prehistory of the region. Even the Romans were impressed by Stonehenge, as the rubbish left behind by tourists of the period has shown.

The cases of Roman finds from Wessex should not be overlooked, however, particularly those describing the excavations by nineteenth-century archaeological pioneer Pitt Rivers at some of the rural settlements. He had exquisite 3-D models created of his digs at Rotherley, Bokerley Dyke and other sites to explain his techniques. These were acquired by Salisbury from his original museum at Farnham, Dorset, when that collection was broken up in the 1970s.

Several cases are devoted to the important New Forest pottery industry, explored and beautifully illustrated in the early twentieth century by Heywood Sumner. More recent finds include a third-century stone sarcophagus from Amesbury, which contained a woman and child; a coin and ring hoard from Bowerchalke and several beautiful metal vessels found near Kingston Deverill. A high-quality mosaic with a central cantharus with dolphin handles came from the remains of a villa at Downton in the 1950s. These are all important reminders of the wealth of the Wessex countryside in the Roman period.

The spectacular site of **Old Sarum** (Sorvoidunum) lies nearly 2 miles (3 km) to the north of Salisbury, in Castle Road (SP1 3SD). This was the centre of settlement from about 400 BC until 1226, when the new cathedral was established at its present site in the city centre. What you see now are the impressive ramparts of the 30-acre (12-hectare) Iron Age hillfort, the eleventh-century Norman motte with outer bailey and the excavated foundations of the first cathedral and cloister of the twelfth century.

There was a Roman settlement here too, outside the ramparts to the east, but nothing of this date can be seen now. The name Sorviodunum has been identified from the *Antonine Itinerary*. It was an important node on the Roman road network, at the meeting point of five major roads to Winchester (Venta Belgarum), Silchester (Calleva Atrebatum), Mildenhall (Cunetio), Badbury Rings (Vinocladia) and westwards towards the River Severn via the Mendip Hills. Occasional Roman events are held within this English Heritage site, so you may strike lucky and see legionaries and auxiliaries going through their paces.

St Hilary, Cornwall *

Inscribed stone

The most complete of the five Cornish inscribed stones (see Breage above) stands in St Hilary Church (School Lane TR20 9DQ). It was found built into the fabric of the church when it was rebuilt after a disastrous fire in 1853, and was then reset into the floor on the left as you enter the church.

Dedicated to Constantine I (the Great), between AD 306 and *c.* 312 when he was ruling as Caesar in the west, it reads:

IMP CAES FLAV VAL CONSTANTINO PIO NOB CAES DIVI CONSTANTI PII
F AUGU FILIO

For the Emperor Caesar Flavius Valerius Constantinus Pius, most noble Caesar, son of the deified Constantius Pius Felix Augustus

Near the altar are painted panels by artists of the famous Newlyn School (1920s), depicting Cornish saints and martyrs. There is a fine Cornish cross in the churchyard.

Inscribed stone
with dedication to
Constantine the Great
in St Hilary Church.
Photo: Dot Smith.

Taunton, Somerset ✳✳✳

Museum of Somerset: Low Ham mosaic; Frome Hoard; stamped lead ingots from Charterhouse.

The Museum of Somerset is housed in the lodge of Taunton Castle (Castle Lodge, Castle Green, TA1 4AA). The Roman section lies mostly along the first floor gallery, which offers a marvellous view of the prize exhibit, the Low Ham mosaic, on the ground floor below.

Flagged as 'the oldest object in Britain to tell a complete story', it has five narrative panels, telling the tale of the doomed love affair between Aeneas and Dido, queen of Carthage. The central panel depicts Venus, who orchestrated the whole episode.

The story of Dido and Aeneas told in a mosaic from Low Ham Villa. *Photo: Somerset Archaeological and Natural History Society and South West Heritage Trust, 2019.*

Projected wall images conjure up an impression of the Roman villa, and a film explains both the story of Dido and Aeneas, and the finding of the mosaic in 1938, when a farmer digging a hole to bury a sheep came upon the first tesserae. Excavations from 1946 to 1955 showed that the mosaic came from the *frigidarium* in the bath suite, dating from about AD 340.

Upstairs are finds from some of the many other villas in the county, including Pitney and East Coker, and the Roman town of Lindinis (Ilchester). Note especially the fourth-century skeleton of a forty to fifty-year-old woman buried with her dog.

There are also several coin hoards. Most spectacular is that from Frome, consisting of 52,503 coins, mostly bronze but five of silver, making it the second biggest hoard found in Britain, and the largest in a single container (the largest, from Cunetio, near Mildenhall, was in two containers). The coins have a date range of AD 253–305, with just over a quarter minted under the central Roman Empire, more than half under the Gallic Empire, and the latest, about 5 per cent, under the renegade British Emperor Carausius, thus encapsulating the history of the second half of the third century.

Also displayed are important finds from the Roman lead mines in the Mendips, including an ingot, or 'pig', with a stamp of the Emperor Vespasian (AD 69–79). Roman features can still be seen at the former mine at Charterhouse on Mendip (above), albeit only as earthworks.

Tintagel, Cornwall *

Two inscribed Roman stones; facsimile of Artognous Stone; earthworks tentatively identified as a Roman signal station.

The spectacular rocky outcrop at Tintagel is one of the most famous sites in Britain, indelibly linked with the legend of Arthur in spite of the lack of factual evidence. The post-Roman village and medieval castle dominate the site, but artefacts found over the years suggest that there was activity here in the Roman period too. Only a few traces from this time are visible, hence the single star rating, but they are worth noting if you are in the area. You do not have to enter the main site to see them.

In the EH visitor centre at the entrance (Castle Rd, Tintagel PL34 0HE) is a facsimile of the famous slate 'Artognous Stone' found here, the original of which is in Truro Museum (below). The earlier Roman part of the inscription reads MAXE, and it has been tempting to see this as a mention of the Maxentius who ruled from AD 306 to 312, co-emperor of Licinius, who is mentioned in the inscription now in the church, but this is far from certain.

A ten-minute walk from the site to the **Church of St Materiana** affords wonderful views over the island and passes some humps and bumps in the ground just outside the churchyard. One area between the churchyard wall and the cliff edge has been tentatively identified as the site of a Roman signal station.

Inside the church, in the south transept, is a stone which was removed from the west churchyard wall, where it had apparently been used as a coffin rest and reap-hook sharpener until 1888, when it was brought into the church for safety. The inscription reads IMP C G VAL LIC LICIN – the name of the Emperor Licinius who was murdered by order of Constantine I in AD 324. The stone has the same possible interpretations as others from Cornwall (see Breage, above), and at nearby Trethevy (below).

A short drive of 1.5 miles (2.4 km) north-east takes you to **Trethevy**, still within the parish of Tintagel. Close to the Church of St Piran, visible in the outer face of the wall of St Pirans House, is another Roman inscribed stone. This one reads IMP C DOMNI N GALLO ET VOLVS, thus naming the Emperors Gallus and Volusianus, who ruled together from AD 251 to 253.

Truro, Cornwall ***

Royal Cornwall Museum: Roman artefacts from Cornish sites.

The museum is housed in two nineteenth-century buildings (a bank and a chapel), making a wonderfully imposing frontage and a fine space for telling Cornwall's story (25 River St, Truro TR1 2SJ).

The Archaeology Gallery is on the ground floor, and the Romano-British section has objects which show that Roman culture was very much in evidence right to the south-west tip of Britain, even if there is not much to see on the ground. The plentiful resources of tin must have been a big draw, and administrators, workers, guards and supplies would have been necessary to ensure its removal and transport.

The excavations at the fort at Nunstallon, to the west of Bodmin, are well-represented by finds and photographs. Occupied from perhaps AD 55 to AD 75, it was then dismantled as its occupants moved on. A stone ornament in the shape of clenched hand was found in 1964 in a stream below the fort. Was this placed at the entrance to the fort to symbolise Rome's power over the locals? A potent symbol if interpreted correctly. The richest finds came from the fort commander's latrine, including a belt, knife, rings and brooches.

The most south-westerly villa so far identified lies at Magor, near Redruth. Excavations in 1931–2 revealed a small winged corridor villa inhabited between *c.* AD 150 and 300, the latest phase perhaps associated with nearby mining activities. The original owners, probably locals, had clearly adopted some aspects of Roman architecture and décor, including painted wall-plaster with a simple design of red tulip or lotus buds and tessellated flooring. There is also information here about Chysauster and Carn Euny (above).

The coins on display have been boosted by recent metal detector finds. The St Levan II hoard, found in 2015, contains 179 copper alloy coins from AD 69–261, perhaps brought over from Gaul as a group of discarded coins ready to be melted down to reuse the metal.

In the post-Roman display is the original piece of slate from Tintagel inscribed with the name Artognous. This inspired cries of 'Arthur!' when it was found, but scholars have pointed out that in the sixth century Arthur would actually have been written as 'Artorius'. At the top of the stone are parts of four larger letters, possibly MAXE, rather crudely inscribed at an earlier Roman date.

On the first floor there are displays of the Romans, Greeks and Egyptians in the Mediterranean world, and the wonderful prehistoric galleries include artefacts from the Bronze Age made of Cornish gold. There is as yet no evidence that the Romans exploited this too, but perhaps it was not worth their while with more plentiful sources in Wales.

3

The Cotswolds to the Great Ouse
Bristol, Bucks, Gloucestershire, Herefordshire, Northants, Oxfordshire, North Somerset, Worcestershire

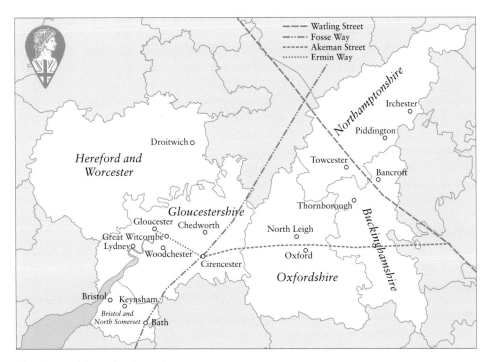

The Cotswolds to the Great Ouse.

The lush farmland of the Cotswolds and the Malvern Hills, across to the wide upper valley of the Great Ouse, ultimately became one of the wealthiest areas of Roman Britain. The Romans wasted no time in advancing in this direction, with the Twentieth Legion Valeria Victrix ('brave and victorious') establishing a fort at Kingsholm near Gloucester by *c.* AD 49/50. There was a brief halt when, according to the historian Tacitus, a frontier was established in the early years along two rivers, traditionally believed to be the Trent and the Severn. The line lies along the Fosse Way, later a great Roman road linking the fortresses at Exeter and Lincoln, and still a major routeway today, running straight through this region. It is not thought to have been a frontier in any physical sense, and onward campaigning soon made it redundant.

The final battle of Boudica's rebellion was fought somewhere along Watling Street, either within this region or in Shropshire, at the head of a valley carefully chosen as a bottle-neck, according to Tacitus, exact site unknown. Various locations between **Towcester** (Lactodorum), Northants, and Mancetter (Manduessedum), Warwickshire, are favourite contenders. The story is well told in **Towcester Museum** of the confrontation between perhaps 230,000 Britons, who became too tightly packed in the narrowing opening, and 10,000 soldiers led by Suetonius Paulinus.

The Twentieth Legion moved on to Chester, and it seems likely that the Second Legion Augusta moved up from Exeter to establish a fortress at Gloucester (Glevum) between *c.* AD 66 and 74, before ending up at Caerleon, which was better placed for campaigning in Wales. No sites representing this military phase are now visible in this region, although excavation have revealed plenty and there are finds in **Gloucester Museum**.

By perhaps the AD 80s **Gloucester** (Glevum) had become a *colonia*, a chartered town with a population that included retired legionaries. This and **Cirencester** (Corinium) were the most important settlements in the western part of this region, the latter being the second largest Roman town in Britain and the capital of the late third-century province of Britannia Prima. Both have some interesting though rather piecemeal remains to visit (including a fine amphitheatre at Cirencester), and good museums, particularly at Cirencester.

Bristol was not a Roman town, though there was a settlement and probably a fort at **Sea Mills** (Portus Abonae), where the River Trym meets the Avon. There is also scattered evidence of villas, at **Kings Weston** to the north-west, and **Keynsham** to the south-east, where there is also thought to have been a small town called Traiectus.

Bath (Aquae Sulis) is the most spectacular Roman spa establishment in Britain, famed for its hot healing springs and elaborate temples dedicated to the water deities. A second heyday in the Georgian period and multiple excavations have resulted in fabulous displays, making it the most visited Roman site in this region. Another temple complex, dedicated to Nodens, can be seen at **Lydney**, Glos. This site also has evidence of mining for iron ore, an important resource in both the Iron Age and the Roman period.

Another natural resource was the salt deposits extracted at Droitwich in northern Worcestershire, from natural brine springs that were as salty as the Dead Sea. The story is told in the Salt Museum there, and more salt towns are described in Chapter 5.

Some of the wealthiest villas in Britain have been found in the Cotswolds. The grandest and best-preserved is that at **Chedworth**, Glos., but there are others well worth visiting at **Great Witcombe**, Glos., and **North Leigh**, Oxon. More of Roman Oxfordshire can be seen in the Ashmolean Museum in **Oxford**.

The villa with the most spectacular mosaics, including the largest of those depicting Orpheus, lies buried and invisible under a churchyard in **Woodchester**. Another wonderful Orpheus mosaic can be seen in Cirencester Museum, and there is one *in situ* at **Littlecote** in Wiltshire (Chapter 2).

In the eastern part of this region you can see the results of extensive excavations at **Piddington Villa**, Northants, in its site museum, and **Bancroft Villa**, Buckinghamshire, is laid out *in situ* for visitors. Not far from here, at **Thornborough**, lies the most westerly of the huge Roman burial mounds which occur more frequently in East Anglia (Chapter 4).

Bancroft, Bucks ***

Roman villa, reconstructed wall foundations including garden; mosaic displayed in Milton Keynes shopping centre.

Walk through North Loughton Valley Park (MK13 0RA) from the car park off Constantine Way, and you will see the low walls and garden of the villa laid out amongst flower beds. These are the reconstructed foundations of the last stage of the house, dating to the fourth century.

The villa site at Bancroft was discovered in 1971, when the Development Corporation of the new city of Milton Keynes employed many archaeologists to monitor the vast building programme for remains. Excavations at the site continued then into the 1980s, making it one of the most extensively examined villas in the UK. It lies in the fertile valley of the meandering Great Ouse, and indeed one of the many tributaries runs through the North Loughton Valley Park, making a green, open setting for the site. A sequence of farmhouses was discovered, from an Iron Age settlement further up the hill to an elaborate fourth-century mansion with formal gardens, thus following the familiar pattern of increasing wealth and elaboration in the Romano-British countryside.

On-site information explains the development from the late first century on. The first winged corridor house was destroyed by fire *c.* AD 170, and a mausoleum or temple was added during the second century, uphill from the main house (now under the Blue Bridge housing estate). A larger house was constructed in the third century, and in about AD 320 this was given a larger, enhanced bath-house, and geometric mosaics were laid in many rooms. The formal garden in front of this has been replanted, including a substantial rectangular fishpond, and a small hexagonal shrine to the south.

A geometric mosaic from a small room adjacent to the principal bath suite can be seen on the wall of Central Milton Keynes Shopping Centre, 3 miles to the south-east: by entrance North 9, alongside Queens Court, in Deer Walk.

Bath (Aquae Sulis), NE Somerset *****

Roman temple and baths around a hot spring, museum.

No exploration of Roman Britain is complete without a trip to the baths, and these are so good that they named the town after them (Stall St, Bath BA1 1LZ). The excellent *Essential Roman Baths* guidebook describes the site as the 'most dramatic public building of Roman Britain' and in terms of surviving architecture, atmosphere and presentation it is hard to argue (although the London Mithraeum might give them a run for their money).

It is also probably the most visited Roman site in Britain, with no restriction on numbers at any one time, so choose your time if you can. Early or late in the day is best, and in the summer you can visit by torchlight late into the evening, which adds to the drama. If you are jostled by multi-national crowds, just tell yourself that this is an authentic Roman experience, as people then travelled far and wide to take the waters and visit the shrine of Sulis Minerva, and the place would have bustled. The audio guide is excellent and is included in the entry fee.

At the centre of it all is a natural phenomenon – the spring of water gushing forth at 46°C (115°F) at a rate of 250,000 gallons per day, rich in minerals and dissolved iron, causing orange staining wherever it flows. The water is colourless when it emerges from the ground, but sunlight and heat encourage algae to flourish, so that the pools, which are now open to the air, have a disconcerting bright green hue. In Roman times they would have been roofed, which would have lessened this effect.

The Great Bath at Bath, still lined with lead from the Mendips.

The Dobunni tribe of the late Iron Age worshipped the deity of the spring as Sulis, who was believed to have curative powers and wisdom when dealing with human problems and dilemmas. The Romans related this deity to their Minerva, and inscriptions suggest that these names became interchangeable, appearing both separately and together. Two contrasting images have pride of place in the museum: a carved stone head with staring Celtic eyes, and snaking hair and beard, which came from the pediment of the temple in 1790, and a gilded bronze head of a woman in Roman style found nearby by workmen in 1727. The former is often presented as Sulis, but it may be a Gorgon, or Oceanus, Neptune or Sol. The latter is likely to be Minerva, as the evidence suggests she once had a tall Corinthian helmet which was her identifying headgear. It may be the head of the life-size cult statue which once stood in the temple. Together they epitomise the cultural fusion of this deity.

Highlights in the museum include the many offerings made to Sulis Minerva and excavated from the spring, including about 14,000 coins, pewter, silver and bronze vessels perhaps used for drinking the water or pouring libations and, most intriguing, messages inscribed on a sheet of pewter or lead, then rolled up and thrown into the spring. Most are curses, asking the deity to inflict horrible punishments on wrongdoers, often including a list of suspects.

As you follow the signs around the baths and museum, it is important to remember that the remains are from many periods. The bath and temple developed on both sides of the sacred spring from fairly simple structures of about AD 75 to something far more elaborate, with many heated rooms and sophisticated treatment areas, by the fourth century. The museum starts with helpful models of both the first and fourth-century complexes. All fell into decay and ruin during the fourth century because of both political and natural instability. Flooding of the River Avon blocked the drains and hypocaust systems, and eventually repairs and maintenance were abandoned.

The spring continued to flow, however. Evidence suggests that the Saxons took advantage of the waters and by the twelfth century the structure known as the King's Bath had been formed within the shell of the Roman reservoir pool over the hot spring, which was then within the precincts of a monastery. A legend, first penned by Geoffrey of Monmouth in the twelfth century, took hold about a legendary Prince Bladud discovering the spring and founding the baths. Look out for his statue and accompanying inscription in the King's Bath today, dated 1699, although the statue is believed to be earlier than that.

The eighteenth century saw a second heyday for the spring, with doctors recommending drinking the water for internal conditions. The first Pump Room opened in 1706, and the first discoveries of Roman remains are recorded from 1727. Major excavations in the later nineteenth century sparked a restructuring and grand opening of the Roman Baths in 1897. The statues of the Roman Emperors overlooking the Great Bath date from this time. Further excavations in the twentieth century revealed much more, and the displays are stunning.

The waters in the King's Bath and Great Bath are no longer considered safe for bathing, as health issues brought this to an end in 1978. You can, however, luxuriate in a modern spa pool using the same hot spring water nearby, built at the same level as Bath Abbey's roof, with wonderful views.

It is enough, though, to stand beside the Great Bath, on original paving worn by Roman feet, beside a hefty lead pipe with folded seam still embedded into the surface, hearing the gushing of the spring nearby. The bottom of the pool is still covered with rectangular lead sheets from the Mendips to seal the hot water in and cold groundwater out, only visible during maintenance clean-ups when the pool is emptied.

There is nothing to be seen of the town which developed around the shrine and its healing cult. Architectural fragments suggest that there might have been a theatre to the north of the temple, and more bath buildings, but no evidence of a forum or basilica has ever emerged. There may have been Roman town walls underlying the later medieval walls and extending to the bank of the River Avon. One tiny glimpse of a black and white mosaic with a Greek key pattern *in situ* used to be possible in the basement of what was once the Royal Mineral Water Hospital – known locally as the 'Min' – to the north of the Roman baths. The site is now being redeveloped into a luxury hotel.

Bristol **

Sea Mills house foundations; Kings Weston Villa; Bristol Museum and Art Gallery.

It may seem surprising that the great port of Bristol was not a Roman city, but its heyday came later as a strategic starting point for voyages to the New World. Excavations in the city have, however, produced scattered evidence that areas of Roman settlement lie beneath the busy streets, a few of which can still be seen.

At **Sea Mills** some low wall foundations, probably of a house, lie fenced in on the east side of the Portway (A4) where it joins the aptly named Roman Way. It has long been known that there was a settlement here called Portus Abonae, towards the western end of the Avon Gorge at the confluence with the River Trym, about 3.5 miles (6 km) north-west of the current city centre. It is a likely spot for a fort, the *vicus* of which grew into a substantial settlement, and work by the Sea Mills Archaeological Research Team continues. Stop by the wall foundations and walk down Hadrian Close to the rivers Trym and Avon, where you get a good idea of the layout of the land and the importance of working with the tides for river-borne traffic. More remains have been found in the allotments nearby, though they are not visible. The ruined harbour wall across the Trym dates from the early eighteenth century.

Kings Weston Roman villa lies not far from Sea Mills, to the north-west, at Long Cross, Bristol BS11 0LH. It is fenced and locked, but the key can be collected any time (in exchange for a deposit) from nearby Blaise Castle or Bristol City Museum.

This is the best surviving Roman building within the area of modern Bristol, found when a housing estate was built in 1947. George C. Boon, later an eminent Roman archaeologist, at that time a young Classics student at Bristol University, noticed the remains of the villa when it had already been partly destroyed, and it became his first excavation. It is still well cared for and partially covered and the useful site information boasts that it includes the only Roman baths in Bristol.

The villa was built about AD 270–300, and various additions and alterations were made before it was abandoned in the late fourth century. The room foundations exposed to the elements include a living room with underfloor heating, with the

Living quarters heated by a hypocaust at Kings Weston Villa, Bristol.

remains of the furnace still visible. The skeleton of a fifty-year-old man, killed by two blows to his head, was found amongst the *pilae* of the hypocaust. Rather than being a Roman murder victim worthy of a Falco story, he was left there after the villa had been abandoned, either in the immediate post-Roman period or the eleventh century.

The site hut covers several well-restored geometric mosaics, one of which is from another probable villa found at Brislington in 1899, used to replace the original much more damaged mosaic from this room. Beside this lies part of the sole Bristolian Roman bath, although the hot part of the suite with hypocaust and furnace was destroyed when the Long Cross road outside was built.

The facilities and explanations cater primarily for school parties, but it is an interesting and well-cared-for glimpse of the Roman landscape beneath the modern housing estate.

The only Roman objects currently on display at the **Bristol Museum and Art Gallery** (Queens Rd, Bristol BS8 1RL) are the 11,460 coins of the early fourth-century Thornbury hoard, found when digging a pond in a back garden in 2004. One of the largest hoards found in Britain, it has a case to itself in the first floor gallery. Everything else from the region, including some marvellous mosaics, remains in the museum stores at present.

Chedworth, Glos. *****

Roman villa with mosaics; museum. NT.

Chedworth villa must have been one of the most impressive stately homes of the late Roman Cotswolds. The beautiful setting, substantial remains, and its history since a gamekeeper digging for his ferret discovered it in 1864 make it unmissable (Yanworth, near Cheltenham, GL54 3LJ).

The Victorian
Museum at
the centre of
Chedworth Villa.

The house was built at the head of the peaceful wooded valley of the River Coln, where there was a natural spring which was incorporated into the design as a *nymphaeum*. The peaceful landscape and views today have not changed much, and a woodland walk up the slope behind the site provides a good overall view in winter, when the trees are bare.

A simple house was built here in the later second century AD, consisting of three detached buildings of a few rooms each and a small bath-house. More than a century later, especially during the period AD 330–380, these were extended and enhanced to form the North and South ranges and the West Wing, the plan of which can be seen today.

In the West Wing, reception rooms and a bath suite with beautiful mosaic floors have been protected within a wooden building, with walkways for easy viewing. Most of the mosaics are geometric in design, but one has mythological figures, including the four seasons in the corners, of which spring, summer and winter survive. This was probably the dining room floor, arranged so that the lively figures could be admired from the communal dining couches. Underfloor heating would have kept the dinner guests cosy.

A gap between the West Wing and the North Range allowed the monumental *nymphaeum* over the spring to be seen from the upper courtyard of the villa. Next to it is another suite of baths, then a long range of rooms whose function is not clear.

The South Range is not completely excavated, but included a kitchen with a latrine opening off it – a common Roman juxtaposition, simplifying water supply and drainage. This part of the complex had timber framed walls in the upper part, which burnt down in the second century to be later rebuilt and extended.

The eastern extent of the complex has not been uncovered.

A decline in lifestyle is evident during the fifth century, with fires lit on mosaic floors and increasing use of the fine rooms for agricultural purposes. It was finally abandoned before AD 600, and over the centuries the walls were robbed for their stone, perhaps for building Cassey Compton House 2 miles (3 km) to the north and probably also to feed a seventeenth-century lime kiln making mortar, also found north of the villa.

The tesserae picked up by the gamekeeper in 1864 were shown to James Farrer, uncle and guardian to Lord Eldon whose family owned the land. He organised workmen to clear the site in the summer of 1865, uncovering everything that is currently visible in a rapid and less-than-perfect way. The Victorian museum in the centre of the site was built that same year, with the innovative idea of displaying their finds on-site, and leaving the structures and mosaics *in situ* for visitors to view. Farrer also investigated the area beyond the villa itself and found two structures believed to be shrines or mausolea, but these are no longer visible.

The site passed to the National Trust in 1924, bought by public subscription for £2,500. Further twentieth-century excavations helped to sort out the building sequences missed by Farrer's men, and excavations are still ongoing.

Cirencester (Corinium Dobunnorum), Glos. ****

Roman town with stretch of wall beside the River Churn; basilica marked out in the modern road; re-erected column base; amphitheatre; Corinium Museum.

Cirencester rather grandly calls itself the 'capital of the Cotswolds', but its considerable charm lies in winding streets, traditional houses and tiny tucked-away arts and crafts shops, rather than any sense of splendour. In the Roman period, however, Corinium

Orpheus Mosaic and Jupiter Column in Cirencester's excellent Corinium Museum. *Photo: Dot Smith, published with kind permission of Corinium Museum.*

Dobunnorum was the second largest town in Britain, at 237 acres (96 hectares), after Roman London which covered 300 acres (134 hectares). Impressively grand architecture, mosaics and wall-paintings of a very high standard have been revealed by excavations over the years, from wealthy houses and public buildings.

During the fourth century Corinium is known to have been a major centre for the manufacture of mosaics. The workshop sites have not been found, but their beautiful products have been identified as locally made. Skilfully worked objects of metal, bone, leather and stone also indicate that there was wealth and patronage for the craftsmen here, no doubt coming from the lush and productive countryside in this part of the world. Perhaps the modern art and craft shops here provide a faint echo of life 2,000 years ago.

In order to see this material wealth and learn the town's history you have to visit the truly excellent **Corinium Museum** in Park Street, as there are only a few fragments of the Roman town left *in situ*. The museum sells a Roman Town Trail guide, which is very useful for hunting these down.

During the Iron Age this was the territory of the Dobunni tribe, who had a major settlement 4 miles (6.5 km) to the north at Bagendon and centres for rearing horses around Lechlade and Fairford to the east. An equine presence continued into the Roman period, as in AD 43 a Roman fort was constructed to house a cavalry unit of 500 men. Two tombstones of cavalry troopers in the museum give us details of Dannicus, from the Raurici tribe (Switzerland), who served for sixteen years, and Sextus Valerius Genialis, from the Fresian tribe (northern Germany), who served for twenty years.

The fort was first built to the west of Watermoor Road, but was moved in AD 49 to firmer ground slightly to the east. It was abandoned in AD 75 when the military moved north, and by AD 80 the civitas capital, Corinium Dobunnorum, was established over the remains of the fort and its *vicus*. A large forum was constructed, now commemorated by the Forum Car Park and shopping area which stands approximately over the site. The main central crossroads of the Roman street plan can still be appreciated from the corner of Lewis Lane and Tower Street. The exceptional Jupiter Column which is displayed in the museum, with carved heads of the followers of Dionysus or Bacchus amongst the Corinthian foliage, was found near here in 1838, and is thought to have once stood in the forum.

The town continued to prosper, and when Britannia was subdivided into four provinces at the beginning of the fourth century, Corinium was made capital of the south-western province, Britannia Prima. This heralded a century of great wealth, coinciding with the rich villas in the Cotswold region and the markets they created for mosaics and other sophisticated goods. During the fifth century, though, its fortunes declined as nearby Lechlade became an important Anglo-Saxon settlement.

The basilica, which opened onto the south side of the forum, was partially constructed over the fort site. It had to be rebuilt in the late first or early second century because the first structure had subsided into the ditches of the fort beneath. The line of its curved apse has been laid out in the road of a cul-de-sac off The Avenue, which helps to orientate the Roman to the modern street plan. This was a very grand building; in the museum look out for the lower half of a Corinthian capital, claimed to be the largest found in Britain, found in 1808 on the basilica site. A good artist's reconstruction is displayed nearby on the museum wall. Another nod to the columned glory of the forum area at the site itself is a column base, looking a little forlorn, re-erected in 1962 by a local business in Hooper's Court on South Way.

The town defences were constructed towards the end of the first century, consisting at this stage of a clay and gravel bank formed from the upcast of a ditch, which was then used as a dyke to divert the River Churn on the eastern side of the town. About AD 140–160 the bank seems to have been heightened to 10 feet (c. 3 metres) and faced with turf, then in the late second century a series of stone gates were inserted, along with interval towers, and the circuit extended all around the town. The north-east Verulamium Gate and the south-west Bath Gate no longer survive, but their position at each end of Lewis Lane, which follows the line of one of the main Roman roads, can still be appreciated. During the third century a stone wall was inserted into the front of the bank. A stretch of wall can be seen beside the River Churn in parkland just north-west of Verulamium Gate. This is the Abbey Grounds behind the Church of St John the Baptist, and the Roman Wall is signposted.

The museum opened in 1938, replacing an earlier museum constructed nearby by the Earl of Bathurst to house two wonderful mosaics, the Hunting Dogs and the Seasons, found in 1849. These are still given pride of place in one of the best Roman exhibitions in the UK.

It is certainly one of the best places in the UK to see mosaics. The second-century Seasons Mosaic, displayed within a furnished room setting, still has five of its original nine octagonal panels. Figures include personifications of spring, summer and autumn, as well as Actaeon being attacked by his own hunting dogs as a punishment for spying on the naked Artemis. A splendid Orpheus mosaic displayed on the wall was found at Barton Farm in Cirencester Park, outside the city walls. The subject of Orpheus charming all the animals with his lyre was a speciality of the fourth-century Corinium mosaicists, with the unusual feature of having the animals arranged in a circle around Orpheus with their feet facing outwards, so that some are the right way up whichever way you are looking.

The military beginnings of Corinium also feature, with burial inscriptions and associated films expanding the imagined lives of the deceased. There is a marvellous array of stone carved deities, especially the cloaked *genii cucullati* and mother goddesses who were so popular in Britain. A famous acrostic graffiti scratched onto second-century painted wall-plaster may also have religious significance. The words read the same across, down and backwards – the straight translation is 'Arepo the sower holds the wheels by his effort', but the fact that the letters of 'Pater Noster' are present twice over have sometimes given rise to a Christian interpretation.

The amphitheatre lies outside the line of the walls to the west, beyond Bath Gate. It is completely covered with grass now, but the elliptical form is still very clear. It was constructed in the early second century, first of timber with dry stone walls. In the later second century this was replaced with a mortared masonry structure measuring about 160 x 135 feet (49 x 41 metres). Around the site Roman quarry scoops can be seen, which were used both for building stone for the town and also for the upcast used for the banks of seating. These areas were later used as cemeteries.

Droitwich (Salinae), Worcestershire *

Salt Museum; Saint Richard's House Heritage Centre.

Droitwich is situated on massive deposits of salt, resulting in brine as strong as the Dead Sea. As with Northwich, Middlewich and Nantwich in Cheshire (Chapter 5), the suffix of the name denotes a salt town, and this is another laying claim to the Roman name of Salinae.

The charming but small **Salt Museum** (22 Victoria Square, Droitwich WR9 8DS) explains the Roman exploitation of this valuable resource, needed for food preservation as well as flavour. Several artefacts found in the area illustrate this, including a Roman barrel in very good condition. Originally a wine cask, the barrel had been put to later use as a salt pan. Also on display are a number of burials, some with facial reconstructions, from the Hampton Road cemetery.

An early wooden fort was built here *c.* AD 60, with the evidence suggesting it was only occupied until AD 68 as military operations moved north and west. A fine section of mosaic from a grand Roman villa built around AD 150 at Bays Meadow is also displayed, and it is possible that the villa owners may have been in charge of the salt production.

The saltwater was employed in more recent times for its health-giving properties, believed to be exceptionally good for aches and pains, especially in the joints. **Saint Richard's House** (WR9 8DS), now the town museum, was the 1930s entrance to a brine baths spa complex, but sadly the buildings behind have now been demolished. A caged-off reconstruction of a medieval salt pit can be found in the nearby Vines Park.

Gloucester (Glevum), Glos. **

Museum of Gloucester with Roman wall in situ; East Gate foundations and wall in Viewing Chamber; finds display in bank.

The Romans were first drawn to the site of Gloucester by its position beside the River Severn, at a point providing a crossing to Wales and the wild west. A *vexillation* fortress, smaller than one for a whole legion, was constructed soon after AD 49 by the Twentieth Legion at Kingsholm, now a northern suburb of Gloucester dominated by its rugby stadium. For some reason, perhaps flooding by the river, this was dismantled around AD 66 and a new fortress was built further south, probably by the Second Legion which had advanced from its base at Exeter (Isca).

When the legion moved on, the site became a thriving Roman town with the status of *colonia*. An inscription found in Rome suggests that this happened when Nerva was Emperor, between AD 96 and 98. Recently this relatively 'good' Emperor was granted the honour of a modern bronze equestrian statue erected in Southgate Street, outside the entrance to the Eastgate Shopping Centre, thanks to a campaign started in 1997, 1,900 years after the foundation of the *colonia*. The full name may have been Colonia Nerviana Glevensis – Glevum for short.

Guided tour of the Eastgate Viewing Chamber, Gloucester, where the Roman wall supports Boots the Chemist above.

The later fortress and the town lay exactly where the city centre is today. Northgate, Westgate, Southgate and Eastgate streets pretty much follow the lines of the main Roman roads, although Westgate has migrated slightly to the north, and Southgate has been extended. Excavations, particularly during the 1960s and 1970s when the shopping centre was being constructed, revealed many glimpses of the Roman town beneath, and small parts can still be seen today.

The Museum of Gloucester in Brunswick Road (GL1 1HP) is the best place to start your visit. A section of the lower courses of the stone city wall is displayed *in situ* in one of the rooms. Another section is visible outside, not far away (below). This replaced earlier earth and timber defences in the AD 80s and high status, beautifully cut Cotswold stone rectangular blocks were used. There is also a timber post on show from the legionary fortress, preserved because it was waterlogged. Two inscribed stones, one a building inscription, the other a tombstone, mention the Twentieth Legion Valeria Victrix, which has led to the suggestion that this legion was based here. There is also a tombstone to Rufus Sita, a horse-trooper who served with the Sixth Cohort of Thracians for twenty-two years. Many beautiful objects of pottery, glass and metalwork are displayed, but keener archaeologists will find the lack of any contextual evidence frustrating, even though the overall story is told well. A corner of a fine mosaic can be seen (the rest is under the carpet!).

A three-minute walk from the museum will take you to a **viewing chamber in Eastgate Street** comprising a glass panel set in the street, beneath which can be seen part of the city wall and one tower of the East Gate of the town, both of which have Roman foundations. The shape of the opposite tower is laid out in coloured stone in the pavement nearby. The best way to see this is on a guided tour, led by a legionary solder who will take you down into the chamber. These happen only occasionally, so ask at the museum for details. A larger section of the beautifully cut Roman wall can be seen, one part of which manages to support the multi-storey Boots store above, the top stone having been cut in the 1970s to provide seating for the metal beam. Many layers of the city's history are visible here.

The only other display available for the very curious is a rather old case of artefacts inside the **Royal Bank of Scotland** at 1 Westgate Street. Found during excavations on the site, they include a rather nice steelyard, or weight balance – quite apt for a bank.

Great Witcombe, Glos. ✳✳✳

Roman villa wall foundations. EH. Open site except bath-house locked.

The villa at Great Witcombe scores highly for its tranquil location, set on a hillslope with wonderful Cotswold views to the south-east. Ermin Way, a short stretch of Roman road between Gloucester and Cirencester, passes less than a mile away. A minor sign-posted road leads from Cirencester Road (heading south-east away from Brockworth) to the car park (GL3 4TW), and there is a short walk uphill past a farm to the villa site.

As you draw near, the sound of running water mixes with the birdsong – particularly apt as the abundant springs in this hillside have attracted people to live here from an early date.

The beautiful Cotswold setting of Great Witcombe Villa.

The walls visible now were largely revealed by the first excavations in 1818, when the site was discovered after the removal of a large tree. There were further investigations in 1938–9 and 1960–72, and consolidation and rebuilding work has allowed the site to be left open. The locked buildings over the bath-house have been reconstructed several times since the nineteenth century.

The villa scores less well for information, as there is very little in the way of signs, just one rather faded notice with a reconstruction painting, which it is just possible to relate to the visible walls. These comprise two wings, each with a number of anonymous rooms, joined by a corridor or gallery which had a tessellated floor, though all surfaces are now covered with gravel. Half-way along this was an apsed room, later converted to an octagon, which may have been a dining room with fine views. Much of the complex would have been at least two storeys high. There was a small detached bath-house beside the south-west range which was later enlarged and incorporated into the main building. The *frigidarium* had a mosaic floor with fish and sea creatures, now covered by a locked building, and nothing can be seen by peeping through the slats.

Iron Age finds showed activity here before the first villa was constructed around AD 200–250. Alterations and modifications continued throughout the fourth century and possibly into the fifth, when it was abandoned. These probably reflect not only a growing standard of living, but also repairs needed because of damage from all the water running through the site.

Surveys by Cotswold Archaeology has shown that the walls we see were only a small part of the whole estate. The villa complex had an enclosing courtyard which extended some way down the slope of the hill, and there was a further range of structures. These include pottery and tile kilns, probably a metalworking area, as well as a possible temple or cult site, perhaps associated with the water, and perhaps a water mill or canalisation of the stream. These peaceful ruins once stood at the heart of a bustling range of activities reflecting the wealth of late Roman Britain.

Irchester, Northants *

Site of Roman town.

Part of the land occupied by Chester Farm (NN8 2DH) was once an important crossing point of the River Nene, and the field to the south of the river has long been known to conceal ruins of a Roman fort, later replaced by a small walled town. This lay on a critical north–south route, and the high status of the walled town may have been because this was the *cursus publicus*, the imperial mail route. A tombstone found here commemorated an imperial official who was a supplier for the imperial mail system.

The last remnants of the stone walls were removed in the eighteenth century, and the town sleeps peacefully beneath the grass. Geophysical survey and excavations have revealed a busy town plan, and there is a major project underway to have walks and exhibitions laid out at Chester Farm to interpret this landscape. This is one to keep an eye on, as leaflets with the walks are available in the car park, but the site itself was closed in 2019.

Keynsham (Traiectus?), NE Somerset **

Roman villa information in Durley Hill cemetery; rebuilt parts of Somerton Roman villa at old entrance to chocolate factory; mosaics under glass at Keynsham Civic Centre.

More and more evidence is showing that there was a thriving Roman community at Keynsham, between Bristol and Bath. The remains of at least two wealthy houses have been uncovered in the past, and the site has been tentatively identified as the town of Traiectus, which is listed in the third-century *Antonine Itinerary*.

Under **Durley Hill cemetery** (entrance off Durley Hill, BS31 2AT) lie the remains of a very large **Roman villa** which was found and much disturbed during the digging of graves and mortuary chapels in the nineteenth century. It was partly excavated in the 1920s, after further remains had been found at the site of the Fry's chocolate factory (see below), and continuing work by the Bath and Camerton

Europa and the bull mosaic from Durley Hill Villa, displayed in Keynsham Civic Centre. *Photo: Dot Smith, published with kind permission of Bath and North East Somerset Council.*

Archaeological Society is revealing evidence for a huge complex, probably with a temple attached to it, dating between *c.* AD 265 and 375. There is only an information board now, amongst the peace of the Victorian and later graves, with a faint hope that part of the villa may be uncovered for public view in the future.

Another complex of buildings nearby, once known as the **Somerton Roman villa**, was discovered in the 1920s when the Fry's chocolate factory, a major Keynsham landmark, was being constructed. It was partially excavated and rather than change the site of the factory, the Roman walls were lifted and moved 300 yards south of their original position to a site just inside the factory gates. Fragments of mosaic and other items were once exhibited in a small museum in the factory, which closed completely in 2010 to be replaced by a large housing development called Factory's View. The road names reflect the Roman past beneath them: Claudius Road, Hadrian Close, Titus Way. The reconstructed walls, with rooms of the villa labelled and identified, are still there inside the gates of the development, at the junction between Keynsham Road and Somerdale Road, just north of Keynsham railway station, alongside architectural fragments of the now-demolished Keynsham Abbey, and memorials both to twentieth-century wars and also to Joseph Fry who started the business here. This is a tranquil corner to ponder Keynsham's past.

Recent surveys in fields nearby show that there is much more as yet unexplored, which may be the town centre of Traiectus.

Mosaic panels from the Durley Hill villa can be seen under glass in the Keynsham Civic Centre (5 Temple St, Keynsham BS31 1HA). Pictorial scenes include Europa and the bull, Achilles hiding amongst the daughters of King Lycomedes and Athena/Minerva reflected in a pool with her double pipe.

Keynsham once had a lot more Roman material on show, as an important Orpheus mosaic was once displayed in the floor of the railway station. Found at Newton St Loe when Brunel's railway was being constructed, it was lifted and laid in the station floor in 1841. Lifted again some years later, it now resides in the stores of Bristol Museum and Art Gallery.

Lydney Park, Glos. ***

Temple complex (wall foundations) and museum. Seasonal opening.

The temple complex at Lydney Park (GL15 6BT) is one of very few Roman religious sites in Britain where there are still visible remains, where the setting is sufficiently unchanged to feel the spirit of the place, and where we even know the name of the deity who was worshipped – Nodens. It is an immensely intriguing site, with complex rituals revealed by early and therefore rather unscientific excavations.

The site lies on a hill which was also an Iron Age promontory fort, with views down to the River Severn, within a spacious park in private ownership since the reign of Charles I. Herds of deer roam freely below, and the rhododendron and azalea gardens along the stream in the valley are beautiful in the spring.

The Bathurst family acquired the estate in 1719, and showed immediate interest in 'Dwarf's Hill', so-named because the area appeared to be a labyrinth of walls and tunnels. Ancient artefacts were revealed whilst hunting for building stone, and in

1805 excavations were carried out by the owner, Charles Bathurst, published many years later, in 1879, by his son. There was a further programme of excavations in 1928–9 carried out by Mortimer and Tessa Wheeler, by which time it was clear that the hill was the site of a 4.5-acre Iron Age promontory fort, as well as mines for iron ore from the Roman and/or the pre-Roman period and a Romano-British temple complex dedicated to the god Nodens. The finds in the museum in the house are from the nineteenth and early twentieth-century excavations. The most famous is a small, exquisite bronze model of a dog, lying down and looking back over its shoulder, now used as the symbol for the park.

The Wheelers were investigating a much-disturbed site, and the stratigraphy was further confused by the fact that parts of the complex had collapsed into both a natural 'sink hole' formed by underground water erosion and an old iron ore mine. Their conclusions on chronology were: Iron Age hillfort from about 100 BC; a Romano-British village for the miners of iron ore during the third century AD; construction of the temple complex in about AD 364–7.

A re-examination of the evidence in the early 1980s, particularly looking at the 8,000 or so coins found, revised this sequence. The idea of the miners' village was rejected and the temple complex was re-dated to the mid-third century, when the Empire was still quite firmly pagan. Repairs and enhancements were made in AD 367 after the collapse of the temple.

Four main structures have been identified, but when you walk up the track to the site, only two are visible today. You will first see the low restored walls of the temple. A model in the site museum shows it with a high *cella* roof surrounded by a lower ambulatory, something of a hybrid between Romano-Celtic and Roman architectural styles. The other visible building is the bath-house, with wall foundations, hypocaust *pilae* and furnaces. Further towards the north-east you can see the remains of a rectangular tank and channel, thought to have been a part of the water supply, which perhaps initially arrived by aqueduct. The other structures, now buried and invisible, were a long building which Wheeler called an 'abaton', providing accommodation for pilgrims, and a large courtyard villa-like structure, perhaps also providing visitor accommodation.

The late alterations to the buildings included at least ten fine mosaics, found during the early excavations in all four of the buildings. None can be seen today, except for a few tesserae in the museum. Some have been reburied, but the most important one has disappeared, and is only known from an illustration in the 1879 publication. It has a design of fish, sea monsters, and red and blue concentric circles with a hole in the centre and a dedicatory inscription:

D [M T] FLAVIUS SENILIS PR RIL EX STIPIBVS POSSVIT O[PILTUL]ANTE
VICTORINO INTER .... I TE

Various readings have been made: 'Dedicated to the god Mars or Nodens, by T Flavius [or Tilvus] Senilis, who may have been superintendent in charge of the rites, or officer in charge of the fleet base [praepositus religionum or praepositus reliquationis], paid for out of offerings of visitors, with the assistance of the dream-interpreter Victorinus'. Some have tried to link Senilis with a fleet at the mouth of the Severn, but most now agree he must have been a priest at the temple. The round hole in the mosaic apparently had a terracotta funnel beneath it in 1805, perhaps for offerings, and the dog may have been found here.

Continue walking and you will see the double rampart of the promontory fort, much entangled with tree roots. The rampart is also visible on the east side of the hill, and a deep hole surrounded by a fence is the entrance to one of the iron ore mines. From the hill you can look down over Little Camp Hill, also within the estate, on which there are the remains of a twelfth-century tower keep castle.

The site museum in the house is an exceptional cornucopia of finds. A great profusion of votive objects in bronze, stone and pottery seem to support the claim that some sort of healing cult was involved here, including parts of the body, more dogs, an oculist's stamps for eye ointment, a figurine of a woman holding her belly, a large number of bone pins and more than 8,000 coins. The inscriptions show that Nodens was associated with Mars, the Roman war god; there are indications of hunting, and there also seems to be a watery association, with sea monsters and fishermen depicted. Nodens may even have been depicted as a dog, given the number of dog figures, often associated with healing because of their habit of licking their wounds. The famous bronze dog displayed here is a replica; the original is in a bank vault.

There are three inscriptions found in the temple, two on bronze and one curse on lead. The bronze inscriptions use two variations of the god's name, Nudens and Nodons, both dedicated in response to fulfilment of vows. There are an additional forty-seven loose bronze letters which are now impossible to interpret.

The lead curse has gained most attention. The inscription reads: 'To the god Nodens: Silvanius has lost his ring and given half [its value] to Nodens. Among those who are called Senicianus do not allow health until he brings it to the temple of Nodens.'

In 1785 a gold ring was found in a ploughed field at Silchester, Hampshire. Its inscription reads SENICIANE VIVAS IIN DE, read as 'Senicianus live in God', a Christian phrase. A 'link' between the name on the ring and the curse had been noted from at least 1881. When Wheeler was publishing his excavations he invited JRR Tolkien, Anglo-Saxon Professor at Oxford University, to contribute a note on the god Nodens. The ring has long been at The Vyne in Hampshire, and in 2013 a special 'ring room' was opened, making much of the possibility that the ring and the lead curse found at Dwarf's Hill may have provided some inspiration for the Lord of the Rings.

Don't miss the marvellous photo album of pictures of the Wheelers' excavations. The room beyond the archaeology gallery is devoted to memorabilia from New Zealand, relating to the great-grandson of the excavating Charles Bathurst who was Governor General there.

North Leigh, Oxfordshire **

Roman villa with mosaics. EH. Open site.

The villa lies in a beautiful location beside the River Evenlode between Witney and Woodstock. It can be a trifle hard to find, being a country mile north-east of North Leigh village itself, but it is worth tracking down (OX29 6QE; take the road leading north from the A4095 through East End, another two right turns to site).

The Villa in its valley at North Leigh.

The walk from the parking lay-by down the hill affords lovely views of the villa and the valley. We were even honoured with the appearance of a Pacific class steam engine pulling a train of Pullman coaches on the railway line a short distance to the north.

An Iron Age settlement here was replaced by a linear Roman dwelling in the first or second century AD, which had two wings added in the third century, partially enclosing a courtyard. These were extended, and the original side rebuilt, in the fourth century. This large courtyard design had four bath-houses, sixteen rooms with mosaic floors and eleven rooms with underfloor heating – quite the country mansion.

The site was excavated in the late nineteenth and early twentieth centuries, and again in the 1970s. Two ranges of the villa are exposed with a covering shed preserving the surviving elaborate third-century geometric mosaic. Although you can view the mosaic through the windows, the building is rarely open for them to be viewed properly.

Oxford, Oxfordshire ✳✳✳

The Ashmolean Museum: Roman finds from Oxfordshire.

Oxford itself was not a Roman foundation, but the Ashmolean Museum in Beaumont Street is a must. The collections of Elias Ashmole were first housed near the Bodleian Library in 1683, making this the world's first university museum, and indeed the world's first museum in the modern sense of the word. The current grand classical structure dates from the mid-nineteenth century.

For the finds from Roman Britain you have to search the cases in the Rome Gallery on the ground floor, since there is no designated Roman Britain room. Artefacts from Oxfordshire and other counties lie cheek by jowl with pieces from around the Roman world.

Look for the figurines and other offerings from a religious sanctuary dedicated to Mars and Venus at Woodeaton; a wonderful array of pottery, bronze and glass artefacts from Shakenoak Roman villa, including a stone column and glass window panes; and a huge bronze steelyard from a weighing device and a pewter dinner service, all found in a late Roman well at Appleford. There is also a very fine, very Celtic-looking bronze bust of Emperor Marcus Aurelius with wide blue glass eyes and a swirling beard. Smaller than life size, it may have been used in Imperial cult processions in a Roman town near Brackley, where it was ploughed up. This is also the home of the wonderful fourth-century Wint Hill glass bowl, with an engraved hunting scene and exhortations in Greek and Latin to live well.

Downstairs in the coin room there are further treasures, with the collections having been swelled, as usual, by metal-detector finds from Oxfordshire. These include the Didcot hoard of 156 gold coins struck between AD 54 and AD 160, and the Chalgrove hoard of nearly 5,000 bronze coins dating between AD 251 and 279, one of which was struck by a hitherto unknown Emperor, Domitianus, whose rule in these turbulent times might have been measured only in days, hence the rarity of his coins.

The coin considered to be the most important ever found in Oxfordshire, though, is a gold coin of Vespasian, found at Finstock in 1850 by 'a poor man whilst ploughing in a field'. It was struck in AD 70 from gold looted from the Temple in Jerusalem, and the reverse bears the chilling legend 'The Justice of the Imperator', referring to Vespasian's son Titus, who had been in charge of the troops.

Having explored the local artefacts, you should not miss the Arundel Sculpture Gallery, collected in the seventeenth century by the Earl of Arundel, and the Cast Room, for further treasures of the Roman world.

Piddington, Northants **

Roman villa site museum. Seasonal opening.

This gem of a museum is housed in an old Wesleyan chapel (Chapel End, Piddington, NN7 2DD), not far from the site of a Roman villa which has been excavated over a period of forty years. Its existence is thanks to the energy and enthusiasm of the excavation directors, Roy and Liz Friendship-Taylor, whose enthusiasm is infectious. Everything on display was found in the excavations. The villa itself is backfilled each season but in August parts are revealed during the short dig season.

A building sequence from about 50 BC has been revealed, from Iron Age round-houses, to a 'proto villa' in *c.* AD 70, to a simple stone-built villa enlarged and enhanced to a winged corridor villa. Unusually, we may even know the name of two of the owners, Tiberius Claudius Severus and Tiberius Claudius Verus, found stamped on tiles now displayed in the museum. A huge stone-lined well has produced valuable environmental evidence, and there were two bath-houses, probably one for the estate workers, the other for the owner's family. A 'squatter' family unit occupied the site for most of the fourth century.

The exhibits include fine examples of Whitby jet, marble from all over the empire, medical implements including a cataract scalpel and fragments of wall painting. One of the best finds was a folding pen knife with a gladiator handle, currently on loan to the British Museum. There is a fine replica on show.

Recent excavations have revealed an early Roman fort close to the villa site, so the story is still unfolding.

Towcester (Lactodurum), Northants *

Towcester Museum: the Towcester Head.

Towcester, on Watling Street, is a charming small town, now famous for its racecourse. It was once a sizeable Roman settlement, walled in the third century, but the last Roman bastion was bulldozed in the 1960s in the name of progress. The marvellous museum, however, has a fine collection of Roman artefacts (White Horse Yard, Watling St, NN12 6BU).

The plan of Roman Towcester has been revealed by excavations over the years, and the museum has a useful model showing what the town would have looked like, accompanied by the obligatory life-size Roman soldier.

The collection includes coins, gaming pieces, pottery and votive offerings but the real delight is the stone carving known as the Towcester Head. This larger-than-life limestone sculpture of a female head on a base has a strikingly intense expression, perhaps owing more to the Wallace and Gromit school of art than high classical realism, but all the more interesting and unusual for it. It may have been part of a funerary monument amongst many others lining Watling Street outside the town. The original head is in the British Museum, but there is an exact replica here.

Boudica's last battle was fought somewhere along Watling Street, and a site close to Towcester is one of the contenders. A great display of 'The Battle of Watling Street' shows the alliance of Britons being defeated at the hands of Gaius Suetonius Paulinus and his legions.

Thornborough Barrows, Bucks *

Two Roman burial mounds.

Two large Roman burial mounds lying in a field north of the A421 near Thornborough (MK18 2AA) are the most westerly of such surviving monuments in Britain, most of which occur in East Anglia (Chapter 4). They can be seen from the road, and there is a footpath from the old road layby if you want to stop and explore. A pretty fourteenth-century bridge over the Padbury Brook, a tributary of the Great Ouse, lies close to the car parking area, and it is a popular summer picnic spot.

The proximity of the brook is likely to have been one of the reasons this site was chosen for the burials, as well as the fact that five Roman roads once intersected close by. The mounds would have been seen by many travellers. More Roman burials, without covering barrows, were found in the 1970s when the new bridge to take the A421 over the brook was constructed.

The two barrows were very inexpertly excavated in 1839 by the Duke of Buckingham's workmen. Both are truncated cones, with flattened areas on top, and are about 40 metres in diameter and 3.5 metres high. One is more oval than the other. The quarry ditches around them can be seen in places. In one of the mounds, although it is not recorded which, remains of a timber burial chamber were found, on a base of limestone blocks. Contained within this was a cremation in a large glass bottle, with another glass bottle, two amphorae, three bronze jugs and a handled bowl, a small lozenge of gold and some red Samian pottery vessels. The burials were made in the second century, and some of the grave goods were decades old when buried, perhaps a collection of heirlooms for a local dignitary. Some of the finds survive in the stores of the Museum of Archaeology and Anthropology at Cambridge.

Woodchester, Glos. *

Villa with mosaic buried beneath churchyard. Open site.

The little Cotswold village of Woodchester, 11 miles (18 km) south of Gloucester, now stands over one of the most magnificent Roman villas ever found in Britain, famed for its fabulous Orpheus mosaic, more than 50 feet (15 metres) square. A rectangular depression in the churchyard in Church Lane indicates where it now lies buried again, the nearby notice bearing a reproduction of an engraving of the mosaic made by Samuel Lysons, the man who first uncovered it in 1793. It is a wonderfully peaceful spot, worth a brief look if you happen to be passing, and a ponder on the theme of 'sic transit gloria mundi' (thus passes the glory of the world).

The mosaic was uncovered again at intervals of several years during the nineteenth century, and less frequently during the twentieth. The last time was in 1973, when so many visitors flocked to see it that the village clogged up completely (if you visit, you will see why). It has suffered some damage because of grave digging and, probably, the revealing and hiding process, and there are no plans to uncover it again. A wonderful replica made by two brothers, Bob and John Woodward, who had seen it in 1973 was sold to a private owner in 2010. This has apparently lain in storage for some years, never making it onto the floor of the Italian villa it was bought for, and has been up for sale again. The mosaic is similar in style to one displayed at Cirencester museum with Orpheus at the centre charming a circle of beast who walk around him, feet facing outward.

There is some information about the mosaic, with an illustration, in the Museum in the Park on the edge of Stroud (Stratford Park GL5 4AF), about 3 miles (5 km) to the north. This has a number of artefacts of all periods, including Roman, found locally.

4

East Anglia
Bedfordshire, Cambridgeshire, Essex, Herts, Norfolk, Suffolk

The area of this chapter covers the bulge of eastern England from the Wash to the Thames (excluding London), from wide open flatlands and the North Sea coast to urban conurbation around the M25, once rolling countryside. This was the territory of the Catuvellauni, the Trinovantes and the Iceni before the Romans arrived, and the interplay between these tribes and the Romans had a strong influence on the invasions and the early years of Imperial rule in Britain.

The site of the first official Roman triumph in Britain was at **Colchester** (Camulodunum) in AD 43, and somewhere to the north was the home of Boudica of the Iceni, who led the most famous revolt against the new government in AD 60/61. Her husband Prasutagus had been established as a client king by the Romans, perhaps with the understanding that his estate would pass to Rome when he died. When he left half to his tribe, the Romans acted mercilessly in taking what they saw as theirs, which included violating Boudica and her daughters. The story is graphically told by Tacitus and Cassius Dio, who then described the retribution wreaked by Boudica and her Iceni and Trinovantian followers, first sacking Colchester, symbol of Roman Imperial rule, then London, the new trading capital, then Verulamium, killing 70,000 Romans and Britons.

The three sacked cities rose from the ashes to flourish as Roman cities and **Colchester** and **Verulamium** are now two of the best-investigated and visually fulfilling towns to visit in search of the Romans. Boudica's army was defeated by the army commanded by Suetonius Paulinus at a battle site of unknown location, somewhere along Watling Street, possibly in our Central England region.

One more town in East Anglia, lying mostly undisturbed beneath the Norfolk fields, is **Caistor St Edmund** (Venta Icenorum), which provides a peaceful walk around its complete wall circuit. Water Newton (Durobrivae) near **Peterborough** is even less visible, but you can walk around the site.

Much wealth came from trade and farming this fertile land. Many farms and villas have been discovered over the years, though there does not seem to have been

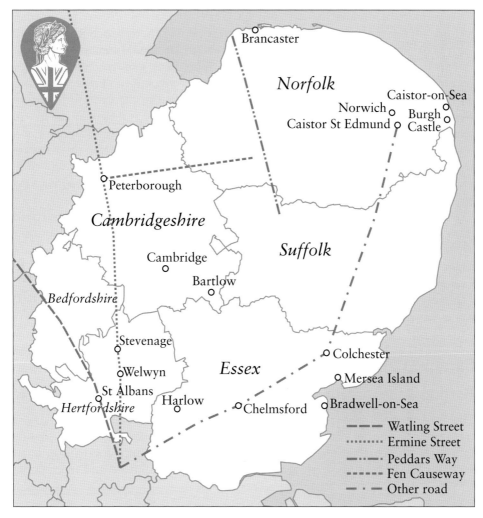

East Anglia.

quite the same level of late Roman luxury as in the Cotswolds and on the south coast. Territory in the fens that had been confiscated from the Iceni became a huge Imperial estate, managed by an official who is believed to have lived in a sumptuous palace discovered under St Kyneburgher's Church, near **Peterborough**. Only the barest glimpse of this is possible now. The only other part of a villa visible in this region is **Welwyn bath-house**, preserved in a vault under the A1.

A continuation of local customs can be seen in the construction of huge burial mounds over wealthy graves, which were a feature of this region. About 150 Roman burial mounds have been noted in Britain, most of them, and certainly the largest and best preserved, lying in East Anglia. Two groups of burial mounds of Roman date can be seen at **Bartlow Hills**, Cambridge, and **Stevenage**, Herts, and a single one at **Mersea**, Essex. Those at Bartlow Hills are spectacularly the largest in Britain, and these prominent landmarks sometimes continued to be a focus for burial in the Saxon period as well.

An important temple site can still be visited at **Harlow**, Essex, now rather forlorn, in a forgotten corner of an industrial estate. There was once a Roman settlement nearby, and information can be found in Harlow Museum.

This is also the area of many of the Saxon Shore forts, constructed in the third century along the east and south coast, first to protect continental trade, and then no doubt to help deter Saxon raiders. Nine are named in the early fifth-century *Notitia Dignitatum*, describing the organisation of the army at the end of the fourth century. Three are in this region and can be visited: **Brancaster** (Branodunum), **Burgh** (Gariannonum?) and **Bradwell** (Othona). Another two forts in this area are believed to be part of the same system of defence, although they are not named in the *Notitia* list: **Caister-on-Sea** and Walton Castle in Suffolk. The latter has long been overwhelmed by the sea due to the encroaching coastline.

Finally, it is possible to walk stretches of the Peddar's Way (the name derived from the Latin *pedester*, on foot), a 46-mile-long footpath in Norfolk from near Thetford to Holme-next-the-Sea, which traditionally follows Roman road and medieval pilgrim routes. The way is straight, without anything tangibly Roman to look at, but through beautiful open scenery and under enormous skies.

In addition to the museums described below, Welwyn Museum has some local Roman finds.

Bartlow, Cambs ***

Bartlow Hills Barrows, large Roman burial mounds. Open site.

This was once a cemetery of seven Roman burial mounds, making it the largest such group in Europe, but only four survive to a substantial height. Park beside St Mary's Church (Bartlow, CB21 4PL) and follow the signed footpath heading south to find them. The most northerly lies within the private and inaccessible

The enormous 50 ft high Mound 4 at Bartlow Hill.

grounds of Bartlow Park, only glimpsed over the fence by the bridge, but the big three are unexpectedly impressive and well worth the walk. The very scant remains of one more can be seen just to the west of the largest.

The conical mounds originally stood in two rows, not far south of the River Granta. The largest, Mound 4, at nearly 50 feet (15 metres) high is the highest burial mound in Britain and, with the steps constructed to its summit, looks something like a Maya pyramid. Excavations between 1815 and 1840 showed that they were made of layers of soil and chalk and may each have had a surrounding ditch. All contained a rich array of grave goods dating to the first and second centuries, including remains of wooden chests, probably burial chambers, decorated vessels of glass, pottery and enamelled copper, and a folding chair made of iron. The remains of flowers, box leaves, a sponge, incense, blood, milk and wine all indicated elaborate burial rites. Unfortunately, most of these were lost in a fire at Easton Lodge, Dunmow, where they were stored, in the mid-nineteenth century. Reading University has recently carried out detailed surveys of the area, but the mounds were not extensively re-excavated.

Bradwell-on-Sea (Othona), Essex **

Saxon Shore fort, Chapel of St Peter on the Wall.

The walk along the straight track to the tiny Chapel of St Peter-on-the-Wall (Bradwell-on-Sea, Southminster CM0 7PN) is truly magical. The chapel stands on the line of the wall of Othona Saxon Shore fort. A religious community has used the Roman name for a retreat nearby, so don't be distracted by signs to this – just keep heading straight towards the chapel and the sea.

The Chapel of St Peter on the Wall on the site of Othona Saxon Shore Fort.

The chapel was built in AD 654 by St Cedd, who was sent to this area to convert the East Saxons to Christianity. It stands on the foundations of the west gate of the fort, reusing the ready-cut Kentish ragstone and tiles clearly visible in the walls. The fort lay beyond the chapel towards the sea, and about two-thirds of the foundations have been eroded, disappearing into the salt flats. If the vegetation is low, you can just about make out the line of the slightly irregular square walls on the west side of the fort as a slight ridge. Excavations in the nineteenth century revealed the rounded corners with circular towers, of which there was another between the gate and each corner. Another trench was dug through the western defences in 1947.

Brancaster (Branodunum), Norfolk *

Saxon Shore fort. NT. Open site.

This is the most north-westerly of the Saxon Shore forts, and one of the earliest, constructed between AD 225 and 250 and therefore later than Caister-on-Sea but earlier than Burgh, the next two around the coast to the east. It replaced an earlier fort on the site, so its strategic position looking over the Wash had already been noted and utilised. It had the typical square plan of the earlier Shore forts, like Caister and Reculver.

Today it occupies a field to the north of the A149, east of Cross Lane (PE31 8XD), behind Brancaster Beach and the North Coast Path, on the edge of the marshes. A National Trust sign with information marks the entrance to the field. The walls stood until the eighteenth century, but now only a few humps and bumps can be made out in the grass (with the eye of faith). A housing estate built in the 1970s to the west of the fort has streets named 'Roman Way' and 'Branodunum', which is one way of immortalising the *vicus* lying beneath it.

Excavations in 1846, 1935 and 1985 produced evidence for occupation continuing during the third and fourth centuries. Finds included a finger ring with Christian symbols and a tile stamped Cohors Aquitorum, suggesting that its garrison at one stage came from Aquitania in Gaul. Aerial photographs taken in drought years have shown features inside the fort and also building activity outside the walls. If you are visiting the beach or walking the coast path it is worth a curiosity stop, especially if you are ticking off the Shore forts, but the visible rewards are slight.

Burgh Castle, (Gariannonum?), Norfolk ****

Saxon Shore fort. Open site.

The estuary setting of the fort at Burgh Castle (Butt Lane, Great Yarmouth NR31 9QB) is beautiful, bleak and much as it would have been 2,000 years ago when it was built as a defensive partner for the fort at Caister-on Sea, 5 miles (8 km) to the north across the water. One of these two forts must have been the Gariannonum listed on the *Notitia Dignitatum*, but it is not entirely certain which. Burgh is now so close to Breydon Water that the western wall and part of the interior have tumbled into the marshes. The surviving parts are exceptionally well preserved, and the lack of a wall on the water side means that there are spectacular views from inside the fort of the open flat landscape, now a nature reserve, under the huge wide skies of Norfolk.

Burgh was built in about AD 260 to support the fort at Caister-on-Sea, built sixty years earlier, to defend the Waveney Estuary. It originally stood on a low cliff above the water, enclosing about 6 acres (2.5 hectares), but coastal erosion has partly eaten it away. The walls around the surviving three sides are splendid, and in some places the flint facing-stones survive on the flint rubble core. These alternate with courses of red brick, giving a colourful aspect to the exterior. There are projecting circular towers at each corner and at intervals along the sides, two of which survive along the best-preserved east wall. These were probably added later. Each has a central hole which may have been for securing *ballistae*, which would have been fired from them, or perhaps to support wooden look-out towers. Little is known of the layout within the walls from excavation, but geophysical surveys have revealed some features.

In the Norman period a motte and bailey castle was constructed in the south-west corner, breaching the wall, but little evidence remains of this now. The fort is managed by English Heritage, but the site was purchased by the Norfolk Archaeological Trust in 1995 and a Lottery grant enabled the 'Life Outside the Walls' project, which started in 2016, looking for evidence for the Roman *vicus* and the development of the village at Burgh. https://sites.google.com/site/burghcastlelifeoutsidethewalls/home.

Caister-on-Sea, Norfolk **

Saxon Shore fort (small section). EH. Open site.

The fort at Caister-on-Sea once stood on a small island in a large estuary formed where four rivers, the Ant, Bure, Yare and Waveney, flowed into the North Sea. The coastline has changed a lot since then. The small excavated section, now visible in a fenced but freely accessible open grassy area, is surrounded by houses which overlie a large part of the fort (Norwich Road, Great Yarmouth, NR30 5RN). A lot of imagination is needed to put the fort back into its Roman context, bustling with life on the estuary. It was built around AD 200, one of the earliest of the Saxon Shore chain. Just 5 miles (8 km) away to the south lies the fort at Burgh Castle, built sixty years later on the other side of the estuary. About 25 miles (40 km) inland lies Caistor St Edmund, the most important town in the area, which would certainly have used the port for trade.

The fort had a mixed garrison of maybe 500–1,000 army, cavalry and sailors, and it is believed that the South Gate, visible today, once led to a beach on the estuary where ships could be loaded and unloaded. It was abandoned sometime in the fourth century, but a Saxon burial ground found in the area outside the walls shows that some activity returned to the area.

Excavations in the 1950s revealed the foundations still open today, neat and well-explained if just a little soulless. These include a stretch of the wall, which fronted an earthen rampart, to the west of the South Gate, and the adjoining gatehouse. This would once have been mirrored on the other side, with a double portal between. Inside, a section of the cobbled road leading to the gate, and beyond it to the estuary, is visible and walkable. There is always something special about being able to walk on a Roman road surface.

A building offering better-than-average fort accommodation, with painted wall-plaster and a heated room with a hypocaust, is close by, built *c*. AD 300 over the top of earlier timber buildings. Perhaps the commander lived here. It burnt down in AD 340, for reasons unknown.

Caistor St Edmund (Venta Icenorum), Norfolk ✳✳✳

Roman town, complete wall circuit. Open site.

This is the only Roman town in Norfolk where there is anything to be seen today. It failed to develop into a later urban centre and now lies in the countryside, on the edge of the village of Caistor St Edmund (4 Stoke Rd, NR14 8QL), 3 miles (5 km) to the south of Norwich city centre. The peaceful spot beside the River Tas is only disturbed by the occasional fast train whizzing by on the other side of the river between Norwich and London, and you can walk around the city walls watched only by the sheep. The only building visible within the walls is the Church of St Edmund in the south-east corner, built in the eleventh century,

The walk around the city wall at Caistor St Edmund.

possibly on the site of an earlier church. No other post-Roman structure is known to have been built on the town site.

Venta Icenorum was the civitas capital of the Iceni, founded *c.* AD 70, a decade or so after the death of Boudica. A large early town of 69 acres (28 hectares) was reduced to half its size, at 34 acres (14 hectares), when the stone walls visible today were built in the third century. The roughly rectangular late town sits in the middle of the earlier trapezoidal one, which may in turn have been built over a short-lived fortress, the triple ditches of which have been noted by aerial photography. This was probably necessary to keep the peace for a while in Iceni territory after the defeat of Boudica's army. The riverside location was chosen at a point where medium-sized ships could bring goods to the town; mooring rings were noted still surviving by the West Gate in the eighteenth century. Although it was not far from the coastal estuary, the terrain here was navigable by road, which was also an advantage.

The walk around the walls is aided by information at intervals along the path. These indicate where buildings once stood, both inside and outside the walls, found by aerial photography and excavation, now hidden under the grass. They include several temples, the forum and basilica, a bath-house, domestic houses and an amphitheatre outside the walls to the south. The deities to whom the temples were dedicated are not known but an intriguing lead curse was found invoking Neptune's help in finding the thief of sundry objects including some leggings, offered as the god's reward in return for the blood of the thief.

The walls are traceable for most of the circuit, better-preserved in some places than others, with tile courses in amongst the dressed flint which faced a rubbly core, which in turn faced an earthen rampart. Just before you reach the Church of St Edmund you can look at the site through a Perspex screen with buildings etched on it, providing a fourth-century view. A visit to the church makes a good end to the visit.

The urban focus switched to Norwich in the ninth and tenth centuries, on the River Wensum rather than the Tas, for reasons which are not entirely clear. Evidence for Anglo-Saxon settlement has been found outside the walls of Venta Icenorum, and the Roman remains seem to have been a focus for both domestic and funerary activity for some centuries, even though people weren't actually living amongst the ruins. Finds from the excavations can be seen in Norwich Castle Museum.

Cambridge (Duroliponte), Cambs ***

Museum of Archaeology and Anthropology Roman Gallery

The opening of the Museum of Archaeology and Anthropology (Downing Street, CB2 3DZ) in 1884 brought together the collections of the Cambridge Antiquarian Society and the University colleges. The resulting cornucopia of objects comes from all over the world, but there are a number of important finds from the small town of Duroliponte, Roman Cambridge, which lay on Castle Hill to the north-west of the city centre. These, and finds from the wider area, are displayed in cases labelled 'Finding Roman Cambridge', and include some beautiful complete glass vessels,

A rude pot from Great
Chesterford. *Photo
Cambridge Museum
of Archaeology and
Anthropology.*

the skeleton of a wealthy woman of the fourth century buried in a lead coffin at
Arbury, who inspired a poem by Sylvia Plath, and a strange rude pot, possibly
Colchester ware, with a relief of women in chariots being pulled by *quadrigae*
of *phalli*.

Chelmsford ***

Chelmsford Museum, Roman Gallery.

Housed in a Grade II listed building in a beautiful park, the Chelmsford
Museum has recently been refurbished at great expense and has a splendid new
archaeology gallery (Oaklands Park, Moulsham St, CM2 9AQ). A market town
called Caesaromagus (Caesar's marketplace) once stood to the south of the town
centre and south of the rivers Chelmer and Can, at Moulsham, halfway between
Colchester and London. Although there is nothing to see *in situ* excavations have
revealed military occupation, defences, a *mansio* and a fourth-century Romano-
Celtic temple, as well as burials with grave goods. The story is told and the finds
displayed in the Roman Gallery, not only from the town but from surrounding sites
such as Witham, to the north-east. Beautiful objects include jet jewellery, a bronze
figurine of a tiger, and a late Roman glass cup from a burial at Chignall.

Colchester (Camulodunum), Essex *****

Roman city: walls with Balkerne Gate; foundations of the Temple of Claudius and Roman Galleries at the Castle Museum; foundations of Roman church; site of theatre; site of Britain's only known chariot racing track; Gosbecks Archaeological Park. Open sites except Colchester Museum and Circus Centre.

If you haven't been to Colchester and this book persuades you to visit, the work involved will all have been worthwhile. The splendidly refurbished Castle Museum holds what is probably the best collection of Roman artefacts in the country; it has the largest and best-preserved Roman city gate extant in Britain and in 2004 the exciting discovery was made of the only chariot-racing circus in the province, in fact one of only two known north of the Alps, the other being at Trier in Germany. In addition, the gargantuan Norman keep, the remains of two abbeys and many lovely medieval buildings make it a city to rank alongside Chester and York.

Camulodunum was the first capital of Britannia until the administrative base was moved to London later in the first century AD. Its importance is reflected in a wealth of Roman remains and artefacts, some uncovered by nineteenth-century excavations, but many revealed by more than fifty years' work by the Colchester Archaeological Trust, led by its director, Philip Crummy.

The pre-Roman native settlement consisted of a sprawling *oppidum*, the centre of the Trinovantes under their King Cunobelinus. Excavations at Gosbecks, to the

Imagined audience watching a chariot race at the Circus in Colchester.

south-west of Colchester, have revealed many features of this settlement, which continued to be used into early Roman times. The area is now designated a protected archaeological park (below).

After Cunobelinus' death his successors started to push the boundaries of their kingdom, annexing lands and upsetting the balance of power in southern Britain, all fuelling a rationale for a Roman invasion to keep the status quo. Camulodunum was thus the priority for the invading army and it was here that Emperor Claudius arrived in triumph, possibly on an elephant (though the evidence is ephemeral), and accepted the surrender of a number of British kings.

A legionary fortress was established in AD 44, but five years later as the troops moved north and west it was converted into a *colonia*, a chartered town populated by ex-legionaries as well as civilians. The name Colchester evolved from Colonia chester to Colne chester to Colneceastre, and the River Colne was originally called Colonia Fluvius, the waterway to Colonia.

This was the first settlement destroyed by Boudica and her followers in AD 60/61, and a destruction layer of red and black burning has been picked up during excavations all over the town. It was rebuilt and enclosed within a defensive circuit, and flourished in the second century, when the circus was built, but then the various crises of the third century took their toll. In the early fourth century a settlement of smaller dwellings seems to have focussed along the High Street, and the Butt Road Christian Church was constructed. The large theatre in the town continued to stand, although it is not known what function it had, and later the medieval St Helen's Chapel was created out of a corner of it.

Life seems to have continued in the town until sometime within the fifth century, albeit in a diminished state. Saxon burials have been found outside the walls, although legends linking Camulodunum with Camelot are fantasies. Roman building materials were reused in medieval structures such as St Botolph's Priory and the Norman castle, and the town carried on.

The walls can be traced around most of the town, sometimes as impressive standing masonry, sometimes in the modern street pattern. The lack of good building stone in Essex meant that fired bricks, flint and septaria, a brittle stone from the Essex coast, were all used in the construction.

Traces often appear unexpectedly out of modern buildings, as along the back of Priory Street car park. The wall was repaired and strengthened by bastions in the late Roman period, but in 1648 the eleven-week-long Siege of Colchester by Cromwell's Roundheads took its toll not only of the people of Colchester but also its creaky old wall, which was left in terminal decline. A heritage information programme around the town has resulted in good information boards at key locations around the walls.

The Balkerne Gate (Balkerne Hill, Colchester CO3 3AA) was the west gate of the city, marking the entry point of the road from London. So well-preserved that it rather splendidly has a pub placed in the top half for thirsty visiting Roman enthusiasts, it is both the earliest and the largest surviving Roman gate in Britain, and was the site of Mortimer Wheeler's first ever excavation in 1917. Its huge size results from the fact that it incorporated the triumphal arch built in AD 49 to commemorate Claudius's arrival (before the walls were built), and it eventually had four arches, two for wheeled traffic and two, smaller, for pedestrians. The wall ditch was extended in front of it in AD 300, effectively blocking it, perhaps because it was a weak point in the defences of the town. The southern pedestrian arch and guardroom are all that survive now – less than a quarter of the original structure. It's a good point to start a walk round the walls, which can be seen along Balkerne Hill, Northgate Street, Roman Road and Priory Street.

The theatre site has been marked out with coloured bricks in the pavement outside 75 Maidenburgh Street. The straight wall can be seen protruding from the base of the north wall of St Helen's Chapel at the end of the street, then the darker bricks show where it continued first south then curved round to the south-west. There is also a window display with some wall remains visible and explanatory boards. Excavations in 1981–2 revealed that it would have seated around 3,000, probably lying on the same site as the theatre destroyed by Boudica and mentioned in the account by Tacitus of the rebellion. Remains of another theatre was found at Gosbecks, now visible as a mound (see below).

The foundations of the **Temple of Claudius** can be seen in the basement of Colchester Castle Museum as part of a very good guided tour. The Norman keep was built over the sturdy vaulted arches that once provided foundations for the temple, extensively reusing Roman masonry. If you take the tour you will hear the fascinating story of these vaults and their remarkable survival. Look closely at the castle walls before you enter and you can see lots of red Roman tiles as well as stone. The huge temple was built to honour Claudius after he died and became a god in AD 54. A potent symbol of Rome's domination, it was attacked and gutted by Boudica's followers in AD 60/61 but was later rebuilt on the same site. It continued to be used until the end of the Roman period, when it was extensively renovated and enhanced, though its purpose then is unknown. The temple was originally fronted by a 131-yard (120-metre) long colonnade with an elaborate central gate. This can be seen displayed under glass in the Claudius Gateway café opposite the castle entrance in Castle Park, recently reopened, and with the added benefit that your coffee and cakes fund a charity to help the homeless.

A short stretch of the wall that was part of a colonnade across the back of the temple precinct can be seen to the left of the path approaching the castle in the Upper Castle Park, and the foundations of a town house of *c.* AD 200 can also be seen behind the castle. This is one of three excavated here by Wheeler.

Colchester Castle Museum itself contains Roman galleries with superb artefacts, including two of the most important funerary monuments in the country, predating the Boudican revolt.

The tombstone of Marcus Favonius Facilis is the earliest known Roman sculpture from Britain. He was a centurion of the Twentieth Legion, and probably took part in the invasion, settled in Colchester in his retirement and died in the AD 50s. The detail of the sculpture clearly shows the uniform of a centurion in the first century, including his reticulated armour, his swords and his badge of office, the vine stick.

The second of the two celebrity tombstones commemorates Thracian cavalry officer Longinus Sdapeze. He held the rank of *duplicarius*, in charge of a unit of thirty-two men, so probably equivalent to a captain in the modern British Army. The tombstone shows Longinus seated on a horse riding down a barbarian. It was thrown down and possibly defaced (literally) during the Boudican revolt. The stone was originally found in 1928, sadly lacking Longinus's face, but when the site was reinvestigated in 1996 the face was found. It caused quite a stir when it was found to fit the tombstone perfectly.

The Fenwick Treasure of gorgeous jewellery, including a woman's gold bracelets, finger rings and earrings and a man's silver armbands, was discovered in 2014 during renovations to a department store in the High Street. It dates to the time of the Boudican rebellion, when it was hurriedly buried in the foundations of a house but never recovered, because the house had been destroyed by fire along with the rest of the *colonia*.

A fine fourth-century mosaic depicting a walking lion was found in excavations of 1974 which also revealed items such as a bed and bedding burnt in AD 60/61. The modern shopping street, called Lion Walk after this mosaic, now has a replica displayed on the wall.

Also look out for the Colchester Vase, with pairs of gladiators vividly depicted on the outside, together with their names; the Colchester Sphinx; the Gosbecks Mercury and the Doctor's Grave assemblage from Stanway.

The **Firstsite Art Gallery** (Lewis Gardens, High Street CO1 1JH) displays the mid-second-century Berryfield mosaic, found in 1923 in a town house just beyond the gallery site, displayed first in the museum and then moved back. Geometric panels alternate with those depicting mythical sea creatures.

The **Roman circus**, the only one known in Britain, was recognised in 2004 during some housing redevelopment work on the site of the Colchester Garrison to the south of the Roman town, beyond the Southway ring-road. It caused great excitement, and it must speak volumes about the importance and sophistication of the town. Approach along Roman Circus Walk (Colchester CO2 7GZ) as car access from other directions is not possible.

Built in the second century, it stood outside the town wall, 450 metres long with seating for at least 8,000 spectators supporting their favourite chariot racing team. The starting gates and the position of the racing track have been located, where the blue, green, red and white teams would have been followed as devotedly as any football team today. It has been calculated that some of the top charioteers were the highest-paid athletes in history, when relative monetary values are considered.

It was used for about 150 years then was abandoned, the stone being reused for other buildings in the town. This means that nothing remains of this great edifice above ground and the foundations are fairly scant. However, a great deal has been made of these, with some excellent interpretative work by the Colchester Archaeological Trust. The outline of the circus has been marked out by a bank in parts, particularly at the west end; creative ironwork and the reconstructed bases of the starting gates can be seen in the garden of the former Sergeants' Mess. The adjacent Roman Circus Centre (seasonal opening) tells you everything about this and other Roman circuses, using models, films, and copies of a glass cup with circus scenes found in Colchester, as well as a bookshop and café.

The site of the city's amphitheatre has not been found, although it is likely that there would have been one.

Butt Road Roman Church is one of the earliest churches found in Britain. Its foundations are displayed not far from the Roman circus on the Maldon roundabout, next to the police station. Excavations have shown that it was constructed *c.* AD 320, and an important cemetery, showing the increase of Christian influence, was found nearby. The splendid grave goods can be seen in the Castle Museum.

Gosbecks Archaeological Park (Stanway, Colchester CO3 0SJ) is a large open area designated to preserve the ancient remains outside the town. It covers 163 acres (66 hectares), just a small percentage of the huge pre-Roman *oppidum* of Camulodunum. Excavations here, 2.5 miles (4 km) to the south-west of the circus, have shown that the settlement continued into the early Roman period, when a Celtic temple was surrounded by a huge Roman portico, and an early Roman-style theatre was built. The sites of these can be seen marked in the grass, with explanatory boards. Grymes Dyke, a 3-mile (nearly 5 km) long earthwork, can also be seen, and there are some lovely walks.

A good Roman town trail, including a walk around the walls, is available at www.camulos.com.

Harlow, Essex **

Roman temple foundations; finds in Harlow Museum.

The spirit of this place must be barely clinging on if it still inhabits this desolate, though surprisingly tranquil, corner of the Temple Fields Industrial Estate (on River Way, Harlow CM20 2EY). To find it, turn left at the big roundabout on the A414 onto Edinburgh Way, then right onto River Way. Park near Westex, find a gap by a gate into a bit of apparent wasteland, and a barely legible sign saying 'Roman Temple' will greet you. The foundations of the temple lie beyond this, marked out in stone and concrete and with battered information boards. One of these declares that this is the site of one of the most important Roman temples in southern Britain. In terms of what has been found, and the fact that the site is still visible and respected, this is quite right.

Excavations in the 1960s and 1980s proved that this spot had been special for a long time. A Bronze Age pond barrow was the first monument, then a circular Celtic temple was built nearby, used for about 200 years until AD 80. A square temple dedicated to Minerva was then constructed, and enclosed by a wooden palisade two or three decades later. Around AD 200 the surrounding sacred wall was replaced in stone, enclosing a larger area, and enhanced with cobbled surfaces and accommodation for pilgrims. By the late fourth century it had fallen into disrepair, but the Saxons also felt the pull of this place and built a wooden structure, possibly a temple, in front of the old Roman *cella*, which was used for about 100 years. It had been a place of worship for more than 500 years, and a focus for burial even longer. The River Stort still runs close by, and this may have been the reason why it was chosen.

Some of the finds from the excavations are displayed in the attractive **Harlow Museum and Walled Gardens**, Muskham Road, Harlow CM20 2LF. This is housed in the former stables of Mark Hall Manor House, a short distance away. There are very good reconstruction drawings of the temple, and figurines of Bacchus and Mercury as well as other objects from the small Roman settlement at Harlow.

Mersea Island, Essex **

Large Roman burial mound.

This huge tumulus stands alone beside East Mersea Road, close to the junction with Dawes Lane, surrounded by railings and partly obscured by trees. It stands 23 feet (7 metres high), with a flat top of 16 feet (5 metres) diameter. The centre was excavated in 1912, and an elaborate burial chamber was discovered. This was made of Roman roofing tiles, two forming the floor, seven courses making the walls, slightly corbelled towards the top, with a single large tile for the roof. The cremated human remains were found in a large globular glass jar inside a lead casket with a wooden lid. Dated *c.* AD 100–120, the burial is exhibited at Mersea Museum when it is open during the summer months. After the excavation a passage was formed to the chamber, and this can still be visited by appointment with **Mersea Museum** (info@MerseaMuseum.org.uk; 12 High Street, West Mersea, Colchester CO5 8QD).

In 2012 the cremated bones were examined by Wessex Archaeology, and various analyses were carried out. This showed that the deceased was a man aged between thirty-five and forty-five, large and robust but suffering from a disease of the joints which would have caused him some discomfort. A sticky substance coating some of the bones was found to be pine resin and frankincense, causing quite a sensation as this would have been imported probably from East Africa. It provides a glimpse of the elaborate and costly burial rites with which this wealthy individual was sent to the afterlife.

The large burial mound on Mersea Island.

Norwich, Norfolk ***

Castle Museum with Roman finds from Norfolk, including cavalry parade helmet and visor.

Norwich Castle (Castle Hill, NR1 3JU) is a dominating landmark of the city, standing high on its mound, which nowadays has a large lift to raise visitors from lower street level. It was built by the Normans in the early twelfth century, but its appearance today has been much changed by an imaginative refacing in Bath stone in the nineteenth century, with added crenellations.

The museum opened in 1894, undergoing several refurbishments since, and entry tickets include access to both this and the castle. A wood-panelled rotunda inserted into the centre of the keep provides the hub, and the gallery devoted to Boudica and the Romans opens off this.

Boudica rather dominates the early part of the exhibition; she is the local heroine, even though there are no sites or artefacts in Norfolk which have an unequivocal known connection with her. The late Iron Age religious site at Gallows Hill, Thetford, may have been somewhere she knew, and a fragment of a bronze horse's leg from Ashill in central Norfolk may have been part of an equestrian statue of Claudius, the head of which was found in the River Alde in Suffolk, possibly looted from Colchester, carried with Boudica's army and then returned to Norfolk. It does make a good story! You can even stand in a chariot with a screen in front and imagine you are travelling with the marauding army.

Many more treasures of Roman Norfolk are well-displayed, including several cases of finds from Caistor St Edmund, and also from Gayton Thorpe Roman villa, as a reminder of the wealth of the countryside in this part of the world. A noteworthy item is a finely decorated third-century cavalry parade helmet and visor from the River Wensum at Worthing. The Anglo-Saxon Gallery is also well worth a visit.

Peterborough, Cambs ***

Peterborough Museum; St Kyneburgher's Church, Castor; Orton Longueville aisled barn; site of Water Newton Roman town (Durobrivae).

The cathedral city of Peterborough lies on the edge of the Fens, where the River Nene drains enough water from the flat land around it to have attracted settlers from prehistoric times on. The famous Bronze Age settlement at Flag Fen, for example, lies just 4 miles (6.5 km) to the east of the city. The remains of Roman settlement are concentrated not beneath the medieval city, but a couple of miles to the west, both north and south of the River Nene.

In order to understand the Roman landscape, you need to visit **Peterborough Museum** (Priestgate, Peterborough PE1 1LF), where the story is told with plans and a fine array of artefacts. Ask for their free leaflet with an illustrated walk through all the sites.

A leaping hare on a fragment of Nene Valley pottery in Peterborough Museum. *Published with kind permission of Vivacity.*

A fort was established at Longthorpe, north of the River Nene, close to a crossing point at Ferry Meadows, perhaps as early as AD 44. It was a *vexillation* fortress of 11 hectares (27 acres), built for half a legion, probably part of the Ninth Legion Hispana, as tiles stamped with its name have been found there. Air photos and excavation suggest that it is one of the most complete such structures in the Empire, though now it lies under a golf course. The troops from here sallied forth in AD 60/61 to challenge Boudica after her destruction of Colchester but were defeated in an ambush on their way to Colchester and returned to their base much depleted. A much smaller fort was then constructed, covering just 4.5 hectares (11 acres), perhaps as a reaction to all those soldiers lost. This was garrisoned until the early 60s AD.

A permanent bridge to carry Ermine Street over the River Nene was built sometime after AD 65, stone blocks of which have been found in the river. These would have supported a wooden superstructure, to the west of the earlier crossing point near Longthorpe fort. Just to the south-east of this, and just north of the A1, lies the Roman town of Durobrivae, named in the second-century *Antonine Itinerary*, meaning 'the fort by the bridge'. Only a few bumps where the walls once stood can now be seen, but excavations in the nineteenth and twentieth centuries, as well as more recent surveys, have shown that this was a significant and wealthy town. An important pottery industry was situated outside the walls, producing colour-coated Nene Valley pottery, with elaborate embossed figurative decoration. There are some beautiful examples in Peterborough Museum; one with a leaping hare is particularly lovely.

The wealth of the area in the late Roman period is illustrated by the magnificent fourth-century Water Newton Treasure, found close to Durobrivae, and also to the modern village after which it was named. It comprises one gold plaque and twenty-seven silver items, including nine vessels and eighteen votive tokens embossed with the Christian *chi-rho* symbol. Found in 1975 in a ploughed field, it may have been used in Christian services, and must have been buried for safety. Peterborough Museum has a few replica pieces, but the national importance of the originals means that they are displayed in the British Museum.

Several wealthy villas have also been found in the area, and the most magnificent of these lies beneath St Kyneburgher's Church in the village of Castor. This was a huge palace, at 317 x 142 yards (290 x 130 metres) one of the largest Roman buildings ever found in Britain, partly excavated in the nineteenth century. It is thought to have been the base of a Roman official in charge of the fenland which had become an Imperial estate after land had been confiscated from the Iceni tribe both before and after the Boudican revolt. There is a model in the museum showing what the palace may have looked like.

This official would no doubt have been in charge of huge engineering projects undertaken in the Fens, including the 85-mile-long (137 km) Car Dyke constructed in the late first or early second century from the River Witham at Washingborough to the River Cam at Waterbeach. Stretches of this are still visible. Its purpose was perhaps to improve the production of the land, as well as providing a canal for moving produce. There was also a gravel road, the Fen Causeway, which was raised above the marshy land. This has been identified running east for 24 miles (39 km) from Ermine Street, near Peterborough, to Denver, Norfolk.

The walk to the site of Durobrivae can be started at **St Kyneburgher's Church, Castor** (PE5 7AX), or you can just visit the church with its beautiful Norman tower, which overlies a huge Roman palace.

The wall of the street outside the church entrance has two huge chunks of herringbone masonry protruding from it. These are the only visible parts of the wall of the eastern range of buildings of the palace, which continue under the church. St Kyneburgher, daughter of King Penda of Mercia, is believed to have established a convent here within the ruins of the Roman palace. Much of the stone of the later Norman church is reused masonry from this building too. In the churchyard there are plans and panels explaining what was found in the nineteenth-century excavations by Edmund Tyrell Artis, and there is a memorial stone to him just outside the main door of the church.

Inside the church are cases of finds from the site, as well as the base of a Saxon cross with intricate design, standing in front of a statue of St Kyneburgher. The cross is likely to be a reused Roman pagan altar.

During the creation of the green and spacious Ferry Meadows Country Park at **Orton Longueville** (PE2 5UR) in the 1970s, just to the south-west of Peterborough, a Roman farmstead was found, overlying a military camp. Take a short walk from the main car park to the edge of Overton Lake, and you will see the outline of

Lynch Farm aisled barn marked out in concrete, with the positions of the supporting posts also marked as circles within it. There was also originally a temple nearby. The barn was used for agricultural storage, as a workshop for metalworking and salt production, and as living quarters. It went out of use after AD 300 because of rising water levels. It is possible to walk around the lake and across the river to look over the golf course where **Longthorpe fortress** once stood.

Stevenage, Hertfordshire *

Six Hills Barrows, Roman burial mounds. Open site.

All six of these large burial mounds survive, albeit rather eroded, making this the largest surviving Roman barrow cemetery in Europe. They reside rather forlornly on an elongated traffic island in an industrial estate, encircled by London Road, King's Road and Six Barrow Way (named after it) and they can be reached from the nearby Asda car park (SG1 2NG).

They are now much the same size as each other, at 60 feet (18 metres) diameter and nearly 10 feet (3 metres) high, but once they would have stood at least 4 feet (1.25 metres) higher. The ditches surrounded them can no longer be seen. They stand in a line alongside a modern cycle track, which is thought to run on the route of the Roman road known as Via Alba, between Verulamium and Sandy, Beds, which was also a Roman town.

All the barrows except one have a tell-tale depression on the summit, indicating antiquarian investigation. These were dug into in the eighteenth century, and nothing but vague reports of bits of wood and iron survives.

St Albans (Verulamium), Herts *****

Entire Roman city beneath parkland, some public, some private. Visible remains include: city wall circuit with gates; house with mosaic; theatre; shops; museum. Open sites except theatre and museum.

Verulamium has the distinct advantage, as far as Roman remains go, of having been abandoned and not built over in the early medieval period. The town moved a short distance over the River Ver to be focussed around the tomb of a martyr, St Alban, leaving the Roman structures undisturbed beneath the ground surface. However, most of the stones above the ground were taken for reuse, and these are now within the fabric of the abbey and other later structures. There is still lots to see, and since Verulamium is proud to be the third largest city in Roman Britain, at 203 acres (82 hectares), after London and Cirencester (Corinium), this makes it unmissable. Car park at Verulamium Museum (St Michael's, St Albans AL3 4SW).

Formal excavations began in the 1930s, directed by Mortimer Wheeler and, more consistently, by his wife Tessa, whose work is commemorated in a large inscription in the museum. The initial plan was to display everything that was

Basilica inscription and mosaics in Verulamium Museum. *Published with kind permission of Verulamium Museum.*

excavated *in situ*, resulting in a sort of British Pompeii, but the practical difficulties of weather and conservation were soon realised, and a few of its monuments were selected for display. Half the Roman town is a grassed public park, beautifully maintained and with various amenities. Long stretches of the town walls, a mosaic floor protected under a modern building, and the site museum (which lies over the Roman forum) can be seen here. The other half is on private land belonging to the estate of the Earl of Verulam, including the theatre, the only one of Roman date still visible above ground in Britain.

Detailed magnetometer surveys have revealed the layout of pretty much all the buildings and streets within the town. Relative dates are harder to discern, but occasional modern excavations necessary when amenities such as pipes are laid tend to confirm the picture portrayed by the survey.

The town was first established as a *municipium c.* AD 50, on the site of Verlamion, the tribal capital of the Catuvellauni. It lies on Watling Street, which followed an important pre-Roman route across the country. There was no obvious opposition from the local inhabitants, and most of the evidence points to a pro-Roman stance. However, metal-detector finds of more than 100 lead sling-shots found scattered to the south-west of the Roman town near Prae Wood, where there was pre-Roman settlement, have been taken by some indicate that the takeover may not have been entirely friendly.

In 1992 the very rich burial of a local chief was excavated in Folly Lane, to the north of the Roman town, which dates to AD 52. His name is not known, but he is thought to have been a client king of the Romans, comparable to Togidubnus and Prasutagus, an ally and friend who was rewarded with immense wealth and left to reign comparatively independently in the early years of the occupation. A huge temple was built next to this burial, finds from which are on display in the museum.

The town was destroyed in AD 60/1 by Boudica and her rebellious hordes, with the characteristic burnt destruction layer appearing here as in Colchester and London. The town was rebuilt, to be destroyed again by fire in AD 155, cause unknown, after which many of the buildings in the town previously made of wood were replaced in stone. There was yet another major fire in the town about 100 years later. Some occupation on the site seems to have gone on until the eighth century, although the main settlement moved across the river. A monastery was founded in 793 dedicated to the third-century martyr St Alban, Britain's first patron saint, replaced by a stone abbey between the tenth and twelfth centuries.

The walls of stone which still stand in the park were constructed in *c.* AD 265–70, after the mid-third century fire, perhaps to strengthen the defences but also to give out a message of strength, civic pride, and to control movement in and out of the town. They were originally more than 16 feet (5 metres) high, topped by a parapet and walkway and completely encircled the town with a length of 2 miles (3.4 km). The stretch through the park reaches about two-thirds of this height in places, and the horizontal brick courses running through the rubble and cement core are still clearly visible. The facing stones have all been robbed for reuse. Look to the left of the path (as you walk along the wall to the north) to see the massive ditch which would have made the circuit even more impressive. The foundations of a circular tower at the northern corner of the walls is visible, and there were probably more of these.

The London Gate straddles Watling Street as it enters the town from the London direction, and was excavated by the Wheelers in the 1930s. The ground plan has been laid out in stone, showing two lanes for wheeled traffic and two for pedestrians; an excellent reconstruction is depicted nearby.

A mosaic floor with hypocaust has been preserved *in situ* in a modern white building in the park. It was probably the reception room of a wealthy town house of *c.* AD 180, part of the ground plan of which is visible outside. The geometric mosaic with sixteen central panels is beautifully preserved, and in one corner there is a glimpse of the underfloor heating system, highly desirable in the British climate. The geometric panels, prefabricated in a workshop, were arranged in alternate identical pairs, but look out for two which break this pattern, since one of them has been rotated through 45 degrees.

The Roman theatre was rediscovered in the late nineteenth century and fully excavated in 1935 by Kathleen Kenyon. It stands on Watling Street as it ran through the town, and the first construction was in *c.* AD 140, with seating for about 7,000.

The bank for the seating auditorium was provided by soil excavated from the area of the circular orchestra. It was further enhanced and extended after the second-century fire, and again in the early fourth century. The stage had three free-standing columns across the back of it, flanked by two half-engaged ones which together formed the façade of the roofed stage building. One of the columns has been reconstructed from excavated fragments, giving a good idea of the original height. The curtain in a Roman theatre rose from a slot beneath the stage, rather than falling from above or from the sides, and this slot is clearly visible.

The raised bank around the outside of the theatre is made of spoil from the excavations and was not part of the original structure. Remains of a temple were found nearby, and it was also linked by a road to the temple near the first-century chief's tomb so it would have had an important religious role as well as providing entertainment. In spite of the renovations in the early fourth century, it went out of use within a few decades, perhaps because of the advent of Christianity and the outlawing of pagan cults. By AD 380 it had become a convenient rubbish dump, providing some interesting material for the archaeologists nearly 2,000 years later.

Houses and shops excavated near the theatre are shown as reconstructed stone foundations. They had been built of wood in the first century and finds showed that some were metal workshops and one was a bakery, burnt down during Boudica's attack. They were rebuilt *c*. AD 100, and this area of the town thrived throughout the second century. A wealthy town house constructed nearby in AD 170 is also laid out. Wonderful panels of coloured wall-plaster, mosaics and possessions of the householders and shop-keepers are displayed in the museum.

Verulamium Museum was first constructed soon after the Wheelers' excavations, over the site of the forum and basilica. A large extension was added in 2000, stylishly built in sympathy with its position at the centre of the Roman town. It houses one of the largest collections of colourful mosaics in the country, and a wonderful array of artefacts from the town, largely arranged thematically to capture the essence of Roman life.

A huge eye-catching inscription has been prominently displayed, fragments of which were found during the forum excavations where the museum now stands, telling us that the basilica was 'adorned' (i.e. extensively renovated and rebuilt in the aftermath of Boudica) in AD 79, just after the death of the Emperor Vespasian, when Agricola was governor of the province. It was once held up by brackets shaped like huge human hands – just one finger survives and is displayed.

Don't miss the case with chainmail and other wealthy grave goods from the cremation of the mid-first-century chief buried in Folly Lane; a beautiful complete glass jug with chain-like handle from a stone coffin found at Kingsbury; and a fourth-century lead coffin decorated with scallop shells. Look out also for a beautiful bronze figurine of Venus (or perhaps Persephone), and the Sandridge Hoard of late fourth / early fifth-century gold coins found by a metal detectorist.

Welwyn, Herts ***

Bath-house of Dicket Mead Roman villa; museum. Seasonal opening.

The modern entrance to the building covering the bath-house of this extensive villa is quite unexpected, looking like a hobbit hole, leading to an underpass beneath the A1. The entrance to the car park is just off a roundabout on the Welwyn by-pass (AL6 9FG).

The bath-house beneath the A1 at Welwyn.

Welwyn has produced a number of rich sites from the late Iron Age and the Roman period. One spectacularly wealthy grave, probably of a local chief, dating between 50 and 10 BC, is displayed in the British Museum. It demonstrates that luxury goods were being imported from the continent between the invasions of Caesar and Claudius. A villa was excavated at Lockleys in the 1930s, and it is known that there was a Roman settlement nearby. It was not too surprising, therefore, when Roman tiles were spotted in the bank of the nearby River Mimram by local archaeologist Tony Rook in the early 1960s. Excavations followed, and the Dicket Mead villa was discovered.

The villa was huge, with at least four buildings spread over a large area, built in *c.* AD 200, with alterations made until it was demolished in the late fourth century. The third-century bath suite attached to Building 3 was particularly well-preserved, and a campaign led to it being conserved and displayed in a vault beneath the embankment of the A1 motorway, which opened as a museum in 1975. All is explained, with models and reconstructions amongst the remains of the various heated rooms showing how the baths would have worked and displays showing artefacts from the excavations.

5

Central England
*Cheshire, Derbyshire, Leicestershire, Lincolnshire,
Notts, Shropshire, Staffs, Warks, West Midlands*

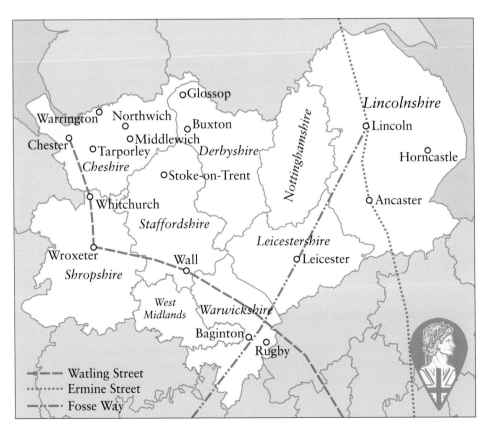

Central England.

Our Central England region stretches from the Welsh Marches and the Wirral to the Lincolnshire Fens and Wolds near the east coast, taking in the Peak District on the way. A number of major Roman roads slice through this territory, including Watling Street, running from London to Wroxeter and then Chester, and Ermine Street, running from London to Lincoln and then York. Part of the Fosse Way loosely marked the frontier of Roman rule in Britain for the first few decades after AD 43, and continued to be an important route, running in a more-or-less straight line from Exeter to Lincoln.

The tribal areas were those of the Cornovii to the west, and the Coritani, or Corieltauvi, to the east, and forts were soon planted at strategic points along these routes, especially where they met rivers that needed to be crossed. These crossing points often also provided riverine navigational opportunities for supplies. A legionary fortress was established overlooking a lake on the River Witham at **Lincoln** (Lindum) by the AD 50s, and this became a *colonia* when the legions moved on in the late first century. On the other side of the country, on the River Dee at **Chester**, a fortress was built by the mid-AD 70s to house first the Second Legion Adiutrix and then the Twentieth Legion. This was a good position for controlling both the restless Ordovices of North Wales and the Brigantes of northern England and may have been intended as a base for an invasion of Ireland, which never happened. Both cities have a great selection of Roman remains to hunt down.

Two more military sites in the region are the unique reconstruction of a wooden fort at The Lunt, **Baginton**, Warwickshire, built over the excavated remains of a first-century fort, and Melandra Castle in the hills near **Glossop**, Derbyshire, where the outline of the fort platform is clearly visible, even from ground level.

Many of the fort sites were replaced by towns, forming a communication and trade network that accumulated wealth as time went on. Along Watling Street there are remains to be seen at **Wall** (Letocetum) and especially **Wroxeter** (Viroconium Cornoviorum) and good museum displays at **Rugby** (finds from Tripontium) and **Whitchurch** (Mediolanum). Salt deposits in Cheshire represent an important commodity in this region, and at the salt towns of **Middlewich**, Nantwich and **Northwich** much Roman activity has been discovered. Although there is nothing to see on the ground, the museums in these towns tell the story of Roman salt-working.

Further east, along Ermine Street the Roman towns to be explored are **Ancaster**, **Horncastle** (Banovallum?) and **Leicester** (Ratae Corieltavorum). Wroxeter and Leicester each have one of the most substantial surviving pieces of Roman masonry in Britain – not to be missed.

Villas were rare in much of this region, particularly the western counties. Just one has been identified in Cheshire, at Eaton near Tarporley, on private land. More have been found to the east, in Leicestershire and Lincolnshire, but nothing can be seen of their riches now except in museums.

In addition to the museums and sites described below, Congleton Museum has information about the Romans in Cheshire, with two coin hoards on display. At Caistor, Lincs, there is a small bit of Roman wall visible in the churchyard wall of St Peter and Paul.

Ancaster, Lincolnshire *

Roman town: scant remains of walls near St Martin's parish church, site of Ancaster Mother Goddesses.

There was undoubtedly once a Roman town where the village of Ancaster lies today, on Ermine Street, the main Roman road between London, Lincoln and York. Alas there is little to see today, although evidence has been found of early marching camps and a stone fort controlling traffic through a gap in the limestone ridge running north–south through Lincolnshire, now known as the Ancaster Gap. The town had developed by the second century and was given stone walls during the third century. Its Roman name is not known; its identification with Causennis, as mentioned in the *Antonine Itinerary*, is no longer generally accepted.

Visible remains are centred around **St Martin's Church** (Ermine Street, NG32 3PW). The line of the town wall and ditch can be seen on the opposite side of Ermine Street to the churchyard. A *Time Team* dig in 2002 revealed part of the wall, and a late Roman cist with a reused slab with an inscription to the god Viridios, perhaps meaning vigorous or virile, who had also been named on an inscription found when digging a grave here in 1961. These are now displayed in the museum known as The Collection, in Lincoln.

On the wall next to the lychgate is a replica of a sculpture of three mother goddesses, the middle one decapitated at some time, found in the churchyard in 1831. Again, the original is in The Collection.

The modern churchyard, a short walk up Church Lane, was also a burial ground in Roman times. About 300 graves have been found here, and two plain Roman stone sarcophagi have been left to illustrate this. There is also a striking modern representation of a legionary standard to enhance the Roman atmosphere.

Inside the church itself there is a small display about the Roman town, including some pieces of sculpture, and there is a good pamphlet for sale at the church and the village post office. A fine Norman font and arcading are also worthy of attention.

Baginton, Warks ***

The Lunt Roman fort, partially reconstructed. Seasonal opening.

The fort known as The Lunt lies in a quiet location on the edge of Baginton (Coventry Road, Baginton, CV8 3AJ). It is the only place in Britain where you can see a reconstructed Roman fort made of wood. The post-holes of its original timber buildings were discovered and excavated in the 1960s, and some were reconstructed *in situ* by a squadron of Royal Engineers, supervised by archaeologist Brian Hobley, using Roman methods and materials wherever possible. The structure of the gateway above the ground plan, for example, was copied from an illustration on Trajan's Column in Rome. It is thus an ongoing experiment in the sustainability of such structures, having already lasted much longer than the originals had to. It opened in 1974, forty-five years ago, so the modern structures have been in use more than twice as long as the originals, which were built *c*. AD 60–61 and abandoned about twenty years later.

Auxiliary soldiers guarding the reconstructed gate of The Lunt fort, Baginton.

The name Lunt is not Roman, but rather the name of the wooded slope where the remains were discovered, derived from the medieval laund or launt. This lies above a crossing point of the River Stowe, close to the junction of Watling Street and the Fosse Way. It was built as part of a militarised zone around the time of the Boudican rebellion in AD 60/61, with nearby forts at Wall (Letocetum), Mancetter (Manduessedum), Alcester (Alauna) and Metchley. The final battle between Boudica's vast army of rebellious followers and the legions under Suetonius Paullinus was fought somewhere in this area, and garrisoned forts were needed to provide supplies as well as troops during and after this.

In AD 64 the fort was reduced in size, with an irregular outline due to the fact that a circular cavalry training arena, or *gyrus*, was included within it. This is the only fort in Europe to have this arrangement, though others had them outside the defensive walls. Finds suggest that cavalry units were stationed here, of perhaps 120 men, along with 480 infantry soldiers, and the *gyrus* would therefore have been put to good use for training purposes. One interpretation put forward for the unusual layout is that many British horses would have been captured after Boudica's last stand, and these would need to be retrained for use by the Roman cavalry. Extra security measures would have been sensible at such a time of increased instability, hence the *gyrus* inside the walls.

It is not entirely certain whether the fort was ever temporarily reoccupied after its abandonment in AD 80. Coins of later date have been found at the site, including a hoard of *c.* AD 200 buried near the eastern gateway and a single later third-century coin found in a gateway post-hole. Do these indicate that people were living here, or were the ruined structures a handy landmark or casual shelter?

Today the reconstructed fort is a wonderful asset for teaching school parties, but it is also fascinating for anyone with an interest in the Romans. The wooden buildings are inevitably showing signs of wear and tear, though there are plans afoot for repairs and reconstruction. The granary has recently been rebuilt, and is an impressive space filled with original finds from the excavations, a fine model of the fort and also replica army equipment for schools and for professional events. The outlines of the headquarters building and six barracks blocks are marked out in concrete on the ground. There is also an attractive garden planted with Roman herbs and flowers. It's a great immersive Roman experience, especially if you coincide with one of their summer events.

Buxton (Aquae Arnemetiae), Derbyshire ***

Buxton Museum and Art Gallery with Roman Gallery

Buxton could have been the Bath of the Peak District, but somehow it has not retained or revealed its Roman heritage quite as generously. The highest market town in England, there was certainly a Roman settlement here, attracted by the hot spring, still rising at a constant temperature of 82°F (28°C). The name Aquae Arnemetiae is taken from the seventh-century *Ravenna Cosmography*, meaning the goddess of the grove, but we know very little about her, not even her name. Although, as at Bath, there was a great resurgence of popularity in taking the waters here in the eighteenth and nineteenth centuries, the Roman structures did not emerge during the building work.

All the evidence today lies in the impressive Victorian building which is **Buxton Museum and Art Gallery** (Terrace Road, Buxton SK17 6DA), built as the Peak Hydropathic Hotel. Roman finds include a hoard of coins, spanning the period AD 70–410, found in 1979 in the mineral baths. These must have been thrown into

The Roman Gallery complete with Legionary soldier, in Buxton Museum and Art Gallery. *Photo: Derbyshire County Council.*

the waters to propitiate the goddess, along with personal objects such as jewellery and thimbles.

In addition to the warm spring, there were other resources to exploit here. The local silver was found to be of disappointingly poor quality, but a number of lead ingots are displayed, some stamped with Hadrian's name, and some with the place name Lutadarum, perhaps their place of origin. This has not been identified with certainty, but it might have been close to the site of Carsington Reservoir, since evidence for Roman settlement and other activity was excavated there prior to its construction. At Poole's Cavern, on the edge of the town, evidence has been found of Roman bronze-smiths making jewellery.

There are also finds from Melandra Castle, Glossop (below) and other forts nearby.

Chester (Deva Victrix), Cheshire *****

Legionary fortress: walls, amphitheatre, other architectural remains, Grosvenor Museum. All open sites except the museum.

Chester is one of England's most attractive cities, with traditional black and white Cheshire architecture, riverside walks and well-kept open spaces. It is proud of its Roman heritage and displays the relics of the period with flair. It has, indeed, recently been dubbed 'Britain's most Roman city', a difficult claim to test, though the echoes of 'sin, dex, sin ...' can often be heard as twenty-first-century legionaries march school parties around the streets. Whether the Romans ever marched to that command, a shortening of the Latin for 'left, right, left', is not known.

It is thought that the Roman presence here began with a fort in the mid-50s, though firm evidence is elusive. By the mid AD 70s a new military base was needed to control the Ordovices of North Wales and the Brigantes of northern England. This site on the River Dee was perfect, as it stood between the two territories, dividing them, and also allowing access to the sea via the river.

The Second Legion Adiutrix ('helper') was dispatched to build the timber fortress, tucked into a bend in the river, with the water running much closer to the west wall than it does now. Some believe that this position was also chosen as a good spot from which to launch a campaign to Ireland, which never happened. The Roodee Racecourse to the west of the city lies over the site of the harbour, and there was a bridge over the river to the south. The name of the fortress and its associated settlement was taken from the name of the river.

The Second Legion Adiutrix left to go to Dacia under Trajan in AD 87, and the Twentieth Legion Valeria Victrix ('brave and victorious') came down from Inchtuthil in Scotland to garrison the fortress. This was rebuilt in stone early in the second century, with a massive stone wall backed by a sand and clay rampart, and a double ditch in front. It was occupied until the late fourth century, with intermittent repairs recorded. The silting of the river and subsequent change of course probably had something to do with its abandonment.

Excavations over the years have produced lots of evidence of the fortress and its associated civilian settlement, all excellently well explained in the Grosvenor Museum. Happily, there is still plenty to be seen on a walk around the city.

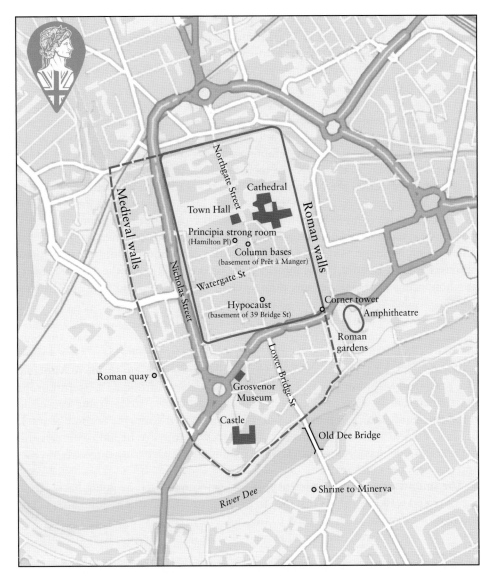

Plan of Roman Chester superimposed on modern street map.

The fortress walls still survive in places, incorporated into the later city walls on the north and east sides. When the city was re-founded as a burgh by the Anglo-Saxons in AD 907, they repaired and rebuilt the Roman walls, but then after the Norman conquest the wall circuit was extended to the south and west to incorporate a castle built overlooking the river. This is the circuit that survives today as a wall walk for most of its length, but less than half follows the Roman line. At various points along the north and east sides, impressive stretches of Roman masonry can still be seen, especially between Eastgate and Northgate, best appreciated by descending from the wall to look at it from the outside. On the west side the Roman wall followed the course of the Inner Ring Road, whereas the medieval walls run closer to the river, along the side of the racecourse.

The *principia*, in the centre of the fortress, lay to the south of the site now occupied by the Town Hall and Tourist Information Centre, in Northgate Street. To the north of the town hall is a small display of Roman relics, including a column and bases, erected to commemorate a 1981 prize given to the city for preserving its historic monuments.

A glimpse of the *principia* can be seen by walking south down Northgate Street, then turn right beside the Dublin Packet pub, towards Hamilton Place, where you will see a window onto the foundations of the strongroom which stood at the north end of the *principia*, once containing soldiers' pay chests and other valuables. The replica legionary standards are there to show that the originals would once have been displayed in the room above. Continue south down Northgate Street to Nos 21–23, currently Pret a Manger, where you can ask to be taken into the cellar to see the massive column bases for the basilican cross hall of the *principia*.

Continue south, crossing Eastgate Street into Bridge Street, where at No. 39 the cellar contains the remains of a **hypocaust of a bath-house**. Until recently these premises were a Spud-u-Like (another relic of the past!), but the new occupiers are honouring the sign on the door which says 'Come and see our Roman remains inside'.

Continue south and cross the river by the Old Dee Bridge, which is the medieval replacement for the Roman bridge that once stood here. Turn right past the Ship Inn onto a footpath into a public park, Edgar's Field in Handbridge. After a short walk you will see an outcrop of rock which still bears a **rock-cut shrine to Minerva**. The carving is worn but this is the only Roman rock-cut shrine in Western Europe that remains in its original location. Within a protective stone frame carved in the nineteenth century, Minerva's outline has survived from the second century, holding a shield with an owl on her shoulder. With the eye of faith you can still make it out. She has been guarding the crossing of the Dee for nearly 2,000 years and is worth the extra walk.

The south-east angle tower of the fortress wall can be seen by going back across the river and walking a short distance to the north-east, to Little St John Street. The foundations lie in a patch of grass to the east of the later Newgate and walls. You can rejoin the wall-walk here, giving a good view down over the Roman Gardens, the angle tower foundations and the amphitheatre.

Outside the south-east corner of the fortress lie the remains of the **amphitheatre**, half excavated and laid out for free viewing, with information boards. It was the largest in Britain and was constructed in stone in the late first century, then rebuilt and much enlarged around AD 200 to seat more than 8,000 people. It remained in use until about 350. A number of excavations have taken place since it was discovered in 1929, most recently and thoroughly by Tony Wilmott and team in 2004–6. These revealed that cock-fighting, bull-baiting and gladiatorial combat were staged to draw the crowds, and that there was a shrine to Nemesis, goddess of retribution, at the north entrance to the arena. Particularly effective is a modern trompe l'oeil mural on the wall of the excavated half of the arena, restoring the appearance of the whole elliptical monument, with a tethering stone for wild beasts at the centre. The arena wall is shown on each side as a ruin, then gradually restored to its former red marble-covered glory in the centre.

Chester amphitheatre with trompe l'oeil frieze, foundations of south-east angle tower of fortress walls in the background.

Chester Roman Gardens lie just to the west of Dee House and the county court, which stand on the unexcavated southern half of the amphitheatre. This was a Festival of Britain project to display Roman architectural fragments found around the city, which were laid out in this public park in 1949, including columns and a hypocaust from the bath building described above in the basement in Bridge Street. They are beautifully maintained and a lovely, peaceful haven.

Grosvenor Museum is a five-minute walk from here west along Pepper Street then Grosvenor Street. Built in 1885 to house the collections of the Chester Archaeological Society, it is a mix of glorious historic buildings, and indeed includes a seventeenth-century house within the premises. The Roman Newstead Gallery, named after the museum's first curator, tells the story of the fortress and its *canabae*, with many artefacts as well as models and reconstructions. There is lots of military equipment, including some for cavalry units, painted plaster and all the paraphernalia of everyday life. 'Stories in Stone' is a gallery full of inscriptions, many funerary, revealing much about the people who lived and died in Deva Victrix. Many of these stones had been used to repair the city wall, probably in late Roman times, this preserving the crispness of the inscriptions. They were discovered and retrieved during repair operations in the late nineteenth-century.

If you walk along the medieval stretch of town wall to the west, overlooking the racecourse, you should look out for a very small patch of the **wall of the Roman quay** which is at the foot of the entrance steps which go down to the racecourse just south of Black Friars road.

Glossop, Derbyshire **

Melandra Castle (Ardotalia?) auxiliary fort. EH. Open site.

Melandra Castle is the only visible Roman structure in the Peak District, so this, and its strategic position, should encourage you to visit (Melandra Castle Road, off A626 Glossop Road in Gamesley, Glossop SK13 6JB). The site overlooks the River Etherow, guarding the route into the Longdendale Valley, and the view north is still as dramatic as it ever was. To the south, though, it now overlooks a housing estate. All the information boards were missing on a recent visit, but it is managed by EH and they will hopefully be restored.

The name Melandra Castle seems to have been used for the site from at least the eighteenth century, when there were still substantial bits of wall showing. The Roman name Ardotalia is a version of a place-name in the seventh-century *Ravenna Cosmography*, which is often used for this site although the association is not certain.

Excavations have shown that the first wooden fort, built *c.* AD 70, was rebuilt in stone in about AD 110. An inscription, now displayed in Buxton Museum, tells us that this was done by soldiers from the First Cohort of Frisiavones, recruited in Germany, commanded by Valerius Vitalis. Evidence for a *vicus* outside the walls of the fort has also been found. The site seems to have been abandoned by the middle of the second century.

The playing card outline of the fort platform is still clearly visible, enhanced by the footpaths worn inside the low banks. The grass-cutters also usually emphasise the position of the main routes through the fort, and the central position of the headquarters building. Occasionally patches of stone can still be seen in the surrounding banks. Finds from the excavations, including the inscriptions, pottery and other artefacts, are in Buxton Museum.

Horncastle (Banovallum?), Lincolnshire *

Roman town: fragments of late Roman walls hidden in modern buildings.

Horncastle doesn't flaunt its Roman heritage, but several chunks of its town walls hidden in unlikely places make an entertaining treasure hunt.

The name Banovallum, meaning 'wall on the River Bain', has been suggested by an interpretation of the seventh-century *Ravenna Cosmography*. It does not certainly refer to Horncastle, but as it has been adopted for a local school and a few businesses it will no doubt stick.

The walled area dates to the late third or fourth century and may have been a stronghold rather than a fully developed town. A larger area of settlement has been identified to the south of this, dating from the late Iron Age into the Roman period, and the relationship between the two areas is not fully understood.

The surviving bits of wall are the best-preserved of the period in Lincolnshire. The easiest place to get your bearings is on the south side of the churchyard of

Roman wall preserved in a bookshop in Horncastle.

St Mary's Church, Church Lane, (LN9 5HW). Here the wall follows the line of houses facing the churchyard in Church Walk. To the west of these, in the lane called St Mary's Square, behind a gate marked 7A & 12, is an enormous section of the core of the wall.

East of the Church Walk houses and around the corner in Wharf Road (LN9 5HL) is Horncastle Library, which was built over another chunk of the Roman wall. This is displayed within, together with information about Roman Horncastle. Outside, on the eastern side of the building, a semi-circular bastion from the south-eastern part of the walls is marked out on the pavement in white stones.

Other glimpses can be had behind the shops near the Co-op supermarket; by the entrance to Banovallum House in Manor House Street, where a section of the western wall is marked with a blue plaque; and most entertainingly, in the back room of the Jabberwock Bookshop at 14 St Lawrence Street.

Leicester (Ratae Corieltauvorum), Leicestershire ***

Roman civitas capital: The Jewry Wall Bath-house and Museum; St Nicholas's Church.

For many years Leicester has not been accorded the attention it deserves, after the city planners of the 1960s built an inner ring road which separated the commercial centre from the River Soar, the castle and the Roman remains. Attempts are now being made to reconnect all the parts of the Roman and medieval city, and since the discovery of Richard III's remains has sparked new interest in the city's history,

The Jewry
Wall in
Leicester, once
the entrance
to a Roman
bath-house.

hopefully the substantial Roman remains in St Nicholas Circle will also attract
more visitors, especially when the museum refurbishment is complete.

This was the civitas capital of the Corieltauvi tribe, whose settlement was
established by the late Iron Age where the Fosse Way crossed the River Soar. This
lies under the area known now as St Nicholas Circle and Bath Lane. A Roman
fort was established here soon after the invasion, and by the second century this
had been replaced by the Roman town known as Ratae, from the Celtic word for
'ramparts'. It flourished, gaining substantial public buildings in the second century
and defensive stone walls in the third century, surviving until the end of the Roman
period. Much archaeological investigation has taken place, making it one of the
most explored Roman towns in Britain, the results of which reside in the Jewry Wall
Museum. Parts of one large public building, a bathing complex, can still be seen.

The most important Roman remains still visible are the **Jewry Wall Bath-house
and Museum** (156–140 St Nicholas Walk, Leicester LE1 4LB). The chance survival
of the Jewry Wall, at 30 feet (9 metres) high the largest surviving Roman masonry
structure in Britain, is due to its reuse as the west wall of the Saxon Church of
St Nicholas. It remained upright after various revisions of the church building,
which still stands nearby. By the early eighteenth century the antiquarian William
Stukeley was referring to it as 'The Jewry Wall', a name thought to derive from
the twenty-four 'Jurats' or medieval borough councillors who held meetings in the
churchyard.

Early ideas on its origins included a Temple of Janus associated with a gate
into the city, and a Roman basilica. Its true purpose, as the entrance to a public
bath-house erected in AD 160, was revealed when, ironically, the site was acquired
for development into a municipal baths in the 1930s. A redundant factory was
demolished and excavations revealed the various foundations of the baths and a
possible Mithraeum to the south, all still displayed today. The museum covering
part of the site was built in 1966 to house the finds from this and other excavations,

including milestones from along the Fosse Way and very fine mosaics, wall-paintings and high-status objects. Many are from excavations of the *macellum* beneath the Travel Lodge in Highcross Street, a courtyard house in Vine Street and beneath the original Shires Shopping Centre. In 2019 the museum is still undergoing extensive renovations.

The Norman **Church of St Nicholas** stands to the east of the Jewry Wall complex, and a circumnavigation will take you down the wonderfully named Holy Bones street. The walls of the church and tower are full of reused Roman stone and tile from the bath-house next door and other nearby structures. A plaque explains all this, and two large sandstone columns are displayed in the churchyard.

Lincoln (Lindum Colonia), Lincolnshire *****

Fortress and colonia: Newport Arch; The Collection; Mint Wall; East Gate, South Gate and Lower West Gate.

Any visitor to Lincoln would be entranced and overwhelmed by the Norman castle and towering medieval cathedral, but you don't have to look much harder to find an astonishing wealth of Roman remains in the city. These are some of the best in Britain.

By the AD 50s a legion of the Roman army had arrived at this point on their march northward, building a fortress on a high hill overlooking a natural lake formed from a widening of the River Witham, now known as the Brayford Pool. This may have been the source of the name Lindum, a Latinised version of a Celtic word for pool. The evidence from tombstones suggests that the first legion to set up camp here was the Ninth Hispana, which moved on to York around AD 71, to be replaced in Lincoln by the Second Legion Adiutrix, before it in turn moved on to Chester. During the reign of Domitian, perhaps *c.* AD 86, the fortress

The Newport Arch, Lincoln, North Gate of the Roman town.

became a *colonia*, a settlement for retired soldiers. The modern name is thus a portmanteau of the Roman Lindum Colonia.

The city expanded rapidly, having strategic importance at the junction of the Fosse Way and Ermine Street, spreading down the slope towards the river, forming a settlement in two parts, an Upper and a Lower Town. Today the main street between them is still aptly named 'Steep Hill'. The castle and cathedral occupy the south side of the Upper Town, the latter representing the zenith of medieval Gothic architecture, for many centuries the highest building in the world.

In the late third century the city was made capital of one of the British provinces, as subdivided by Diocletian, probably Britannia Secunda, though some think Flavia Caesariensis.

The **Newport Arch** was the north gate of the Roman town, still substantially complete, and the only Roman gateway in the country still used by modern traffic. Alas, this has meant the arch has had a few scrapes with modern technology, having been nearly demolished in the 1960s by an errant lorry, having two more stuck beneath the arch in the early 2000s, then recently narrowly avoiding a similar event fuelled by Satnav.

The stonework dates from the early fourth century, when the gate was enhanced to reflect the status of the city as a provincial capital. It would originally have had a second pedestrian archway flanking the large central arch for traffic. An excavated area beside the arch shows the original street level, which would have meant the arch was 26 feet (8 metres) high, some 12 feet (3 metres) higher than it appears today. Even more impressive, it would have had a second storey and would have been flanked by semi-circular towers.

From the Newport Arch at the top of Bailgate a small intervallum road named East Bight leads past a stretch of the north **city wall**, in front of which the base of a **Roman water cistern** can be seen marked out in the grass. This is all that remains of a sophisticated water supply system, bringing water by aqueduct from a spring called 'Roaring Meg' to the north-east of the city, having raised its level by some form of water tower with pump or bucket and chain, to give it the height to run along the channel. Various lengths of lead and ceramic pipes have been found during excavations over the years, as well as a bath-house near this site, which would have made use of a lot of the water.

Heading south on Bailgate, you see the circular positions of nineteen columns of a colonnade marked out in the cobbles of the street. These made up the eastern portico of the **forum**, which lay more or less in the centre of the Upper Town. The remains of the columns were mostly discovered in 1878 when a sewer was dug along this street. Some of the bases still survive in shop cellars, though these are not open to the public.

Nearby are smart metal railings surrounding a Roman well that was located in the forum, partially excavated in 1984 and now covered by glass for safety.

Behind the Castle Hotel on West Bight is an impressive stretch of Roman walling, 16 feet (5 metres) high and about 66 feet (20 metres) long, still encapsulated by later buildings. It is a rare survival in that it was not defensive, but rather the north outer wall of the basilica, the Roman town hall and law court. It has been known since the eighteenth century as the **Mint Wall**, presumably from an erroneous belief that it once formed part of the town mint.

The Victorian **Church of St Paul in the Bail** that once stood on the site of the forum was demolished in the early 1970s, allowing the area to be excavated before a new church was constructed. This revealed that a whole series of churches had stood on the same spot, perhaps going back to the fourth century, which would make it one of the earliest church sites in Britain. The second church on the site dated from the seventh century, and the position of this is marked out in the paving beside the modern church.

Walk east along Eastgate to the **Roman East Gate** in the Upper Town, the north tower of which is well laid out and displayed in the forecourt of the Lincoln Hotel. Behind the hotel, through a car park, is a long section of the eastern town wall running north of the East Gate, somewhat obscured by foliage but still visible.

No visitor to Lincoln should miss the cathedral, and even here there is a Roman treat: a section of a **fine geometric mosaic**, discovered in the cloisters in 1793 and moved to its current position at the bottom of a staircase near the coffee shop.

At the top end of Steep Hill the site of the upper town's **South Gate** can be seen both as part of the wall of the shops on the west side and again opposite inside the shop at No. 44. Steps leading up the hill to the gate were revealed by excavations but are not visible today.

The major remains to see in the Lower Town are a significant stretch of **town wall in Temple Gardens**, to the east of the Bishop's Palace and the **Lower West Gate** near the Lincoln City Offices in Orchard St.

There is also a fine **Roman altar** in the **Church of St Swithins** in Bank Street, in the south-east corner of the Lower Town. It was found when the church was built in 1884, and still stands inside it. The altar was dedicated to the Fates, goddesses and the spirits of the deified emperors by Gaius Antistius Frontinus, who was a curator, i.e. someone who looked after something, probably finances, perhaps of a burial club.

The new city museum, called **The Collection** (Danes Terrace, Lincoln LN2 1LP), is really superb. The lion's share of the collection is Roman and includes mosaics, pottery, coins, tombstones and milestones. Of particular note are lead cisterns, which might be early Christian fonts, the Tattersall Hoard, and an erotic knife handle. An impressive model of a legion at full strength on parade reminds us what a formidable fighting force this must have been.

A really nice touch is the cast of a dedication stone from Mainz in the main reception. The stone was set up by Marcus Minicius Marcellinus, who was the most senior centurion (Prima Pilus) of the Twenty-Second Legion. The stone relates that Marcellinus was from Lincoln and therefore he is earliest known person from the city.

The Collection runs tours of Roman Lincoln during the summer months which are well worth joining, and a Roman walk is also marked out with signs around the city.

Finally, south of the city and over the River Witham are three more bits of Roman archaeology preserved in three different churches.

Less than 200 yards (182 metres) south of the river lies the eleventh-century **Church of St Mary le Wigford** (3 St Mary's Lane LN5 7AR), and just beside the door, set into the west face of the tower, is a **Roman tombstone** which was reused and re-inscribed in the Anglo-Saxon period, the new inscription having been squashed into a triangle at the top of the stone.

The Roman tombstone was dedicated to a man called Sacer, son of Bruscus of the Gaulish Senones tribe, as well as his wife Carssouna and his son Quintus. The dedication begins DIS MANIBVS NOMINI SACRI, to the spirits of the departed and to the name of ....

The Saxon inscription, reading from bottom to top, reads 'Ertig had me built and endowed to the glory of Christ and St Mary', and may well be the dedication stone of the church, dating from the eleventh century. Why Ertig chose to use, but not deface, the older stone is a mystery – perhaps the wording suggested a Christian faith, although the words are in fact typically pagan.

A further 700 yards (640 metres) south, at the junction of High Street and Sibthorpe Street, is the **Church of St Mary's Guildhall**. Beneath a glass panel inside, a **section of Roman road** can be seen, probably the Fosse Way, close to its junction with Ermine Street.

Right next to St Mary's is the **church tower of St Peter at Gowts**, and high up above the lancet window on the west face, and therefore very difficult to see, is a very worn **carving of a lion-headed human figure**, believed by some to represent the Mithraic god Arimanius. It has been compared to a similar figure from York, in York Museum.

Middlewich (Salinae or Condate), Cheshire *

Auxiliary fort and salt town: Library display, including the Middlewich Diploma; fort platform, Roman town heritage trail, King Street.

The 'wich' suffix in place names has its root in the Anglo-Saxon denotation for a salt-producing town, and Middlewich lies, as its name suggests, between two others, Northwich and Nantwich, to the north and south respectively. The rock salt deposits beneath the Cheshire basin were a valuable commodity to the Romans, since the water running over these provided inland brine that could be extracted and heated to produce salt through evaporation. This was a vital ingredient in the preservation of the food needed to feed the army, and indeed all those who served the Empire. It is often said that the word salary derives from the part of a soldier's pay either made in salt or set aside to buy salt.

The Roman name for the settlement at Middlewich may have been either Salinae or Condate ('confluence' or 'watersmeet'); the debate has occupied scholars for many years. Support for the latter might be suggested by the name of the main Roman road north through the town: King Street, previously known as Kind Street, perhaps derived from Condate.

Middlewich Library (Lewin Street, CW10 9AS) is the best place to start, with displays of archaeological finds and the start of a heritage trail to the site of the Roman fort in Harbutt's Field.

All sorts of artefacts are on show, and more specific to this area, an example of a lead salt pan, in which the brine would have been heated to extract the salt. Excavations have revealed many features such as brine pits associated with the industry, as well as the sites of the timber buildings in which the salters lived and worked. Tim Strickland's marvellous book on Roman Middlewich is for sale here.

There is also a bronze discharge diploma given for twenty-five years of service as an auxiliary soldier in the army, conferring Roman citizenship on a trooper of the Ala Classiana, a cavalry regiment. The diploma dates to AD 105, during the reign of Trajan, and we know that the regiment, originally raised in Gaul and Thrace, was mentioned in dispatches for its war service in northern Britain. It has been suggested that this retired soldier may have used his capital to set up a private saltworks at Middlewich.

The heritage trail takes you to **Harbutt's Field**, on a flat area of high ground to the south and east of the confluence of the River Wheelock and River Croco. A fort was built here in the AD 70s as part of Agricola's campaign of expansion in the north of England. The lines of the fort walls and the streets within have been marked out by modern pathways, giving a sense of the scale of the structure.

The associated *vicus*, which developed into the town once the fort was abandoned, lies under modern housing, but information boards give details.

Heading north from Middlewich towards Warrington, the road follows the line of the Roman road, King Street, and is a delight of straight-line driving for a good few miles.

Northwich (Condate?), Cheshire *

Auxiliary fort and salt town: Lion Salt Works and Weaver Hall Museum.

This is another possible candidate for the Roman place-name Condate (see also Nantwich), since it lies at the confluence of the rivers Weaver and Dane. Excavations have produced evidence for a fort established in the late AD 70s, at about the same time as the fortress at Chester, along with a *vicus* which developed into a civilian settlement. Nothing can now be seen of these, but there is much to be learnt about the Roman salt industry here.

Roman salt pan in the Lion Saltworks, Northwich.

The Lion Salt Works (Ollershaw Lane, Marston CW9 6ES) is the site of the last open pan salt works in Cheshire, which closed in 1986 and was then transformed into a museum to tell the story of the Cheshire salt industry. Much of the Victorian equipment and machinery is preserved, and the enterprise has won heritage awards. It begins with the evidence for Roman activity, and a few of the most important finds from the salt towns have been displayed here. These include pieces of kiln from Middlewich and a lead salt pan inscribed with the name Veluvius, presumably the salter, from the fort at Castle, Northwich. There is also a piece of a medieval wooden salt ship from Nantwich – a large wooden trough designed to store brine as part of the production process. A leaflet sold here on Roman salt-making discusses the evidence for both Imperial and private enterprise in this commodity.

Other Roman finds from the town can be seen at the **Weaver Hall Museum and Workhouse** (162 London Road, Northwich CW9 8AB).

Rugby, Warwickshire ***

Rugby Art Gallery and Museum.

Amongst the artworks and the library in the modern **Rugby Art Gallery and Museum** (Little Elborow Street, CV21 3BZ) is a collection of Roman artefacts excavated from the town of Tripontium, 3.5 miles (5.5 km) to the north-east. This lay just off Watling Street, at a point where three bridges were needed to cross the River Avon and two of its tributaries, hence the name, which is listed in the *Antonine Itinerary*. Gravel extraction has destroyed some of the site, but a large bath-house, administrative building and a *mansio* have been identified.

The displays include reconstructions of market stalls and other aspects of Roman life, but also a good range of artefacts excavated by the Rugby Archaeological Society. These include a fine decorated buckle which has been used as the society's logo. Graffiti on tiles has revealed the name of the local tribe, the Corieltauvi, and also a fragmentary Roman alphabet.

The Roman gallery shares the top floor with an exhibition of British twentieth and twenty-first-century art. Paintings by Stanley Spencer, L. S. Lowry, Paul Nash and Graham Sutherland rub shoulders with the rather fine drawings of finds from Tripontium by Eamon O'Kane.

Also in the building is the Rugby Hall of Fame for those with an interest in the *Azzurri*, more modern Italian combatants.

Enamelled brooch from Tripontium.
Photo: Rugby Museum and Art Gallery.

Stoke-on-Trent, Staffs * *

The Potteries Museum and Art Gallery: Staffordshire Moorlands or Ilam Pan, the Lightwood Hoard, finds from Rocester and Chesterton.

One would expect the Potteries Museum (Bethesda Street, Hanley ST1 3DW) to house a world-class collection of ceramics; it also has an exceptional art gallery, the odd Spitfire or two and a stunning collection of archaeological treasures. A new gallery has recently been introduced to display the breath-taking collection of Anglo-Saxon jewelled sword fittings and other precious metal objects known as the Staffordshire Hoard.

Another superstar item can sometimes be found here, courtesy of the chance discovery in the county of the Staffordshire Moorlands or Ilam Pan, described in the entry for the Tullie House Museum in Carlisle, its other occasional home. The small enamelled bronze bowl would have been a souvenir of Hadrian's Wall.

There are also artefacts from the forts and settlements at Rocester and Chesterton and a coin hoard found in a garden in Langton in 1960. The late third-century Lightfoot Hoard contains more than 2,000 coins, including a large number of barbarous radiates, and some silver snake bracelets.

It is pleasing to note that the first pottery kilns known to have existed in this metropolis of ceramics were Roman.

The enamelled Ilam Pan, a souvenir of Hadrian's Wall. *Photo: The Potteries Museum, Stoke on Trent.*

Wall (Letocetum), Staffs **

Roman town: baths, mansio and museum. EH.

This was once an important staging post on Watling Street, between London and Wroxeter. The same route is now more or less followed by the A5 and the M6 toll, though rather than running through the village of Wall, built on the ruins of Letocetum, the main road loops around it, resulting in a surprisingly quiet oasis.

A fort was built here *c.* AD 50, the settlement around which developed into a prosperous town by the second century. At its largest it spread for about a mile along Watling Street, but when the walls were built in the fourth century they enclosed a much smaller area. Traces of a temple (beneath the church), a large granary, an amphitheatre (now a depression in a field), houses, defences and burials along Watling Street have all been identified at various times.

In the post-Roman period the focus of settlement moved from here to Lichfield, 2 miles (3 km) to the north. Parts of the late Roman town walls were still standing in the nineteenth century, providing the inspiration for the name of the new post-medieval settlement.

The visible remains at **Wall Roman Site** (Watling St, Lichfield WS14 0AW) are now limited to the foundations of a bath-house and a *mansio* laid out beside the road still named Watling Street. Most of the floor plan of the baths is complete, together with the associated exercise hall. The hypocaust system can clearly be seen. Various periods of excavation, beginning in 1912–14, have revealed a long and complicated history of perhaps five phases, beginning as a first-century military establishment, and enhanced and modified until the fourth century.

The walls of Wall (Letocetum) Roman town on Watling Street. *Photo: Sioni Davies.*

To the north-west of the bath-house lies the *mansio*, an official government coaching inn offering accommodation to important travellers. It was constructed in stone in the mid-second century, replacing two earlier consecutive wooden structures on the site. The bath-house may have been a part of this complex. Both structures were destroyed by fire in the late third century, and this area was excluded from the circuit of walls surrounding the smaller late Roman town.

The site museum (seasonal opening) is small but delightful, run by helpful volunteers. Amongst the many finds displayed is some beautiful plaster work, a segment of a milestone and a lead statuette of a wrestler.

Warrington, Cheshire *

Roman town site; Warrington Museum, including the Warrington Actor's Mask; Roman road.

Warrington is the home town of one of the authors and although its visible Roman remains are scant they provided the inspiration for this book.

Warrington was, until modern times, the lowest bridging point on the River Mersey, controlling much of the north–south transport route on the west side of the Pennines. No evidence for a Roman bridge has yet been discovered, but there was clearly a crossing as King Street, the Roman road that passed through Middlewich and Northwich, also passed through Warrington on its way towards Carlisle.

It is thought that an Agricolan fort was built north of the river, close to St Elphin's Parish Church, on the same spot as the later Norman motte and bailey castle. The main Roman settlement, however, was south of the river in the area of Stockton Heath, often referred to as Wilderspool in the literature, although this name is no longer in common usage.

The site of an extensive Roman industrial town was first discovered when the Bridgwater Canal and Greenall's Brewery were constructed in the late eighteenth century. This is canal country and the Old Quay Canal and the gargantuan Manchester Ship Canal have also criss-crossed the site, revealing its Roman past. Continuous building and man-made changes to the line of the River Mersey make it a difficult site to interpret. The only indication of the centre of the settlement, where Morrison's supermarket is today, is a blue plaque on the adjacent handsome eighteenth-century brewery buildings. South of the ship canal a small street called Roman Road disappears under Stockton Heath Primary School. Recent excavations revealed the line of the road together with kilns and wells; the road has been preserved and displayed and can be viewed by appointment.

Warrington Museum is a real Grade II listed treasure, a rare survivor of an early Victorian Museum with fitted display cabinets full of mummies and shrunken heads. Only a small number of local Roman items are on display. The most unusual is a very rare actor's mask, made of pottery and with attachment holes on each side of the face, found at Stockton Heath and donated to the museum in the 1870s. Pottery was an important industry in Roman Warrington, so was the mask a local product intended for use elsewhere or did the town have an as-yet-undiscovered theatre of its own?

Whitchurch (Mediolanum), Shropshire *

Roman town site: Whitchurch Heritage Centre.

Whitchurch still stands on Watling Street, but for the story of the fort succeeded by the town called Mediolanum you have to visit the Heritage Centre (12 St Mary's Street, Whitchurch SY13 1QY). Excavations have suggested that its history is linked to that of Wroxeter, as it lies halfway between that fort and Chester, both about 20 miles away.

The displays in the museum include some impressive complete pots, mostly from burials found along the High Street, which would once have been outside the town. The Sedgefield bronze mirror, dating to about AD 150, also came from a burial site.

Wroxeter (Viriconium Cornoviorum), Shropshire ****

Civitas capital: the 'Old Work', reconstructed town house, St Andrews Church. EH.

The arrival of the railways in Shropshire in Victorian times brought a rush of interest in the lost Roman city of Viriconium (off the B4380 north of Wroxeter village, SY5 6PJ). Excavations in the mid-nineteenth century generated one of the largest collections of artefacts in Roman Britain, including an extremely fine silver mirror, bronzes and enamels. There were no less than three guide-books to the site with advertisements for hotels, livery stables and local grocers and information on everything one would need to organise a trip, picnic in the picturesque ruins and see the latest discoveries.

The Roman town had been left in ruins as the centre of population migrated during Saxon times to a more defensible site at Shrewsbury, a few miles along the River Severn. Unusually, a sizeable chunk survived the stone robbers and the whole site is dominated by the 'Old Work', the gargantuan remains of the basilica wall adjoining the bath suite. Similar in scale to the Jewry Wall in Leicester but without the modern buildings to impinge on its majesty, the Old Work is one of the most imposing pieces of Roman masonry surviving in Britain.

A legionary fortress was built here, at a strategic crossing point of the River Severn, in about AD 60, replacing an earlier auxiliary fort to the south. The fortress underlies the town, and was garrisoned first by the Fourteenth Legion Gemina, then the Twentieth Legion Valeria Victrix, before it moved on to Chester in the late AD 70s. It was then downgraded to a supply depot, and the military nature of the site ended towards the end of the first century. It became the civitas capital of the local Cornovii tribe, whose territory had previously included the nearby Wrekin hillfort, which seems to have been stormed and burnt by the Romans when they first arrived in the area.

The extent of the subsequent city is enormous, covering some 192 acres (78 hectares), making it the fourth largest in Britain. The line of the city walls can be clearly seen in the surrounding countryside as it is followed by modern field boundaries of ditches and hedgerows. These defences were built in the second century and comprised a turf and timber rampart, which was enlarged in the fourth century.

The area of the site open to the public is only a very small part of the city centre, including a rectangular basilica hall, with a central nave and two aisles, which was the exercise hall of the bath-house. One of the long sides, which contained the main entrance to the complex, survives to a whopping height of 23 feet (7 metres), called the 'Old Work' from at least the seventeenth century. The hypocaust system of the heated rooms of the enormous bathhouse is also well laid out and there are two shops and a *macellum*, adjacent to these. Unusually, it seems that the bath complex was maintained into the fifth century, before being systematically demolished. Building platforms for houses and other structures were then built over the ruins, and some form of town life seems to have continued until the sixth or seventh century, when the site was abandoned.

Opposite the large standing wall was the entrance to the forum, and an inscription once displayed above this dates its completion to AD 129–130, during the reign of Hadrian, and includes the name of the town. A cast is in the site museum, which also has decorated wall plaster, intriguing votive items and oculist materials which might suggest that Wroxeter was a centre for the treatment of eye diseases. Other finds from the site, including the silver mirror and tombstones, can be seen in nearby Shrewsbury Museum.

Across the road from the museum is a reconstructed town house. Built in 2010, it is useful in gauging the scale of the buildings in the town.

The hidden jewel of Wroxeter is the **Church of St Andrew**. When the main part of the town was abandoned, a small village grew up at the south end, and the north wall of this church is Anglo-Saxon in date, perhaps ninth to eleventh-century, built out of reused Roman stone blocks. Built into the south side of the church is an eighth-century carved cross from the time of Offa, King of Mercia. The church gateposts comprise two Roman columns with capitals, and the font is also carved from the base of a massive column.

Roman Columns from Wroxeter reused as the Lych Gate for the church.

6

Wales

There was no delineation between England and Wales until several centuries after the end of Roman rule, the name deriving from the Anglo-Saxon word Wealas, meaning foreigner. Before the Romans arrived, much of the territory in the north was dominated by the Ordovices tribe, and that in the south by the Silures, occupying the higher ground to the west of the Welsh Marches.

The early advance of the army into the west began under Ostorius Scapula between AD 47 and 52 and continued until Boudica and her followers drew the attention of the legions away in AD 60/61. By this time there had been many skirmishes, and the druidic priesthood had been pushed back to their stronghold and sacred centre on Anglesey (Mona). There is a vivid description by Tacitus of the desperate hordes of men and women along the shore of Anglesey facing the Roman troops under Suetonius Paulinus, who soon cut them down and desecrated their sacred groves. Tacitus ends the episode with 'While he was thus occupied, the sudden revolt of the province was announced to Suetonius' – all eyes were then on what was happening in East Anglia and beyond.

Despite this near-catastrophic disruption of the Roman advance, the Silures tribe was overcome by forces led by Julius Frontinus in AD 74, and the Ordovices in the north had been subdued by Julius Agricola by AD 78. A strong military presence was considered a continuing necessity in this volatile region – a host of marching camps, forts and fortlets has been recognised by survey, aerial photography and excavation all over Wales, some of which are visible today from the ground. Between forty and fifty military sites are known in this region, of which twelve are described here because there is something tangible to visit. Many more are visible to some degree as earthworks, and could be hunted down by those who are very keen. Many have 'Caer' or 'Gaer' as part of their name, the Welsh word for camp or fortress, showing that a memory of what they had been lingered on in the Welsh landscape.

Pre-eminent amongst the military remains in Wales is the legionary fortress at **Caerleon**, which became the base for the Second Legion Augusta in AD 75, after it had moved from Exeter and then Gloucester, retaining a presence here until about AD 300. It is the best surviving fortress in Britain since much of the ground has not subsequently been built over, and many features are laid out for visitors, including an excellent site museum.

Wales.

This region was rich in natural resources which the Romans were quick to exploit. Gold was mined at **Dolaucothi**, and the National Trust site here makes a great visit. There was also Roman extraction of copper on Anglesey, silver and lead on the north coast and in Gwent, and coal near Pontypool. Later mining activity has often obscured Roman evidence at the sites, but finds of ingots, analysis of artefacts and physical traces recognised during excavation reveal that the ores were being extracted before the Romans arrived, and that mining intensified under their industrial organisation.

Many of the forts would have guarded the trade routes of these commodities, and a network of roads served the mines. Confusingly, a number of these Roman roads are known as **Sarn Helen**, reflecting a traditional belief that St Elen of Caernarvon ordered roads to be built through Wales. Helen, or Elen, was the wife of Magnus Maximus, fourth-century Emperor of Britain, Gaul and Spain, known in Welsh as Macsen Wledig, whose dream is the title of one of the tales of the twelfth or thirteenth-century *Mabinogion*. These legends saw him as the ancestor of several early medieval Welsh kings. Some of the most scenic, relatively easy walks along these routes go through the Brecon Beacons.

Settlements soon grew around the forts and fortresses, and two civitas capitals have been recognised in Wales. **Carmarthen** (Moridunum), Britain's smallest Roman town, was wealthy enough to have its own amphitheatre, still visible today. **Caerwent** (Venta Silurum) has lots to see, including some of the best Roman town walls anywhere in Britain.

Much of the population continued to live in fortified collections of circular houses, just as in other more remote parts of the province such as Cornwall and the north. Examples include **Din Lligwy** on Anglesey and the spectacular hillfort at Tre'r Ceiri on the Llyn Peninsula in Gwynnedd.

At least thirteen villas have been identified in Wales, showing that some farmers did adopt Roman architecture and comforts, although nothing approaching the wealth of the Cotswold villas has yet been found. Most are in the south and the west; the most northerly yet recognised is Abermagwr in Cardiganshire. A number have been excavated and published, but it is only at Ely, Cardiff, that there are any visible traces, and this is only an unmown rectangle of humps and bumps next to a playing field in Trelai Park.

There has been some debate about whether a system of late shore defences was constructed along the west coast of Britain to match the Saxon Shore forts further east. There is not much evidence for this in south Wales, but a fort at **Cardiff** was rebuilt in stone in the late third century, probably to guard the Severn Estuary. Those at **Caernarfon** (Segontium) and **Holyhead** (Caergybi) in the north-west would have provided protection against raids over the Irish Sea. There may have been naval fleets based in these areas but no conclusive proof of their presence has yet been found.

In addition to the museums described below, the Radnorshire Museum in Llandridod Wells, Bangor Museum and Powysland Museum in Welshpool also show Roman finds from nearby excavations. Brecknock Museum in Brecon also has a Roman collection, undergoing refurbishment in 2019.

Brecon Gaer / y Gaer (Bannium Cicucium), Powys ***

Auxiliary fort: stone walls and gates. Cadw.

Turn south-west off the road between Cradoc and Aberyscir, and the site lies on private land at the end of a narrow tarmac access road to Y Gaer Farm (LD3 9NT). Walk through the farm buildings and through a gate to the footpath around the fort. This is an open site.

The West Gate of Brecon Gaer fort, pivot holes visible in the threshold stones. *Photo: Dot Smith.*

A first glimpse of Brecon Gaer makes two millennia seem no time at all: a deserted Roman fort still standing in the Welsh hills, robbed here and there for building stone, but with much of its outline intact. This clarity has been aided by the excavations of Mortimer Wheeler in 1924–5 and the subsequent care of Cadw.

It lies on a ridge close to the confluence of the Usk and Ysgir rivers, on a route through Silurian territory, between other forts and marching camps. The first timber and earth fort was built *c.* AD 75–80 and manned by a 500-strong cavalry unit from Vettones in Spain. This was replaced by a stone fort built and manned by a detachment of the Second Legion Augusta in *c.* AD 140. This lasted until *c.* AD 200, and there is evidence for two subsequent reoccupations during the third and fourth centuries.

The stone fort had walls 10 feet (3 metres) high and a tower at each rounded corner. Three of the gates, on the east, west and south sides, have been excavated and consolidated, each with two lanes for traffic and two gatehouses. At the west gate the pivot holes for the gate are still clearly visible. The stonework of the curved north-east corner is beautifully well preserved. On the north side farm buildings overlie the defences, making use of the Roman stone.

Wheeler's excavations revealed barracks, a bath-house, and the HQ building within the defences, all now under grass with grazing cows. There was a *vicus* for families and traders outside the north wall.

The finds are in Brecknock Museum in Brecon. One of the most poignant is a tombstone of 'Candidus, trooper of the Cavalry Regiment of Vettonian Spaniards, Roman citizens ... aged 20, of 3 years' service'.

Caerhun (Kanovium), Gwynedd *

Auxiliary fort platform. Open site.

Hidden at the southern end of the estuary of the River Conway, Caerhun nestles a few miles to the south of Edward I's great castle at Conway. Travelling south from Conway on the Llanrwst road to the west of the river, Caerhun fort lies on the left just before reaching the village of Tal y Bont (Caerhun, Tyn y Groes LL32 8UG). The only indicator is a signpost to the thirteenth-century church of St Mary.

Take the track to the church and the fort platform will appear in front of you as a grassy earthwork. St Mary's church lies in the north-east corner of the fort and the small parking area has an information board. Good plans of the fort can be found on boards in the lychgate and inside the church, which was built using the handy stone from the fort.

Initially a fort of earth and timber was built in the mid-70s AD for a garrison of 500 auxiliary soldiers. It was rebuilt in stone in the early second century. Periods of abandonment are evident but activity continued into the fourth century.

The ramparts on the south-eastern corner are impressively high and the south wall and gate are well worth a look. Evidence for a *vicus* north of the fort has been found, as indeed have the remains of the bath-house between the fort and the river.

The pretty church of St Mary was constructed in the thirteenth century, now surrounded by ancient yew trees overlooking the stunning Conway valley.

A very fine example of a Roman milestone, now in the British Museum, was found not very far away in Llanfairfechan, marking 8 miles from Kanovium, on the route to Caernarvon. The inscription shows that it was dedicated to the Emperor Hadrian and it can be precisely dated to AD 120–121 by his honorific titles.

Finds from the excavations of the 1920s are in the Roman Room at the Llandudno Museum.

Caerleon (Isca), Gwent *****

Legionary fortress: amphitheatre, barracks, bath-house and museum. Cadw; open site except bath-house and museum.

Caerleon is the 'must-see' military site in Wales, much-excavated, and with lots still visible, including an amphitheatre (the best-preserved in Britain), barracks blocks (the best-preserved in Europe) bath-house and its own Roman Legion Museum. It is sometimes referred to as Isca Silurum, to differentiate it from Exeter (Isca Dumnoniorum), but the local tribal name would not originally have been used for a fortress.

This was one of the three permanent legionary fortresses in Roman Britain, along with Chester and York, established after the manoeuvres of the first-century campaigns and before the construction of the northern frontier. It is the only one not lying beneath a modern city, which is why there is so much to see.

It was founded in the mid-70s AD after the campaigns of Julius Frontinus against the Silures and Ordovices in south and north Wales respectively, as a base

The amphitheatre at Caerleon, which would have seated the fortress garrison of 5-6000.

for the Second Legion Augusta, which had moved on from Exeter and Gloucester. Caerleon had the advantage of access from the sea, via the River Usk, to keep supplies coming in.

It continued to be occupied until the end of Roman Britain, but after the end of the first century it was a long way from the main action. Much of the garrison actually spent most of the second century building and controlling Hadrian's Wall and, briefly, the Antonine Wall, but the south Welsh base was maintained.

Most of the main structures of a fortress have been identified by excavations – barracks blocks, the central *principia* and *praetorium* and a huge legionary bath-house. Most of these structures were first made of wood but were replaced in stone in the second century. The exception was the bath-house, where risk of fire meant that it was stone-built from the beginning. The early earthen defences were strengthened by the addition of a stone wall in the second century. The site of the hospital has also been identified, as well as a huge metal workshop and granaries.

Excavations by Cardiff University in Priory Fields to the west and south of the amphitheatre have revealed evidence for a port on the River Usk, with associated courtyard buildings and a bath-house. In addition, the large sprawling settlement, the *canabae legionis*, surrounding the fortress has been discovered in places, where traders, families and general hangers-on resided. It all presents one of the most complete pictures of fortress life anywhere in Britain, well explained in the superb site museum.

The amphitheatre is impressive, standing just outside the fortress walls to the west. The arena is clearly defined, the walled bank surrounding it sliced into eight sections by passageways giving access to both the arena and the seating above. Large post-holes found during excavations in the bank suggest that the seating was arranged on a wooden superstructure. It would have been able to seat the whole garrison of 5–6,000, and was used for military training and demonstrations as much as for entertainment. The parade ground lay just to the north-west of it, now under a sports field. The amphitheatre was excavated in 1926 by Mortimer and Tessa Wheeler – financial sponsorship coming from the *Daily Mail* – and this showed that it had undergone several modifications before being abandoned, probably in the third century.

The foundations of the **barrack blocks** can be seen if you walk north-west around the fortress defences. Four have been marked out, but only the one nearest the rampart was fully excavated, which is why it is at a lower level than the others. Each had twelve *contuberniae* or sleeping rooms for eight men, possibly in bunk beds. Ten of these would have housed a century of eighty men, so the two spares might have been for new recruits, slaves, or for storing equipment. The drain of a communal latrine is clearly visible in the nearby corner of the fortress.

The legionary bath-house is on the High Street (NP18 1AE), north-east of the barracks. The remains have been partially roofed over, with museum displays of objects found here, explaining how the baths were used. The projection of water into the plunge pool, with swimmers playing, is wonderfully atmospheric, and red light in the hypocaust shows how hot this would have been.

The nearby **Roman Legion Museum** has more finds from the bath-house, including many exquisitely carved gemstones which must have been loosened by the hot steamy air and lost down the drains, to be retrieved by archaeologists two millennia later. Note the beautiful facet-cut bath-flask, which would once have held oil for massage, with a copper strigil, fine examples of essential bath-time kit. Excavated armour, alongside reproductions, illustrate the kit of both legionary and auxiliary, and many important inscriptions tell the stories of individual soldiers who lived and died here.

Much of the garrison finally left the fortress in the turmoil of the late third century, *c*. AD 287–296, perhaps moving to the new stone fort at Cardiff which was built about this time. Many of the buildings were abandoned or demolished, although there is evidence of occupation in some of the barracks continuing to the fourth century – a much reduced military presence perhaps, after the reforms of Diocletian?

The history of Caerleon then became embroiled in the legend of King Arthur, recorded by Geoffrey of Monmouth in the twelfth century and embroidered ever since, most beautifully by Mary Stewart's novels for children. The amphitheatre was identified for a long time as Arthur's round table.

Caernarfon (Segontium), Gwynedd ***

Large auxiliary fort. NT and Cadw.

Segontium is the first Roman site co-author Mike visited as a young boy, where he first caught 'Roman Legionnaire's Disease'! Lying in a prominent position above the Plantagenet town of Caernarfon, it is a strange oasis of calm just off the bypass and on the road to Bedgellert (Llanbeblig / Constantine Rd, Caernarfon LL55 2LN). The rather lovely Edwardian museum was closed at the time of writing, which is a real shame.

The fort itself is impressive. It is split in two by Llanbeblig (Constantine) Road, with the east side having the lion's share of the exposed areas of the fort. Signage is

Segontium Auxiliary Fort in Caernarfon, the largest in Wales.

a little sparse but the granaries, barracks, commandant's house and *principia* make themselves fairly clear. The steps down to the strong room in the *principia* are very crisp and evocative.

Segontium was the largest fort in North Wales and is estimated to have had a garrison of 1,000 auxiliaries, probably part-mounted troops. It is interesting to reflect that Edward I's strategy of subduing Wales by creating garrisons at Caernarfon, Harlech and Conway had already been used by Agricola 1,200 years before. Segontium was the major link in the chain of forts that included Caerhun, just south of Conway, and Tolmen y Mur, just north of Harlech. Built on higher ground than Edward I's later castle, it commanded a good view of the Menai Straits. Perhaps one of the purposes of the garrison was to guard the valuable minerals being mined on Anglesey.

The building sequence followed the usual pattern of first-century timber structures replaced in stone during the second century. The garrison was reduced at this time – an inscription suggests that there were 500 men here in AD 120, from the First Cohort Sunicorum who were originally from Gallia Belgica, in the north-east of Roman Gaul.

During the third and fourth centuries there were continuing reductions, and the role of the garrison was probably primarily to protect from piratical raids. The coin evidence suggests the occupation continued to the end of the fourth century. The legend of Macsen Lleldig tells us that Macsen and Elen ruled the empire from a castle at Caer Seint – claimed to be Segontium. The stone was later plundered for Edward I's castle.

The ambience of Segontium benefits from the foresight of an early member of the National Trust, who planted Mediterranean pine trees around the perimeter. On the scorching hot day when we visited it felt as though we were in a select corner of Pompeii.

Caerwent – Venta Silurum, Gwent *****

Roman civitas capital with magnificent walls, forum-basilica, temple, shops, houses. Cadw. Open site.

If Caerleon is the pre-eminent Roman military site in Wales, Caerwent is the best Roman town, and it is fortunate indeed that they lie less than 10 miles (16 km) apart, making a perfect Roman day out. This is not just a coincidence – founding the civitas capital of the Silures tribe in about AD 75 under the protection and watchful eye of the nearby legionary fortress was a very sensible move. Nowadays the A48, which more or less follows the route of the Roman road from Gloucester to Carmarthen via Caerleon, runs around its north wall, so it is not hard to find. A few modern buildings now stand either side of this road, but much of the interior of the town is grassland, and the walk around the walls has beautiful views over the countryside. Excavations over many years have revealed Roman building foundations, now laid out with signs.

'Small but perfectly formed' is a good description – the stone walls enclose 44 acres (18 hectares), so the town was only about one-fifth the size of Cirencester, not so far away. The car park is at West Gate Barns (NP26 5AU), near the west gate.

The walls are the finest of their kind to be found in Britain, standing more than 17 feet (5 metres) high in places, and they can be traced for the whole circuit of 1 mile (1.6 km). The modern road through the village cuts the wall where the East and West Gates once stood; the gatehouses have been largely destroyed. Excavation has shown that they had double portals flanked by large rectangular towers. As you walk, look out for areas where only the rubble and cement core survive and stretches where the neat rectangular facing stones are still in place. The junctions between the work of different gangs of builders can also be detected. Originally there would have been a wall walk on top fronted by battlements.

The walls of Caerwent, Roman Isca Silurum.

The large external polygonal towers on the north and south sides were added in the mid-fourth century. The construction of the walls themselves, inserted into earlier earthwork defences, has been dated to AD 330 by a coin thought to have been associated with building work, but many think they may actually be third-century in date, which is when many other town defences were strengthened.

Two inscribed stones reside in the porch of the Parish Church of St Stephen and St Tathan, to the south of the main road through the town. You can take a short cut from the walls to the interior through the churchyard. One is an altar dedicated to the god Mars Ocelus, a fusion of a Roman and a Celtic deity, by a grateful optio: 'To the god Mars Ocelus, Aelius Aegustinus, optio, willingly and deservedly fulfilled his vow'.

The other is dedicated to Paulinus, who commanded the Second Legion Augusta, then held two governorships in Gaul, and became governor of Britannia Inferior in AD 220. Since this latter post is not mentioned on the inscription it must date to just before this.

'To Tiberius Claudius Paulinus, legate of Leg II Aug, proconsul of (Gallia) Narbonensis, imperial propraetorian legate of Gallia Lugdunensis. By decree of the ordines for public works on the tribal council of the Silures'. It is a rare confirmation in writing of the status of the town as tribal capital of the Silures.

A Romano-Celtic temple lay across the road to the east of the church. The foundations are laid out as excavated: a square within a square, the inner being the shrine of an unknown deity, all within a rectangular *temenos* (sacred enclosure). An altar for sacrifices and offerings was found, and an ornate entrance building which may have housed rituals. It dates to AD 330, surprisingly late in the history of such buildings, at a time when Christianity was becoming established elsewhere.

The forum and basilica lie nearby, the administrative and commercial centre of the town, built in the early second century in a grand style with a large hall with two rows of massive Corinthian columns of local sandstone. Excavations have shown it went through a substantial rebuild in the third century, perhaps because of subsidence, and stopped being used *c.* AD 330.

A large courtyard house stood to the west of the forum, with many rooms of high status laid out around two courtyards. Painted wall plaster, mosaic floors and fine artefacts were found during excavations in the 1980s, some of which can be seen in Newport Museum. It stood in splendour during the fourth century, the culmination of improvements first from a late second-century/early third-century timber house on stone foundations, then from a larger stone-built house on the same site. Other courtyard houses have been found at Caerwent – a model in Newport Museum shows what these would have looked like.

Houses, shops and workshops excavated in the 1940s stand nearby, just north-east of the car park. The foundations include a pottery kiln and a smithy, and there were many changes to the layout over the life of the town.

Other structures have been found which are no longer visible, including a large oval to the north-east of the basilica, which may have been an amphitheatre, though some think it may have been a cattle market. There was also a bath-house to the south of the forum and other temples. An important second-century inscription was found reused in a later wall dedicated to a Rhineland god, Mars-Lenus, equating him with a Celtic god, Ocelus Vellaunus, showing how deities moved with their devotees and were matched with locals. This can be seen in Newport Museum.

Cardiff, S. Glamorgan ✱✱✱✱

Cardiff Castle incorporating Roman fort walls, reconstructed gate.

Cardiff city centre is dominated by its castle and surrounding park, with wild beasts of stone leaping over the walls, playing or snarling at passers-by (Castle St CF10 3RB). These are part of the transformation brought about in the nineteenth century by William Burgess for the 3rd Marquess of Bute, turning the family mansion into a Gothic Revival extravaganza.

As you approach the castle entrance look at the walls to your right, and you will see patches of stonework low down which are demarcated in red Radyr stone. These are the surviving remnants of a stone Roman fort built during the second half of the third century. This glimpse is available without going into the castle, but a full visit to appreciate the complexity of the site is well worth the entrance fee.

This was the fourth Roman fort on this strategic site near the River Taff, not far from the Bristol Channel. Traces have been found of three predecessors of timber and earth, the size and position of which varied with time. The first, dated by coins to the AD 60s, was the largest, and the castle (which shares the late fort walls) now lies completely within its boundaries. Two much smaller forts of the second and third centuries followed, now lying beneath the north wall of the castle. A plan displayed beside the long stretch of Roman wall by the gift shop shows their relative positions. This stretch was the lower internal face of the south wall of the fort, which would originally have been protected by an internal bank. It was never therefore visible or exposed to the elements until it was excavated in the late nineteenth century, hence its excellent state of preservation.

Archaeological excavation and survey have shown that the late stone fort was built hastily and rather inexpertly. Rather than a neat square, it has been described as an 'irregular nine-sided polygon', probably built as a response to the instability of the late third century. It seems to have been abandoned before the fourth century ended.

Reconstructed North Gate of the Roman fort which preceded Cardiff Castle.

The exposure and rebuilding of the Roman walls was thanks to the 3rd and 4th Marquesses of Bute in the late nineteenth and early twentieth centuries. The Normans had enhanced the abandoned Roman defences at the end of the eleventh century by covering the remains of the walls with a huge earthen bank. This formed the bailey of the large motte constructed in the north-west corner of the fort. Nearly 900 years later Lord Bute's workmen were tunnelling into the east bank to build a new tower and extend the grounds of the castle when the ancient stone walls were rediscovered. The walls were then uncovered and substantially restored to their former glory.

In fact, the whole circuit was rebuilt, with the addition of a covered gallery within, added so that Lord Bute and his guests could walk and remain dry whatever the weather. These vaults within the walls provided shelter from air raids for the people of Cardiff during the Second World War.

The twin-towered North Gate was also rebuilt from its original Roman foundations, demarcated by red stone, to mimic the Roman original. The first, late nineteenth-century, version was criticised for being too high, so it was altered in 1922. It certainly looks impressive.

The internal buildings of the fourth-century fort have not been discovered. The wall running from the Norman motte across the green was constructed by the Normans to form an inner and outer castle ward. It was demolished, along with many other historic features, in the eighteenth century when the landscape gardener Capability Brown was hired by the 1st Marquess to transform the mansion gardens. Roman levels in some areas have been removed by this and later gardening activity.

The fifteenth-century mansion, later enhanced by Burges's Gothic towers and fabulously exotic interior decor, is also well worth a visit.

Carmarthen (Moridunum), Dyfed **

Civitas capital: amphitheatre and museum.

The Roman presence at Carmarthen began with a timber fort built *c.* AD 75 north of the River Towy, where there was a crossing point. A smaller stone fort was built in the north-east corner of this one a short time later, before the garrison moved away soon after AD 120.

Moridunum then became Britain's smallest Roman town, the civitas capital of the local Demetae tribe. It developed from the *vicus* outside the fort to the north-east. The second-century defences, consisting of an earthen bank fronted by two ditches, enclosed only 32 acres (13 hectares), so it was even smaller than Caerwent. Later these were replaced in stone, and the line of the walls is more or less followed by Richmond Terrace, Little Water Street and The Parade. The site of the Roman town thus straddles Priory Street (A484). Over the years, particularly since the 1970s, excavations in various parts of this area have produced evidence of domestic and commercial buildings, a Romano-Celtic temple and, in summer 2018, the probable site of the forum, rich with finds, just off Priory Street. There is nothing to be seen of any of the town within the walls, however, except as displays in the Carmarthenshire Museum.

The amphitheatre at Moridunum (Carmarthen), Britain's smallest Roman town.

The amphitheatre is the only visible monument, lying 200 metres outside the walls to the north-east, on Priory Street, not far from the site of Merlin's Oak, marked by a large notice board. This was recognised in 1944 when the surrounding housing was being built, and preserved as an open area. It was excavated in 1968, and part of the stone arena wall and entrance passage have been rebuilt for display. The surrounding grassy mound would once have been covered with timber seating. The site is an open park.

The town was still being maintained and rebuilt into the late fourth century. Later it was associated with the legends of Merlin.

Carmarthenshire Museum is housed in the former Bishop's Palace at Abergwili, around 1.5 miles (2 km) to the east of the town centre, just off the A40. It has a number of displays packed with Roman finds from the town, a little old fashioned but wonderful to see. There is lots of military metalwork from the site of the forts, and pottery and glassware of good quality. Only one inscription has so far been found in the town – from St Peter's Vicarage in the western part, and probably of fourth-century date. This reads BONO REIPVBLICAE NATO – 'to him who was born for the good of the state', an admirably loyal sentiment expressed in this remote corner of the Empire. There are also finds from Dolauchothi and Pumsaint, and other sites in the region.

Din Lligwy, Anglesey ✳✳✳

Fortified Romano-British farmstead. Cadw. Open site.

This has to be the closest you will get to the full *Game of Thrones* or *Lord of the Rings* experience on a Roman period site in Britain... Walk past a ruined medieval chapel, down through a field with wide spectacular views of the coast and then a

Roman-British farmstead at Din Lligwy, a site with atmosphere.

climb through a dark wood to the skeletal jagged remains of a cluster of buildings made of monumental stone slabs. The woods give a sense of what a sacred mistletoe grove of the Druids might have felt like before their destruction by Paulinus's legions, but in fact they post-date the occupation of the site by many centuries. During the later Roman period the landscape was open, and the inhabitants would have enjoyed wonderful views across Lligwy Bay.

The settlement consists of an intriguing pentagonal enclosure with two roundhouses and at least four rectangular Roman-style buildings, all built of large irregular slabs of the local stone. Coins and other artefacts found during early twentieth-century excavations showed that there was occupation here in the third and fourth centuries. Local people were apparently continuing to live in their traditional circular houses, building rectangular structures for housing animals and for workshops. The latter were probably for iron working, since slag and smithing hearths were found within. There are some good on-site reconstruction drawings.

Nearby is a Neolithic burial chamber with a capstone weighing 25 tons supported by uprights, visible from the road as you approach the layby from the south-east. The ruined chapel dates from the twelfth century, with additions made in the fourteenth and sixteenth centuries.

(Moelfre LL72 8NH.) Park in a layby on a minor road leading north-west from the A5108 / A5025 junction. An information board in the layby describes all three sites.

Dolaucothi, Carmarthenshire **

Gold mines; museum and organised underground tours. NT.

The gold mining complex at Dolaucothi, in the Cothi river valley near Pumsaint, lies just off the A482 between Llanwrda and Lampeter in south-west Wales (Llanwrda, SA19 8US). It is the only source of gold in Britain where firm evidence of Roman exploitation has been found, and excavations and surveys have revealed information about how this was done.

The mines were once again active in the late nineteenth century, until mining stopped in 1938, not because the gold had run out completely but because it was too expensive to extract from the rock. The estate was acquired by the National Trust in 1941, and there is now a visitor centre, with organised tours which take you underground (hard hats and other safety gear provided). At ground level the 1930s mining equipment and vehicles have been preserved and displayed, some of it from this site, some from other mines, and the Roman activity is explained as part of the tour, rather than being a visible feature, reflected in the star rating. It is an awe-inspiring glimpse of Roman organisation and technological expertise, revealed by several periods of archaeological investigation by teams from Cardiff and Lampeter Universities.

A fort was established at nearby Pumsaint, north of the River Cothi, during the AD 70s, probably to protect the mining activities. This was occupied until sometime in the second century, but mining continued after the troops were withdrawn, and the mines may well have passed into civilian hands. An associated civic settlement is indicated by bath-house remains found south of the river in the nineteenth century.

Recent work has suggested that the gold may already have been mined by surface working in the prehistoric period, and the Romans simply took this over and then intensified it by extending underground. Evidence has been found of an extensive water-driven system which must have aided mining operations. At least four leats (water channels) have been identified, one tapping the Cothi River nearly 7 miles (11 km) upstream, and others tapping the headwaters of the Annell and Gwenlais and tributaries of the Cothi at various distances from the site. These could have brought 3 million gallons (nearly 14 million litres) of water to the mine daily, feeding holding tanks identified above the mines. It is tempting to see this being used in the way described by the first-century writer Pliny, perhaps inspired by the mines at Las Medulas in northern Spain, for washing away the soil to reveal the rock with gold-bearing veins, a system known as 'hushing', but the evidence for this is not yet conclusive. Alternatively it might have been used for driving heavy hammers to crush the ore, or for washing the gold out of the crushed ore. The remains of a large wooden waterwheel of Roman date found in one of the underground galleries was most likely used for lifting water to the surface. Since this was 12 feet (3.5 m) above the gallery floor, it was probably one of a series.

A huge stone, known as Carreg Pumsaint, which stands near the entrance to the site, has been interpreted by some as an anvil used with a heavy hammer for crushing the quartz – it has several large hollows up each side which might have been formed by this activity, with the hammer being moved when the hollows got too deep. Local tradition tells of the hollows being made by the heads of saints who sought shelter beneath it in a storm, giving the name Pumsaint ('five saints') to the nearby town.

Gelligaer, Mid Glamorgan*

Auxiliary fort platform and information panels beside Church Road; practice camps on Gelligaer Common.

The fort at Gelligaer was built in a commanding position on a ridge between the valleys of the rivers Taff and Rhymney, one of a line of forts between Cardiff and Brecon Gaer (Church Road, CF82 8FW). Much excavation has taken place here, revealing lots of the structures within and around the military complex, but all that can be seen now is the grassy square of the later stone fort, surrounded by a low broad bank, with some information panels in a layby beside Church Road.

A first-century timber fort to the north-west was replaced by a stone one in the early years of the second century. The discovery of three inscriptions dedicated to Trajan provide a date for the construction, the largest being on display at the new St Fagans Museum of History. The grandeur of the fort can best be appreciated by looking through a transparent panel with outlines of the main buildings to get an idea of scale. An annexe was added to the south east, containing a huge bath-house, and a tile kiln was discovered south-east of this when digging one of the graves in a nearby churchyard. The garrison soon moved on, however, perhaps as soon as AD 130, but there is evidence of reoccupation in the late third or early fourth century, perhaps as a response to unrest.

If you want real insight into the life of a Roman soldier, continue north-west after visiting the fort, taking a right fork onto Heol Adam. This is the Roman road heading straight from Cardiff to Brecon – take the first right after about 1.5 miles to bring you back in a loop through Gelligaer Common. Five rectangular practice camps can be spotted as faint earthworks at intervals along this road if the light is good. These would have kept the troops busy when they had no campaigning to do, becoming experts in the speedy digging of camp enclosures.

Holyhead, Anglesey **

Caer Gybi, late shore fort and Caer y Twr, naval base and signal station. Cadw.

Holyhead is a port town inextricably linked with trade and transport to and from Ireland. It is the terminus of the A5, which follows the major Roman highway of Watling Street for most of its route, having been transformed by Thomas Telford in the early nineteenth century as the quickest route to Dublin. Holyhead has fallen on hard times and is now only a shadow of its former self, although it is possible to spot some very fine buildings in the town, some of which are undergoing renovation.

The ancient church of St Cybi (Stanley St, LL65 1HG) is a peaceful spot just off the High Street, well worth a visit for its fabulous perpendicular porch. The main attraction for us is the three side walls of the church yard, once the defences of a late third-century shore fort, **Caer Gybi**. It is similar to, if much smaller than, those of south-east England, and probably worked in conjunction with nearby Segontium to defend against sea-borne raiders.

The impressive walls are herringbone-patterned, rising above 15 feet (4.5 metres) in places. The protruding round corner towers are equally substantial but may have had some restoration in the late eighteenth century. The open side to the south-east is thought to have opened onto a stretch of beach where ships could load and unload, and there may have been two projecting walls extending down the cliffs to protect this.

Above the town, on the summit of Holyhead mountain, are the remains of a signal station at **Caer y Twr**, built within the ramparts of an Iron Age hillfort. It lies next to the triangulation point and could benefit from some signage, but can be found by walking from the South Stack Cliffs RSPB centre visitor centre (LL65 1YH). There are fantastic views out over the harbour of Holyhead to the east.

The tower was built between the second and fourth centuries, when sightings of hostile pirates or raiders could be signalled to the shore fort below and to the large fort at Segontium (Caernarvon) 20 miles to the south. Nothing remains of the superstructure, but it is likely to have incorporated a flaming beacon of some sort. Just below the tower is a group of enclosed hut circles, which may have been contemporary with it.

Margam, West Glamorgan*

Stones Museum. Cadw. Seasonal opening.

This former Victorian schoolhouse of Stones Museum (Abbey Road, Port Talbot SA13 2TA) houses an important collection of Celtic stone crosses and other memorial stones of the sixth to sixteenth centuries. Only one, though, is relevant to our survey: a sixth-century memorial stone to Cantusus, son of Paulinus. This had made use of a sandstone monolith with a Roman inscription by turning it upside down and putting the new inscription on the reverse side. The original inscription reads: IMP C FLA MAX MINO INVIC TO AV GVS (now partly missing).

This may translate as: 'For the Emperor Caesar Flavius Valerius Maximinus, the Unconquered, Augustus'.

Maximinus II ruled as (disputed) Emperor in the East from AD 310 to 313, and like the inscribed stones in Devon and Cornwall this may be a milestone or it may be an expression of loyalty.

It was found, in six pieces, in 1839 at Port Talbot on the route of the Roman road from Neath (Nidum).

Neath (Nidum), West Glamorgan *

Auxiliary fort: foundations of two gateways.

The Roman auxiliary fort at Neath was first discovered and excavated in 1949 when a housing estate was constructed over its southern half. It lies south of Neath Abbey Road (A474), on the residential loop road called Roman Way. The foundations of the **South-East and the South-West Gates** have been displayed, firmly hemmed in by railings, between the houses on the road. The former lies to the east by the railway embankment, the latter to the north, between Roman Way and Neath Abbey Road. Not far beyond the railway to the east is the River Neath (Welsh Nedd), and the fort was positioned to guard the crossing point on the road to Carmarthen (Moridunum). Neither site has any surviving signage, though they are well maintained within their cages. Both passages of the South-East Gate can be seen between square towers, and the outer ditch is also clearly visible; the footings of a guard chamber and a doorway represent the South-West Gate.

The fort was almost exactly square, enclosing 6 acres (2.4 hectares), and the north part lies to the north of Neath Abbey Road under school playing fields. Excavations in 2011 revealed remains of a timber and earth fort built in the first century under Frontinus, and also of the civil settlement which grew outside the north-west gate. The fort was rebuilt in stone in the early second century in a slightly different position. There seem to have been periods of abandonment and reoccupation until the early fourth century.

Newport, Gwent ****

Newport Museum in Central Library.

The Roman Gallery here is something of a hidden treasure, upstairs beyond the Central Library in a modern building in the centre of a shopping arcade (4 John Frost Square NP20 1PA). There are many cabinets packed with high quality finds from the excavations at Caerwent, particularly those of the early twentieth century. These are arranged around a central space that holds a mosaic from one

Wall plaster fragment from a Caerwent house. *Published with permission of Newport Museum and Art Gallery.*

of the houses, originally showing busts of the four seasons, of which Summer and Winter survive, the latter wearing a typical British hooded cloak. The central figure may have been Orpheus, charming the animals, some of which are depicted around him in rather naïve form.

A multitude of finely crafted items of shale, glass, pottery and metalwork are displayed, as well as painted wall plaster and architectural fragments. One of the star objects is the Chi-Rho Hoard, found buried in large potter jar in a Caerwent house, including a pewter bowl with an engraved Christian *chi-rho* symbol. It is thought to relate to a communal Christian meal known as the 'agape' and is perhaps the earliest evidence for Christianity in Wales at *c.* AD 370.

There is also information and a model relating to the late third-century Newport boat, found in waterlogged conditions at Barlands Farm, Magor. Made of oak, using traditional Celtic construction methods rather than Roman, it is a rare surviving example of such a vessel.

Prestatyn, Clwyd *

Bath-house. Open site.

Lying just off the Prestatyn to Ruddlan road, down a cul-de-sac of modern houses are the remains of a suite of Roman baths, discovered in 1934, and excavated and displayed when the housing estate was built in 1984 (42 Melyd Ave, LL19 8RT).

It is still uncertain whether the baths were attached to a nearby fort or a civic settlement, but it is likely that they were built by the Twentieth Legion based at

Prestatyn Bath-house, probably built by the Twentieth Legion based at Chester.

nearby Chester. A number of tiles, from its workshop at Holt, were found with the stamp LEG XX VV and the legion's boar insignia. The date of construction is *c*. AD 120, and they were extended in about AD 150. A cold plunge-bath at the east end was fed by a local spring by means of a wooden aqueduct channel, supported by pairs of alder wood posts found during the excavations. The warm and hot rooms with *pilae* for the underfloor heating are well preserved, as is the channel from the furnace.

In addition to the baths, evidence for a number of timber buildings and three bronze-smiths' workshops were found nearby, with debris from making brooches, sword and dagger chapes and other items.

The settlement and the baths are likely to have had links with the local lead industry and the nearby port, which would have been closely managed by the military. North Wales, in particular Flintshire, was rich in lead and many examples of lead pigs bearing the name of the local Deceangli tribe have been found at various locations, some of which are exhibited at the Grosvenor museum in Chester.

St Fagans, South Glamorgan **

National Museum of History.

For ninety years from 1927 the archaeology galleries of the National Museum of Wales were housed in the grand building in Cathays Park in central Cardiff. There was a wonderful array of treasures and everyday artefacts of all ages on display, from sites all over Wales. This building still houses the National Art Gallery and exhibitions.

In 2018 the new buildings which are now the home of Welsh archaeology opened at St Fagans National Museum of History, in countryside to the west of the city (Cardiff CF5 6XB; signposted from the M4, though you have to keep your eyes peeled at country junctions).

This was previously the Welsh Folk Museum, opened in 1948 to express the rich cultural heritage of Wales, including historic buildings that had been moved and rebuilt here. The buildings have been expanded to include reconstructed Iron Age round-houses, the medieval prince's court of Llys Llywelyn and a Bronze Age round barrow, as well as every imaginable kind of historic building from smithy to prefab. Fantastic adventure playgrounds for children have been added and the setting is still beautiful woodland. It makes a great day out, especially for families and schools, but what it lacks, sadly, is an archaeology gallery.

There are some of the best-known treasures from the old museum in the 'Wales is ...' gallery in the main building. This traces national identity from the Palaeolithic to the modern day, through themes such as 'Wales is ...sacred places'. Some of the metalwork hoard from Llyn Cerrig Bach in Anglesey is shown, deposited in a lake between 300 BC and AD 100 and including weapons, gang chains and horse gear. 'Wales is ...partly Roman' has a few wonderful pieces such as a late first-century bronze cup from Abergavenny, with a leopard with inlaid silver spots clinging to the rim and shoulder to form a handle. There is a terracotta roof antefix of the Twentieth Legion from Holt, with boar standard; gold coins from Caerleon; an inscription to Trajan from the fort at Gelligaer, a wax tablet and a huge grinding stone for flour. It provides a cross-section, but only a tiny part of the artefacts which were once on display.

In another huge new building further round the park – Gweithdy (workshop) – there are explanations of how different materials were worked and exploited through history. Stone displays include a mosaic panel from Caerwent and inscriptions of Roman date as well as prehistoric flints and later items. Complete Roman pots from Holt lie alongside Bronze Age burial urns. Metalwork of different periods is similarly displayed together. Whilst there is a sort of logic to the technological approach, you have to look hard for anything Roman.

Tomen Y Mur, Gwynedd ***

Auxiliary fort: amphitheatre, reconstructed wall, Roman roads and Norman motte. Open site.

Tomen Y Mur ('the mound in the walls') is a veritable smorgasbord of the Roman military. It is set in the glorious scenery of the Snowdonia National Park, and the site is very exposed to the elements. It lies near Maentwrog, Blaenau Ffestiniog (LL41 4RE), with access from a minor unsignposted road east off the A470, just south of the junction with the A487.

The layout is a little complicated to understand at first, not least because the Normans built a motte and bailey castle in the centre of the fort, reusing the Roman

Reconstructed fort wall at Tomen y Mur.

fort walls as the bailey defences, hence the name of the site. Further confusion is caused by a later farmer's dry-stone wall running parallel to the long wall of the fort up to the motte. However, the signage on the site is plentiful, informative and well laid out. Ironically, there are no signposts from the main road so finding the monument might prove the biggest challenge.

The fort was built in two stages: the first larger, timber structure dates to AD 78 under Agricola for a 1,000-strong cavalry unit. The second was built of stone in *c.* AD 120 and was reduced in size, housing 4–500 infantry. This would have been due to part of the garrison being moved elsewhere, perhaps to build Hadrian's Wall. Only about fifteen years later, in *c.* AD 135, the fort was abandoned.

The outlines of both forts are easily discernible, one inside the other, the earlier fort an earthwork, the later walls made of slate. They might benefit from a bit of professional consolidation but they are still impressive.

Inscribed centurial stones believed to be from this site were found reused in Harlech Castle, and are now in Segontium Museum (closed in 2019). These commemorate the unit that built stretches of the fort wall, and the length in paces. One facsimile, reading IULIA PERPERTVI.P.XXXIX (the century of Julius Perpetuus built 39 paces), has been built into a reconstructed stretch of the wall standing at the north-west corner of the later fort. A cow-house built into the wall of the fort was, bizarrely, hit by a bomb in the Second World War, and in 2007 the pile of reused Roman stones was utilised again to reconstruct the fort wall, showing what it would originally have looked like.

Outside the fort, excavations in the nineteenth century revealed a *vicus*, a parade ground, the line of an aqueduct, a *mansio* and a bath-house complex. The Roman roads leading to and from the fort are particularly well-defined and emphasise the strategic importance of the site where four roads met.

A highlight of the complex is the amphitheatre, which would have been used in the main for military training rather than gladiatorial combat. This had timber seating on a bank of earth, which is hard to see in parts because of a late stone wall built on top of it, and the remains of a nineteenth-century quarry railway which crosses it.

Tomen y Mur is another site which features in the medieval tales of the *Mabinogion*, as the legendary palace Ardudwy.

Ystradfellte, Powys **

Sarn Helen Roman road, inscribed standing stone of Maen Madoc.

Sarn Helen is the name given to several stretches of Roman road in Wales. One route runs for 160 miles (260 km), rather meandering in places, from the south-west (Carmarthen) to the north-west (Aberconwy). This sometimes underlies modern roads, and sometimes sets off as a track through the countryside; stretches of the latter are worth seeking out for an enjoyable walk in the footsteps of the Romans. It is popular as a long-distance cycle route and a hiking route, with some flexibility employed for practical reasons.

Inscribed stone
at Maen Madoc
beside Sarn Helen
Roman Road,
near Ystradfellte.
Photo: Dot Smith.

Another route runs north-east between Neath and the fort of Brecon Gaer. This
has several enjoyable walking stretches which can be done quite easily, passing
through the Brecon Beacons National Park.

One easy stretch can be found signposted 'Sarn Helen Roman Road' on the left
from a minor road which leads north from Ystradfellte, just past Aber-Llia. This
track goes through a Forestry Commission plantation, and as you emerge from
the trees (heading south-west) you will see a standing stone in a field to your left,
marked on OS maps as Maen Madoc. It may originally have been a prehistoric
grave marker (the base is surrounded by deeply embedded stones) but it was
later given a Roman inscription up one side: DERVAC(IVS) FILIVS IVSTI (H)IC
IACIT – 'Of Dervacus, son of Ivstus. He lies here'. It is a very pleasant stroll, about
forty-five minutes there and back.

There is another good walking stretch north-east of Neath, between Resolven
and Banwen.

7

Northern England

Co. Durham, Cumbria, Greater Manchester, Humberside, Lancashire, Merseyside, Northumberland, Tyne & Wear, Yorkshire

This region covers a huge area, from the urban conurbation of Manchester to the glorious landscapes of the Lake District, crossing the Pennines to the Yorkshire Moors, right up to the current border with Scotland.

We have excluded the Hadrian's Wall frontier (which is, of course, not the present-day border with Scotland), to describe it separately in Chapter 8, including all the structures on the Wall, those on the Stanegate line south of it, and the fortifications along the Cumbrian coast down to Maryport.

Much of the land south of the frontier was the territory of the Brigantes tribe prior to the Roman expansion north. Their queen in the mid-first century AD, Cartimandua, 'ruled by right rather than through marriage' according to the historian Tacitus and was loyal to Rome. In AD 51 the rebel Caratacus, originally of the Catuvellauni, asked her for sanctuary after being defeated in Wales by the Roman general Ostorius Scapula, but she handed him over in chains. In 57 the Romans helped her win a conflict against her divorced husband Venutius, but in 69, a year of great instability within the Empire, Venutius tried again to seize power. This time the Romans could only send limited help, Cartimandua disappeared from the historical account, and the Ninth Legion Hispana was sent north to deal with the rebels. The hillfort believed to be the stronghold of the Brigantes until about AD 70/71 is at Stanwick, 10 miles south-east of Barnard Castle, and can be visited.

This is the date, AD 71, when the fortress at **York** (Eboracum) was founded by the Ninth Legion, and a network of supporting auxiliary forts spread over this whole region. Many were established in the late 70s AD under the Roman Governor Gnaeus Julius Agricola, father-in-law of Tacitus, who therefore documented his activities exceptionally well. We have described the twenty best-preserved auxiliary forts and other military sites below, but there are many more known from excavations and survey. They stood particularly along the main roads north, at river crossings and other critical points, a day's march apart, those

Northern England.

closest to the Wall being regarded as outposts in the frontier system. The two main Roman routes north are still used today. **Dere Street** runs from York to Corbridge east of the Pennines, and the route through County Durham is more or less that of the modern B6275, and that of the A68 further north. There can be few greater motoring experiences for Roman devotees than joining this just north of Scotch Corner and heading straight as an arrow for the North. After it passes through the Wall north of Corbridge, it still follows the line of the Roman road, going up and down like some early version of a big dipper. An unnamed Roman road took the western route from Chester, via Manchester to Carlisle, with further roads linking these two routes across the country.

Some of the forts are spectacularly located, especially **Hardknott** and **Whitley Castle** in Cumbria, the latter the highest in England, possibly safeguarding the mining of lead and silver. Castlefield Fort in **Manchester**, by contrast, has survived the thousand cuts of continuing urban life above it, and makes a good display in spite of its limitations. The camps at **Cawthorn** may have been used for real manoeuvres or for practicing strategy.

Two milestones more or less *in situ* can be hunted down in this region, at **Middleton** and **Temple Sowerby** in Cumbria. Two evocative stretches of metalled road, once ascribed to the Romans, have now, rather sadly, been reassigned to other periods and uses: Blackstone Edge in Greater Manchester and **Wheeldale Moor** in N. Yorks.

The Ninth Legion Hispana based at York inspired Rosemary Sutcliff's bestselling novel *The Eagle of the Ninth*, based on the conjecture that its disappearance from York and from Britain, never properly explained by the historians, meant that it was wiped out in a battle here. Peripheral evidence from inscriptions suggest that it is far more likely that it moved elsewhere, and was perhaps split up, but the controversy lingers. In any case, the fortress garrison at York was replaced by the Sixth Legion Victrix, which remained there until the end of Roman Britain.

All these forts, as well as the fortress at York, drew substantial civilian settlements around them. That at **York** became a *colonia*, which coexisted with the fortress, and was luxurious enough to entertain three Emperors, playing an important role in the larger politics of the Empire. **Aldborough** became the civitas capital of the Brigantes, a place of wealth and culture, revealed by the mosaics and other finds in the site museum and in **Leeds Museum**. In some parts of Cumbria and Northumberland people continued to live in settlements unchanged from those of the Iron Age, with a lifestyle not altered much by the Roman presence except for the use of pottery and artefacts. At Ewe Close in Cumbria the outlines of an enclosed settlement of circular houses can still be seen and finds suggest that habitation continued into the fourth century.

Cultural wealth has also been revealed at villas and country estates. Although scarce on the west coast, they were fairly plentiful around York, with sixteen having been identified in North Yorkshire. Only one of these has anything to see *in situ* now, at **Beadlam**. Others have left a glorious legacy of mosaics, some of them with mythological figures in a particularly idiosyncratic local style, such as those from Rudston in **Hull Museum**.

During the late Roman period a series of installations usually known as signal stations was established along the east coast, constructed later than but in contemporary use with the Saxon Shore forts further south. The most visible of these is at **Scarborough**, N. Yorks, though it is not really understood how the signal system would have worked.

In addition to those described below, there are Roman collections at Doncaster Museum and Barnard Castle Museum, the latter including finds from nearby Maiden Castle fortlet and Greta Bridge fort (Maglona).

Aldborough (Isurium Brigantium), N. Yorkshire ***

Roman town with landscaped site including walls, mosaics, sculpture and museum; Mercury relief in St Andrew's Church. EH. Seasonal opening.

The modern village of Aldborough largely inhabits the same space as that of its Roman predecessor, Isurium Brigantium, civitas capital of the Brigantes. This was a rectangular walled town of 22 acres (9 hectares), to the south of the River Ure, 17 miles (27 km) north-west of York. It lay on Dere Street, the Roman road leading from York to Hadrian's Wall and the North, which actually turned a right-angle in the centre of the town. This must have been an important trading post on the route. Inside St Andrew's Church, which stands within the square of the Roman forum square, is a relief of Mercury, identified by his winged helmet. It was found long ago, and it seems fitting that it this god of merchants, travellers and thieves should still stand at the centre of the town. The church itself has much reused Roman stone in its walls.

There was a military presence here from the time of the foundation of the legionary fortress at York in *c.* AD 71. A fort has been found just to the west of Aldborough at Roecliff, and two of the Vindolanda tablets of the late first century mention Isurium, associated with travelling expenses between York and the frontier. Tiles with the stamp of the Ninth Legion have also been found here.

At some stage, date uncertain, the military presence developed into a town, which was given stone walls in the late second or third century. The course of these can still be seen along field boundaries around the village, and to the south the shape of an amphitheatre can just be made out to the east of Front Street, lying unexcavated on private land.

The accessible remains, at **Aldborough Roman Site** (Front St, YO51 9ES), lie in the south-western corner of the Roman town. The entrance lies inside the spot where

Geometric mosaic *in situ* at Isurium Brigantium Roman town, Aldborough.

the South Gate once stood. There is a small museum with some exquisite finds, and a sign-posted walk through gardens where stretches of wall, various sculptural pieces and geometric mosaics protected by covering buildings can be seen. Much of the land is still owned by Aldborough Manor, and it was a nineteenth-century owner, Andrew Lawson, who encouraged the excavations. He also landscaped the gardens around the ruins and built the first museum to entertain visitors. There was further exploration in the twentieth century, and now the town is being studied by a team from the University of Cambridge.

Some unusually elaborate figurative mosaics have also been found, although these are not on show at the site. One with Greek lettering depicting the nine muses on Mount Helicon is reburied *in situ* with its find-spot marked in the ground. A wonderful grinning wolf standing over the twins Romulus and Remus is now in Leeds Museum (below). These both show the wealth and the classical aspirations of the owners of the wealthy town houses of Isurium.

Alnwick, Northumberland***

Alnwick Castle Museum of Antiquities: the Rudge Cup, the Corbridge Ring, the Prudhoe Hoard.

Alnwick was not a Roman settlement, but the Castle Museum (NE66 1NG) is the repository of a fine collection of Roman items from Northumberland, the rest of Britain and Pompeii. In particular, it is the home of one of the great treasures of Roman Britain, the Rudge Cup.

The castle is the seat of the Dukes of Northumberland, and the Percy family has included keen collectors of antiquities since the early eighteenth century. Various members have been presidents of the Society of Antiquaries in London and in Newcastle. Alnwick Castle was Hogwarts School in some scenes in the Harry Potter

The Rudge Cup, souvenir of Hadrian's Wall, in Alnick Castle Museum. *Photo Northumberland Estates.*

films so it has become something of a pilgrimage destination for muggles from all over the world. Weave your way through them to get to the Postern Tower, where the Museum of Antiquities is housed over two floors.

The Rudge Cup is an enamelled bronze bowl found in 1725 down a well on the site of a villa at Rudge, Wiltshire, part of the family estate. Beneath the rim the names of five forts on the west side of the wall are inscribed: MAIS (Bowness-on-Solway), ABALLAVA (Burgh-by-Sands), VXELODUM (Stanwix), CAMBOGLANS (Castlesteads) and BANNA (Birdoswald), with a representation of a crenellated wall below. Two similar, though far from identical, vessels have been found, one in Amiens in France, the other in Staffordshire (see Carlisle, Tullie House Museum, Chapter 8). These were all presumably souvenirs of the wall, possibly made around AD 130, or perhaps after the retreat from the Antonine Wall in the 160s, when Hadrian's Wall was completed in stone for its entire length. The original cup and a rather splendid facsimile are in a display case on the ground floor.

There are some other great pieces in the collection, including a contemporary looking ring from Corbridge, the Prudhoe Hoard of silver denarii, and many items from High Rochester fort (Bremenium), which was dug by the 4th Duke around 1850.

Ambleside (Galava), Cumbria **

Auxiliary fort with praetorium, principia and granaries; NT, open site.

It is hard to think of a more idyllic place for a fort than the site at Ambleside (LA22 0EN). Situated in a park called Borrens Field at the top end of Windermere, there are spectacular views of the lake and the surrounding fells.

The first wooden fort on the site was built in the late first century AD and housed a garrison of 200. It was abandoned, but a larger stone fort was built in the early second century, and these are the remains that are visible today.

The second fort had a garrison of 500 auxiliary infantry, and there is evidence that a large civilian *vicus* developed to the north and east. This, together with the huge granaries discovered within, may suggest that it played a major role in supplying the troops to keep the Lake District under control. There is evidence that it was occupied through to the late fourth century and beyond, and it may have been taken over as a stronghold by a local warlord as Roman rule came to an end.

The East Gate, the Porta Praetoria, and the South Gate are exposed to view, with pivot holes for the massive wooden gates in the threshold stone of the latter. This gate leading to the lake may indicate that the Romans had transport boats on Windermere.

The central area of the fort is uncovered so that the foundations of the *praetorium*, *principia* and granaries can be seen. The strong-room of the headquarters is well defined.

Finds from the fort can be seen in the attractive Armitt museum in Ambleside (LA22 9BL).

The idyllically situated auxiliary fort at Ambleside.

Beadlam, near Helmsley, N. Yorkshire *

Romano-British farm. EH. Open site.

Beadlam villa lies in the valley of the River Riccal, nestling under the escarpments of the North York Moors. The remains are now visible as low walls surrounded by sheepfold fencing as if to stop them wandering off further down the valley. They lie in a field to the south of Linkfoot Lane (A170), just west of crossroads with Wykeham Dale and Burn Lane (YO62 5HY).

Excavations have revealed a Romano-British farm comprising three buildings around a central courtyard, part of one of which can be seen. Finds, including mosaics, tesserae, tiles and pottery, demonstrate a good standard of living, and date the occupation to the third and fourth centuries, though there may have been some earlier activity on the site.

The digs have also revealed an unexplained female skeleton, either cut into the floor of the north range or laid on it and covered. Many villas became a focus for burials after they had gone out of use, and this may be the explanation, rather than some macabre conflict.

The idyllic medieval market town of Helmsley with its magnificent Norman castle lies just a mile or two to the west.

Bewcastle (Fanum Cocidi), Cumbria **

Auxiliary fort, Hadrian's Wall outpost to north; eighth-century cross, medieval castle and Church of St Oswald.

The golden rule for Roman forts, until the late third century at least, is they are playing card shaped – oblong with rounded corners. Bewcastle does everything except conform. It is an irregular hexagon that follows the contours of a small, naturally defendable plateau.

The Roman name has been identified as Fanum Cocidi (the Shrine of Cocidius) from a series of six altars dedicated to this local deity. The name is also recorded in the *Ravenna Cosmology*.

The 6-acre (2.4-hectare) fort is a frontier outlier, situated 10 miles north of Hadrian's Wall and connected to Birdoswald Fort by the Maiden's Way Roman road. The forts were also connected by a communication system and the foundations of two stone signalling towers have been found between them. Garrisoned by the First Cohort of Dacians from modern-day Romania, the fort was originally built of turf when the Wall was being built.

It was abandoned when the frontier moved to the Antonine Wall, then rebuilt in stone and reoccupied on the move back to the Hadrianic frontier. The new garrison was the First Cohort of Nerva, a double unit of 1,000 men, part infantry, part cavalry. It is thought that there were two traumatic episodes when it was overrun and destroyed, first in AD 343 and again during the Great Barbarian Conspiracy of AD 367.

Today the ramparts can clearly be seen; the interior is shared with later structures, namely the Norman castle ruins, the ancient Church of St Oswald and an important eighth-century Anglo-Saxon cross.

There is a small museum in the churchyard (CA6 6PS), telling the history of the fort, the cross and the village. Finds, including the Cocidius altars, can be seen at Tullie House Museum in Carlisle.

Binchester (Vinovia), Co. Durham ***

Auxiliary fort, Hadrian's Wall outpost to south, with praetorium and commander's bath suite. Seasonal opening.

Binchester (Vinovia) lies on Dere Street in a sequence of surviving forts a day's march apart, starting about 10 miles (16 km) south at Piercebridge, then Binchester, Lanchester and Ebchester (all below), leading to Corbridge (Chapter 8), then through Hadrian's Wall and on via High Rochester (below) into Scotland. It lies in an elevated position within a bend of the River Wear just to the north of Bishop Auckland, where Dere Street bisects the modern town and is traceable in the modern road system before evaporating a mile or so before the fort. (Binchester, Bishop Auckland DL14 8DJ).

The first fort was built *c*. AD 80 only to be replaced about eighty years later by a smaller stone fort which remained in use throughout the Roman period. It was garrisoned by a number of auxiliary cavalry regiments including the Ala Vettnum from Spain and the Cuneus Frisiorum Vinoviensium from Frisia in Holland, the latter perhaps here for some time since they took the fort's name.

The central part of the fort is displayed, with the *praetorium* baths providing the centrepiece. One of the foundation stones of the *praetorium* bears a curious carving of an animal, sadly now missing its head, so it may have been a cat or a dog. It would have been invisible below ground level, so perhaps a dedication stone. The bath suite is one of the best-preserved in Britain with high walls, hypocausts and wall flues. The range of rooms is shown with appropriate tableaus. Excavations at the site are on-going.

Outside the *praetorium*, a section of Dere Street is displayed and is well worth a look.

Brougham (Brocavum), Cumbria **

Auxiliary fort platform, museum in Brougham Castle. EH.

Brougham Norman castle stands proud on a river terrace above the confluence of the rivers Lowther and Eamont, with the picturesque village lying below (Moor Lane, Penrith CA10 2AA). It occupies the north part of a Roman fort, which provided ready-made outer bailey walls and a source of building stone, too tempting for the Norman builders to ignore. The gate house of the castle even has a Roman tombstone set into its ceiling.

The strategic importance of the site in Roman times was not only due to the defensive properties of the hill and the rivers, but also because three major routes crossed here, heading south to Manchester, west to Ravenglass and south-east to York. No excavations have been carried out on the fort site, but it is believed to have been founded in the 70s AD and occupied until at least the late third if not the fourth century. The outline of the ramparts is particularly distinct at the approach to the castle by the crossroads from the south.

The small museum in the ticket office and shop has a good array of inscribed stones including some fine tombstones and a third-century altar set up by a soldier of the Stratonician cavalry, from modern-day Turkey. Several altars have been found in the area dedicated to the local god Belatucadrus, who was associated with Mars.

Another example of a Roman fort even more obscured by a Norman keep can be seen at Brough (Verteris), Cumbria, 20 miles (32 km) to the south-east.

Castleshaw (Rigodunum?), Greater Manchester **

Auxiliary fort and fortlet, earthworks.

The site is situated on the south side of Dirty Lane, directly to the south of Castleshaw Upper Reservoir. The earthworks here are unusual in that they show two rather different military establishments on the same site. First, there is the almost square outline of an Agricolan auxiliary fort, established *c.* AD 79 as part of a line of forts along the road between Chester and York. This was one side of the high Pennine crossing point, and the fort at Slack was on the other. This was abandoned around AD 90 as part of a general military reorganisation.

Fifteen years later, under Trajan, a smaller fortlet was built inside the original structure, reusing the southern rampart. This was one-fifth of the size of the 1-hectare (2.5 acres) earlier fort. Limited excavations have established the presence of internal structures such as barracks and granaries in both, and the earlier fort also had a *praetorium* and *principia*, as well as stables.

The earthworks are clearly visible, and the views are good, although the landscape was transformed in the late nineteenth century when the two nearby reservoirs were constructed to provide water for industrial Oldham, luckily leaving the fort untouched between them. There is detailed on-site information, and the Friends of Castleshaw ensure that there are ongoing investigations.

Cawthorn, N. Yorkshire **

Roman camps (earthworks).

This makes a gorgeous 1-mile walk through the North York Moors National Park, and a booklet can be obtained from park information centres with details of where to go and what to look for. The site lies 5 miles north of Pickering; take Cropton Lane to Cropton, turn right onto High Lane, then left onto a track leading to a car park just south of the earthworks. The track to the forts is signposted with Roman helmets.

A series of earthworks lies along the crest of a south-facing slope at the north rim of the Vale of Pickering. These are still recognisable as one square fort, which partly overlies an unusual polygonal camp, and another fort with an attached annexe to the east of this. Activity here seems to span the first to second centuries, and traditionally these have been identified as training and practice camps, constructed as part of military exercises. However, more recent thoughts suggest that they were in fact permanently occupied and garrisoned forts, part of the network across northern England. Recent excavations have recorded buildings based upon turf-built dwarf walls. There are beautiful views from the top of the crest, and nearby is a stretch of medieval trackway known as the Portergate.

Chester-le-Street (Congangis), Co. Durham**

Auxiliary fort: part of commandant's house; the Church of St Mary and St Cuthbert.

The market town of Chester-le-Street lies at the confluence of the rivers Wear and Cone, 8 miles (13 km) south of Newcastle. Now perhaps best known as the home of Durham county cricket ground, it has a name deriving from Anglo-Saxon terminology, meaning the fort on the road. The route, later known as Cade's Road, linked the fort at Pons Aelius (Newcastle) to the legionary fortress at York (Eboracum), and the modern Front Street still follows this line.

Remains of the fort can be seen in and near **St Mary and St Cuthbert Church** (DH3 3QB) on the east side of the town, built of stone from the fort. Lewis holes, made by the Romans for lifting the blocks into place, can still be seen on some stones. Opposite the church and a little to the north at the bend in the road is an excavated section of the commandant's house. Built by the Second Legion Augusta around AD 120, the fort is understood to have been garrisoned by the cavalry unit Ala Secundae Asturum Antoniniana.

The church itself has a fine collection of mutilated fourteenth-century tombs and an anchorage. This rare survival was a small space for an anchorite, who would have been bricked in, with a small squint hole allowing sight of the church services and a window for the receipt of food. This space has been turned into a small museum containing inscribed stones and a very splendid pinecone finial from the Roman fort.

Ebchester (Vindomora), Co. Durham *

Auxiliary fort, Hadrian's Wall outpost to south; St Ebb's Church, bath-house on private land.

The fort at Ebchester lies half-way between Lanchester and Corbridge, on Dere Street. The modern village overlies it, leaving much to the imagination, aided by an information board. This is to the right of the post office in Vindomora Road, close to the centre of the fort, and there is a footpath from here to the earthworks of the northern defences.

St Ebba's Church (7 Vindomora Road, DH8 0PW) stands in the south-west quadrant of the fort, and it is possible to discern the break of slope of the fort platform on the south and west sides of the churchyard. The church itself houses some inscribed stones including an altar to Jupiter Greatest and Best (IOM). There is also an excavated commandant's bath-house on private land, but permission is needed to visit this.

Hardknott, Cumbria ****

Auxiliary fort with bath-house, parade ground and tribunal. EH.

The fort of Hardknott lies at the top of its eponymous pass controlling the passage of Eskdale and guarding the road from the Roman forts of Ravenglass to Ambleside (Holmrook CA19 1TH). Its situation is majestic, and the views down to the Irish Sea and over the Scafell range from the lofty walls are wonderful. Did this make it a great posting or did the garrison wish for some R&R down the valley in Ravenglass?

Its remote position has meant that the reuse of its stones has been limited to nearby dry-stone walls. The fort walls are therefore impressively high, particularly seen from the outside, forming a square with rounded corners. Clever consolidation with a stratum of slate indicates the height before renovation and a layer of displaced Roman stones caps and protects the walls.

Hardknott auxiliary fort, high in the Lake District.

In the centre of the fort the main buildings, including the commandant's house, headquarters building and granary, are easily discernible, as are the square internal towers.

The fort was built under Hadrian in the AD 130s and a fragmentary inscription found at the South Gate tells us that the garrison included the Fourth Cohort of Dalmatians, originally from the Balkans. It was once identified as Mediobogdum, named in ancient sources, but this is now thought unlikely. The garrison left whilst the Antonine Wall was being built but the fort was reoccupied in the AD 160s. It was finally abandoned, perhaps at the start of the third century, though finds suggest that travellers continued to take shelter here.

Outside the south gate of the fort, close to the road, are the remains of the military bathhouse including a circular *laconicum*. Beyond the north wall lies the best-preserved parade ground in Britain, terraced out of the uneven ground, looking like a cricket pitch and known locally as the 'Bowling Green'. On one side a natural outcrop of rock was flattened to form a tribunal where commanding officers could review the troops as they trained.

Hardknott can be reached from Ambleside via the Wrynose Pass or from Ravenglass up Eskdale although both can prove difficult in winter. Those with a love of steam trains should catch the Ravenglass & Eskdale Railway to Dalegarth station and hike up the rest of the valley, but this is not for the faint-hearted or weak-kneed.

High Rochester (Bremenium), Northumberland ***

Auxiliary fort, Hadrian's Wall outpost to north; Roman roadside mausoleums; ballista balls.

It would be easy to miss the wonderful Roman remains here as the main road skirts to the west of the old line of Dere Street and passes by, oblivious to the history of the place.

High Rochester (NE19 1RB) is the most northerly fort in England, lying just a couple of miles below the Scottish border. It lies at the end of the aptly named Bremenium Way, which forks to the right off the A68. The wall circuit, up to 9 feet (nearly 3 metres) high in places, now encloses a small number of farm buildings and cottages. The West and North Gates are particularly well preserved, with springer arch stones still in place.

The fort differs from many other in the north by having large platforms to place artillery, dating from the third century. These would have been the catapult machines such as *ballistae* or the smaller *onagri*. Look out for the *ballista* balls, presumably found locally, incorporated as gable decoration in the cottage at the junction of the A68 and Bremenium Way. More reused Roman stone is evident in the drain stones cladding its outside walls.

On the opposite corner to the cottage stands a First World War memorial in the style of a small wayside Roman temple with Doric columns. Half way between this and the fort, to the east at the top of the high ground, is a Roman burial ground

Re-used Roman stone in a cottage near High Rochester auxiliary fort.

with an extant mausoleum, a very rare occurrence in Britain. Only three or four courses of this circular monument survive but it is nonetheless a remarkable sight.

The fort is part of the Duke of Northumberland's estate and was excavated in the mid-nineteenth century. Many of the finds are in the museum at Alnwick Castle, including a rather fine dedication stone from the East Gate. This depicts Mars and Hercules and the inscription shows that it was built by a *vexillation* of the Twentieth Legion Valeria Victrix.

Hull, East Yorkshire ****

Hull and East Riding Museum: the Rudston Venus mosaic, the Horkstow chariot race mosaic, Yorkshire and Lincolnshire villa mosaics.

One of the great delights of hunting down the remains of Roman Britain is finding them in unlikely places. The old port of Hull (or Kingston upon Hull) has no Roman history of its own, the nearest Roman port town being at Brough, a few miles west up the Humber. However, it is a four-star site courtesy of the Hull and East Riding Museum (36 High St, Hull HU1 1NQ) and its fabulous collection of late Roman mosaics, from what must have been very elegant and affluent villas in the region.

Located in the Museum Quarter in the narrow streets of the old town, it sits next to other museums of transport and maritime interest.

The collection is breath-taking. The Venus mosaic from the villa at Rudston, just to the south of the Yorkshire Wolds, is perhaps the most famous, notorious more for the naivety of its execution than its beauty. You can't help but smile when you see it, with Venus triumphantly displaying the apple she has won after the judgement of Paris. The superb charioteer mosaic from the same site shows a driver in his *quadriga* in the central panel.

The Chariot Mosaic from Rudstone Villa, full of excitement and life. *Photo: Hull and East Riding Museum.*

The chariot theme is repeated in another grand mosaic from a villa at Horkstow Hall, in North Lincolnshire, discovered when digging a vegetable garden in the late eighteenth century. Three huge panels survive, one depicting Orpheus, another resembling a 'painted ceiling', but it is the chariot race that is the most complete and vibrant. The central spine of the circus is depicted with turning posts at each end. Around these, chariots are racing at obvious speed sporting their team colours, one having lost a wheel, all adding to the excitement. The only known circus in Britain is that at Colchester (Chapter 3).

More mosaics, along with other artefacts found at Brough (Petuaria), have been set into imaginatively reconstructed houses from the settlement.

Ilkley (Olicana), W. Yorkshire **

Auxiliary fort platform; the Manor House Museum; the Verbeia Stone.

Ilkley Manor House stands on one corner of a Roman fort which once stood at a crossing point of the River Wharfe. The core, built in the fourteenth century, was extended in the seventeenth century into a typical Pennine sandstone manor, looking every inch a model for Wuthering Heights. Inside, the wooden beams and stone walls provide an atmospheric setting for a small art gallery and the **Ilkley Manor House Museum** (LS29 9DT).

Tombstones and altars found locally make up the bulk of the displays. Of particular interest is a memorial stone for a thirty-year-old woman originally of the of the Cornovii tribe in present-day Shropshire.

One inscribed altar has been responsible for much debate on the ancient name for Ilkley. It was dedicated to Verbeia, thought to have been the river god of the Wharfe. However, some believe that it may in fact be the name of the Roman settlement here, rather than Olicana as identified from the early seventeenth century. More evidence is needed to decide either way.

Behind the museum part of the fort platform is clearly visible and a stone with a bronze plaque marks the site of the North Gate. Part of the west wall of the fort has been left exposed, and the west wall of the manor house was built straight on top of the sixth course of Roman masonry. Excavations have revealed that the fort was occupied from *c.* AD 80, with five phases of building and rebuilding until the end of the fourth century.

Lancaster, Lancashire ***

Auxiliary fort: Wery Wall and bath-house; Lancaster Museum with Reiter Stone.

Lancaster is a fine northern town with some very impressive architecture and a real buzz on market days. It lies on the River Lune, a short distance from the west coast, and as so often happened, the hill on which the original fort was placed was

Reiter stone from Lancaster,
rich in propaganda, displayed at
Lancaster Museum.

also chosen by later generations for their major constructions. Thus, the splendid medieval Lancaster Castle and the Priory Church lie over Lancaster's successive Roman forts, and the town over its *vicus*.

Visible *in situ* are the **Wery Wall** and adjacent earlier **bath-house**, the remains signposted from Lancaster Priory (Priory Close LA1 1YZ), lying at the end of the footpath down the slope. The large chunk of wall still standing by the enclosing railings is all that is left above ground of the last fort in the Roman sequence, constructed fairly hurriedly in *c.* AD 330, probably as a defence against sea-borne raiders. It is on a different alignment from the three successive earlier forts beneath, built between *c.* AD 71 and AD 140–60. The adjacent bath-house, with part of the heated rooms and furnace exposed, was contemporary with the third fort, of second-century date. The V-shaped ditch of the final, fourth-century fort can be seen cutting right across the hypocaust of the *caldarium*. We know that other chunks of the late fort wall stood until the eighteenth century, as the antiquarian William Stukeley described the effort needed to clear them out of the way. The complicated sequence is described on site.

Lancaster City Museum (Market Street LA1 1HT) has a fine Roman gallery. The ground floor holds an imposing Hadrianic milestone from Artle Beck showing its distance of 4 miles from Lancaster, although without mentioning the name of the town.

The main Roman gallery is on the first floor with a good collection and two show-stoppers. The first is the tombstone of Insus, a first-century cavalry officer in the Ala Augusta troop, who came originally from Trier in Germany. This is a known type of Reiter or 'rider' stone, showing the cavalryman riding down an already decapitated local native warrior. It is so similar to one found at Ribchester (below) that they are believed to be by the same sculptor. The stone was found face down in 2005, meaning that the carving was protected and therefore remarkably crisp.

The other treasures are the Burrow Carvings, a group of stone heads and animals which are probably from a temple, shrine or mausoleum of the third century. Found during the building of the Lancaster Canal in 1794, they are unique in Britain and are brilliantly displayed on a reconstructed Doric façade.

Lanchester (Longovicium), Co. Durham **

Auxiliary fort, Hadrian's Wall outpost to south; All Saints' Church, Durham Cathedral Treasury and the Lanchester Roman Navy Diploma in Palace Green Library.

Lanchester fort is the next one north on Dere Street from Binchester, 12 miles away. It lies on high ground above the River Browney to the south-west of the present village.

A lay-by on the south side of the B6296 provides parking next to the well-defined fort platform, which lies on private land with no public access. Nevertheless, one can get a good idea of its size and area from the roadside, and there is an interpretation board to help. Although overgrown, the rampart walls stand to a good height.

All Saints' Parish Church (Durham Road, Lanchester DH7 0LJ) has a display of artefacts from the fort including a monumental altar and other inscribed stones in the south porch. The columns holding up the North Aisle are also thought to have come from the fort.

Many other altars and inscribed stones from Lanchester lie in the collections in **Durham Cathedral Treasury.**

The rarest of the treasures from Lanchester was found by a metal detectorist in 2016 and is displayed in the **Palace Green Library at Durham University.** This is a copper alloy Fleet Diploma, granted to a sailor after twenty-five years' military service, the first complete such diploma to have been found in Britain, and so far unique in recording the discharge of a sailor with the Roman Navy. It would originally have been two rectangular plates attached together with metal wires, but it was found broken into eight pieces and neatly stacked, perhaps having been divided up for his various descendants to keep as proof of their identity and rights as Roman citizens.

The diploma was issued during the reign of Antoninus Pius in *c.* AD 150 to Tigernos, a native of Lanchester. Intriguingly, he had not served with the local fleet, the *Classis Britannica*, but with the *Classis Germania*, based in the Rhineland, in present-day Holland and Germany. It has provided fascinating details about his career and those of his commanding officers.

Leeds, North Yorkshire *****

Leeds City Museum, wolf and twins mosaic.

It is likely that a fort, possibly called Cambodunum, lies somewhere beneath the streets of Leeds, since there is a gap here on the road between Manchester and York. This remains to be discovered, but many objects have come to light over the years in and around the city, displayed in the historic City Museum (Millennium Square LS2 8BH).

Painted wall plaster and mosaics from Dalton Parlours Roman villa are particularly fine, as is a milestone from Castleford, which once stood 22,000 paces from York (Eboracum). It bears two inscriptions, the first dated AD 249–51 by its dedication to Emperor Decius, the second AD 251–3 to Gallus, a real sign of the rapidly changing times of the third century. The wonderful mosaic from Aldborough showing a grinning wolf with tiny twins below it is here, as are other finds from that site (above). An altar from Adel, Leeds, was dedicated to the local goddess Brigantia, often identified with either Victory or Minerva.

Mosaic of cheerful wolf suckling Romulus and Remus, from Aldborough, displayed in Leeds Museum. *Photo: Leeds Museum and Galleries / Bridgeman Images.*

Malton (Derventio or Delgovicia?), North Yorkshire **

Auxiliary fort site and museum.

The fort at Malton lay just north of the River Derwent, 18 miles north-east of York, in a rural landscape in the south-west corner of the Vale of Pickering. It would have guarded the river crossing, its origin linked to the establishment of the legionary fortress at York. The first construction was of wood and turf at the end of the AD 70s; it was rebuilt in stone in the early second century, lost much of its garrison to Hadrian's Wall, but activity continued here right into the fifth century. An inscription tells us that in the middle of the second century an auxiliary cavalry unit raised in Gaul was garrisoned here – the Ala Picentiana. A number of villas have been found scattered around it, including that at Beadlam (above) and evidence has been found for civilian settlement both around the fort and to the south of the river at Norton. Both Derventio and Delgovicia have been claimed as the Roman names for Malton, but until an inscription is found clinching the argument, it remains ambiguous.

The fort site lies in Orchard Fields, to the right of the B1257 as you head east out of Malton. There are paths laid out here through Lady Spring Wood and along the River Derwent, and the banked outline of the fort is clearly visible in the grass. Excavations have revealed the South Gate, nearest the river, with a late Roman town house outside it, but these are no longer exposed.

Malton Museum (36 Yorkersgate, YO17 7AB) contains the best glimpses of life at the fort and the civilian settlements. It is small but has some exceptional objects on display. Those of a military nature include bits of chain mail, a copper alloy mess tin with the owner's name, Lucius Servenius Super, punched on the back of the handle and stone and lead ammunition. There is also a lovely little jet amulet of a bear, from an infant's grave, and an inscription asking for good fortune for a goldsmith's shop, the only reference to such an establishment so far found in Britain.

Manchester (Mamucium), Greater Manchester **

Castlefield auxiliary fort with reconstructed gate and walls; Manchester Museum Roman Galleries.

This once down-at-heel area of Manchester is now up and coming with trendy bars, restaurants and apartments, and the old covered market has become part of the Science Museum.

The Castlefield Fort Site (106 Duke Street, M3 4RU), now part of an urban heritage park, does indeed feel very urban, with no fewer than five railway viaducts, two canals and the River Medlock running across it. This was part of a chain of forts along the road between York and Chester, between Castleshaw to the east and Northwich (Condate) to the west. Built of timber in AD 79, it was then rebuilt three times, in *c.* AD 90, AD 160 and AD 200.

The park contains foundations of some of the *vicus* buildings and a fabulous full-scale reconstruction of the North Gate of the fort. Behind the fort gate,

Reconstructed fort wall and gate at Manchester (Mamucium).

next to the viaduct and down a Victorian cobbled street is a similarly reconstructed west wall to the fort. Although modern, these two sections of wall offer the rare opportunity to walk a battlement on the same spot as a Roman soldier would once have done. They certainly look the part as they are made out of the same local sandstone as the originals.

Most of the finds from the fort and *vicus* are held at the **Manchester Museum** (Oxford Rd M13 9PL), part of the University of Manchester. The Roman gallery is a little spartan but includes a number of altars, one found near the fort quite recently, upside down with crisp lettering. In addition, there is a wordsquare with part of the same inscription as that found on a tile in Cirencester (Chapter 3). Dated to the second century, it is sometimes interpreted as evidence of early Christianity. Other items of interest are stone carvings from a Mithraeum, and a bronze citizenship diploma from Ravenglass, granted to a soldier originally from Syria after twenty-five years' service.

Middleton, Cumbria *

Milestone.

The Roman milestone at Middleton in Lunesdale, north of Kirby Lonsdale, has a history of moving around a bit. It was discovered in this small village in the nineteenth century, buried beside the line of the Roman road from Ribchester to the fort at Low Borough Bridge.

It was then re-erected on a small rise in a field just south of the church, about a hundred yards from the present-day road. Over the years it proved too irresistible to cattle for use as a scratching post and eventually toppled over. Until recently it remained lying on the ground, looking very unloved indeed. Thankfully a group of interested guardian angels, including the playwright Alan Bennett, rescued it and it is now situated with head held high within the churchyard of the Holy Ghost Church, near to the south wall, and close to where it was originally found.

There are two inscriptions on the stone. The first, of Roman date, reads MP LIII, presumably showing the 53 miles from or to Carlisle. The second Victorian inscription records its discovery and re-erection by a William Moore in 1836.

Old Penrith (Voreda), Cumbria **

Auxiliary fort, Hadrian's Wall outpost to south.

The Roman road from Chester via Manchester to Carlisle does not have a popular name but, like Dere Street, was an important supply route to the frontier. Heading up the western side of England to Carlisle, it more or less follows the route of the A6. Forts are known to have stood at regular intervals along this but, as it approaches Hadrian's Wall, only Old Penrith (Voreda) has anything visible today.

This is a fort 'in the wild', 5 miles (8 km) north of Penrith and 13 miles (21 km) south of Carlisle, lying next to the A6 on the left (heading north), immediately beyond Castlesteads Farm. This is private land, but the fort outline can be seen easily from the pavement on this side of the road. The ramparts and ditches are obvious and the stones of the East Gate are partially exposed to view. The fort of Voreda was occupied from the second to the fourth century, and for most of that time the garrison was the Second Cohort of Gauls.

Piercebridge (Morbium?), Co. Durham **

Roman bridge; auxiliary fort, Hadrian's Wall outpost to south. EH. Open site.

Piercebridge is the southernmost of the forts along Dere Street often interpreted as outliers of the Hadrian's Wall frontier. The road here kinks to the west to accommodate the modern bridge over the Tees, but just before this, on the right-hand side if you are heading north, lie the skeletal remains of the Roman bridge over the river.

A short walk from the car park (DL2 3SW) will take you to where the landlocked foundations of the bridge lie exposed like the spine of an enormous dinosaur, due to the change in the course of the Tees. The enormous stones of the south abutment excite immediate admiration for Roman engineering. Many have metal inserts and Lewis holes, indicating how they were moved into position. It was built in the early third century to replace an earlier wooden bridge upstream, halfway between the modern bridge and this one. All these changes in the position of the bridge meant that Dere Street had to move several times too.

Across the river, a third-century fort once stood beneath the modern houses which now lie on both sides of the B6275. It is assumed that this too replaced an

Gigantic tumbled stones from Roman bridge at Piercebridge.

earlier fort, though proof is still elusive. The visible remains are to the right of the road, and consist of the north-east corner of the fort, barrack blocks and a latrine, along with some of the *vicus* outside the east gate. On-site information is plentiful and finds displayed at Bowes Museum include a spectacular North African type head pot and an early fourth-century milestone.

Ravenglass (Glannoventa), Cumbria **

Walls Castle Roman military bath-house, fort platform. EH.

Ravenglass has a huge natural harbour carved out by the confluence of three rivers: the Mite, the Esk and the Irt, which form a large common estuary. The Roman fort here, Glannovanta, may have been the final part of the Cumbrian coast defensive system, or may have simply guarded the harbour. Some think there must have been a Roman fleet based here, but no conclusive evidence for this has yet come to light. However, at one time the First Cohort Aelia Classicus was based here, an infantry unit whose name suggests it was recruited from a fleet (classis) in Hadrian's time, taking his family name. Only the platform of the fort is visible now, but its external bath-house has survived much better.

A walk along the main street, through the site of the medieval market place to the shore, gives a great view of the sheltered anchorage. **The Roman Baths** (Walls Drive, CA18 1SR) can be reached either by continuing around the shore and under the railway arch, or by following the signs from the car park of the Ravenglass & Eskdale Railway.

The baths stood outside the north-east corner of the fort and now have some of the tallest surviving walls from Roman Britain, standing to 12 feet (nearly 4 metres)

Walls of the bath-house at Ravenglass (Glannoventa).

in places. They have the look of a sculpture park, with some slightly improbable overhangs, and one can understand why the monument became known locally as Walls Castle. It was incorporated into domestic buildings in the medieval period, hence the unusually good survival, including a statue niche still visible in one wall.

To the north and east of the fort and bath-house evidence of a large *vicus* has been found. The fort appears to have been in constant occupation until the late fourth century, when the barracks were rebuilt after a fire. After this it may have become a base for a local warlord and his followers.

Ribchester (Bremetennacum), Lancashire ***

Auxiliary fort; Edwardian museum with Reiter Stone; bath-house and granaries.

Ribchester lies on the north bank of the River Ribble, on the road north from Manchester towards Hadrian's Wall. The meanderings of the river over the past 2,000 years have taken their toll and about a third of the fort, established in the early AD 70s at a crossing point, has been lost to erosion. The fort was occupied into the fourth century, and a large civilian settlement or *vicus* grew around it, more or less covering the same area as the modern village. The charming museum lies near the river and the church, close to the original centre of the fort next to the *principia*.

Ribchester Museum (PR3 3XS) owes its existence to Margaret Greenall of the Warrington brewing dynasty and opened in 1915. It displays objects found during the nineteenth-century excavations, including pottery, organic objects such as leather tent segments and inscribed stones. There are some fine altars and, most

Column and Corinthian
capital standing outside
Ribchester Museum.

importantly, the Ribchester Reiter Stone. Possibly made by the same mason who
sculpted one from Lancaster (above), it shows a Roman cavalryman riding down
and killing a barbarian. The fort was manned in the later second century by a
cavalry unit of Sarmatians, raised in Hungary but originally from Iran, and the
distinctive armour on the tombstone suggests that it depicts a soldier from this
regiment. A painted replica next to the original reminds us how brightly coloured
the stone once was.

The other great treasure from the fort is the Ribchester Hoard of cavalry armour
and equipment, found by a boy playing by the riverbank in 1796. The most
spectacular piece is a cavalry sports helmet, made of bronze and heavily decorated,
that would have been worn in displays of cavalry skills known as the *Hyppika
Gymnasia*. The Ribchester Helmet spends most of the time in the British Museum
(Chapter 1) but occasionally has an outing to Ribchester, and there is always a fine
replica on show here. Less splendid but revealing items include nit-combs complete
with the remains of nits between the teeth.

There are exposed Roman ruins elsewhere in the village, mostly excavated during
the nineteenth century, including some **granaries** next to the church, itself obviously
built with Roman dressed stone, and a **bath-house**, to the east of museum, in a
garden behind some houses.

The substantial Doric columns of the **White Bull Inn** are thought to have originally come from the *principia*, though they were retrieved from the riverbed opposite the church. Opposite is a fine millennium memorial in the style of a section of Trajan's column.

Risingham (Habitancum), Northumberland **

Auxiliary fort, Hadrian's Wall outpost to north; West Woodburn milestone.

The fort of Risingham (Habitancum) lies about 10 miles north of the Wall, just south-west of the linear settlement of West Woodburn in Redesdale, and south of the River Rede. It is actually on private land and permission should be sought to access the site, but the view from the road leading left off the A68, high above the fort, is exciting enough. The playing card shape of the circuit walls is very clear, with visible stonework and multiple ditches on the eastern and southern sides. Very little excavation has been done here, so it is not clearly understood, but several phases of rebuilding seem to have taken place between the second and fourth centuries.

The name Habitancum occurs in an altar inscription from the site. Various regiments of auxiliaries are known to have provided a garrison, including the First Cohort of Vangiones and a detachment of soldiers from Raeti from modern-day Germany and Switzerland respectively.

If you resume the journey north on the A68, cross the river and stop again a short distance north of West Woodburn, where there is a crossroads with a farm track. On the left just before the crossroads you will see a standing stone, identified as a Roman milestone. The inscription has long faded but a more modern stone plaque set up by the Redesdale Society denotes its Roman heritage.

Scarborough, North Yorkshire *

Roman signal station. EH.

Scarborough Castle is impressive for both its Norman keep and its position on the cliffs overlooking the town and surveying the North Sea.

Even more rewarding, on the east side of the outer bailey, right on the cliff edge, are the foundations of a Roman signal station. Erosion over the years has led to the loss of the east side of the defences, and at first the low walls look a little confusing, with the rectangular outline walls of a Norman and medieval chapel overlying those of the Roman period.

The Roman remains comprise the foundations of a central square base for the signal tower, now a grassy bank, surrounded by an enclosure wall and deep cut ditch. The enclosure wall has evidence of D-shaped corner towers, a feature of later Roman military architecture. There is a reconstruction drawing on site to help you make sense of it.

The remains of the signal station at Scarborough, overlain by the walls of a chapel.

The station appears to be part of a chain of similar structures down the Yorkshire coast. Others are known to have existed at Filey, Huntcliffe and Goldsborough, and they are often seen as being allied to the shore fort defensive system along the south-east coast. They were once ascribed to Theodosius, the Count of the Saxon Shore around AD 370, but recent thoughts are that they may be later, perhaps the work of self-proclaimed Emperor Magnus Maximus in the 380s AD. It seems to have been used until the early fifth century.

The mechanics of the signal station system are not clear. If they were part of a more extensive signalling system along the east coast, there must be more sites still to be discovered. Was the intention to gather a naval and/or land borne military response to raiders or were they warnings directed at settlements inland? Studies are ongoing.

Temple Sowerby, Cumbria *

Milestone in situ.

On the A66 just outside Temple Sowerby, to the east of Brougham, is a rare example of a Roman milestone in its original position, 1 modern mile west of the fort of Bravoniacum (Kirkby Thore). Brougham Castle (Brocavum) lies to the west, and both mileages may once have been inscribed here, now completely worn away.

This milestone used to be a very forlorn sight as pantechnicons roared down the trunk road only feet away from it, but the building of the Temple Sowerby bypass has freed it from heavy traffic. The picturesque village, with its Knights Templar connections, has benefitted greatly from the new road, but alas the milestone hasn't done so well. The now marooned lay-by, its home for so many years, is being used as a storage site by the Highways Agency. Although the milestone is surrounded by protective railings, with a small descriptive sign, it would benefit from some more space and its own brown sign.

Wheeldale Moor, N. Yorkshire *

Wade's Causeway, supposed Roman road.

This length of irregularly paved road on the eastern slopes of Wheeldale, above Wheeldale beck, leads apparently nowhere out onto the North York Moors (nearest postcode YO22 5AP). It has long epitomised a sense of past glory, changing fortunes and enduring Roman workmanship. Unfortunately for the romantics amongst us, recent research has pretty much destroyed hopes that it is Roman in date. It was first recorded as a Roman road on a map of 1720, and cleared and exposed in the early years of the twentieth century, so that until the late twentieth century it could be followed for 1.25 miles (2 km) as an exposed paved surface, with an apparent covered drain along the centre. Its further route was traced with the eye of faith for 33 miles from Amotherby, near Malton, to the coast north of Whitby.

A section put across the paved section very recently confirmed that it does not have the camber, surface or depth of a typical Roman road, and its context does not fit in with other known routeways in this part of the world. It is probably some sort of territorial boundary of unknown date. However, that need not stop you walking along the monument, still signposted as a Roman road, much of it now covered again with vegetation, and pondering past glory. Like Blackstone Edge Long Causeway in Lancashire, a supposed Roman road now known to be an eighteenth-century turnpike or packhorse route, this is one that is now lost to Roman Britain.

Whitley Castle (Epiacum), Alston, Cumbria ***

Auxiliary fort with some of the best-preserved ramparts in the Empire.

Whitley Castle feels like a five-star site waiting to happen, bursting with archaeological potential. This once-hidden gem of Roman Britain is now well sign-posted as Epiacum, the name taken from Ptolemy's *Geography*, with a car park (on the A689) and also information for walkers on the Pennine Way trail. It lies at Castle Nook and Whitlow Farm, nearest postcode CA9 3BG.

These improvements have been possible thanks to the great enthusiasm of the landowner, Elaine Edgar, and the Heritage Lottery Fund. Investigations and events are broadcast on their website www.epiacumheritage.org. A short but steepish climb takes you from the car park up to the East Gate of the fort, past the remains of a medieval fortified bastle house. The various features have

The extraordinary defences at Whitley Castle (Epiacum), the highest stone-built auxiliary fort in Britain.

been numbered, appropriately in Roman numerals, and described in a pamphlet available at the car park.

This is the highest stone-built Roman fort in Britain, at over 1,080 feet (330 metres) above sea level. It lies just north of Alston, England's highest town, overlooking the South Tyne Valley, midway along the Maiden Way Roman road which runs from Kirkby Thore to Carvoran, on Hadrian's Wall. Excavations have suggested that the stone infantry fort was built in the early second century, though there may have been an earlier fort or settlement, yet to be found. An inscribed altar found here suggests that it was garrisoned in the early third century by the Second Cohort of Nervians from the lower Rhine in modern-day Belgium.

Rather than being rectangular like other forts, it was squashed into a lozenge shape to fit the available flat ground. The internal features, including six barracks blocks, had to be similarly distorted to fit the frame. Instead of having a single bank and ditch around it, there are four around the three sides on the hill spur, and no less than seven on the uphill side. No other known fort in the Empire has such complex defences – the soldiers stationed here must have got sick of being told to 'dig another ditch'! It has long been thought that the fort might have been the centre of lead and silver mining operations in the Alston area, and this hypothesis is continuing to be investigated.

The boggy ground around the fort and its associated *vicus* could well be hiding more organic treasures, since several Roman leather shoes were retrieved from a rubbish pit when a drainage ditch was dug in 1825.

York (Eboracum), North Yorkshire *****

The Yorkshire Museum, The Multangular Tower and legionary fortress walls, York Minster Undercroft Museum, the Roman Baths Pub & Museum.

Roman Eboracum is unique in Britain in that it is known to have played host to three Roman Emperors and their families, Hadrian, Septimius Severus and Constantius I, all using it as a base whilst wall-planning or campaigning further north. Two of them died here, and Constantine the Great was declared Emperor in the city by the army.

It continued as one of England's most important cities, becoming capital of post-Roman Northumbria, the effective capital of the Viking Danelaw, and is now the seat of one of the two archbishoprics in the England (the other being Canterbury). The Roman name Eboracum evolved through a complicated pattern of bastardisations including the Anglo Saxon Eforwic and the Viking Jorvik to present-day York. The Archbishops of York still sign themselves with the surname Ebor.

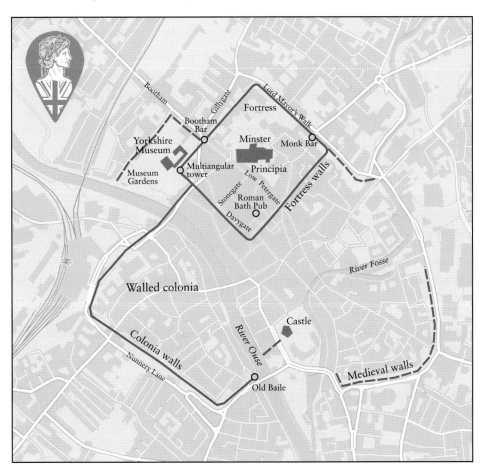

Plan of Roman York superimposed on a modern street map.

The city today is beautiful, with the Minster, medieval churches and narrow streets, epitomised by the Shambles, adding to the pleasure of seeking out the sites where Roman Eboracum can still be seen.

The foundation of the military presence here came after Cartimandua had been driven out of Brigantian territory by her ex Venutius in AD 69, making a strong base necessary to maintain stability.

The Ninth Legion Hispana moved north from Lincoln and built a great fortress on the north bank of the River Ouse, close to its confluence with the Foss, around AD 71. The Ninth was replaced in Britain around AD 120 by the Sixth Legion Victrix, who then garrisoned York for the remaining period of Roman occupation.

Unusually for Roman Britain, York had two very distinct parts: the legionary fortress north of the river and the walled civilian settlement to the south. The latter was given the status of *colonia* in the third century, probably by Septimius Severus, the Emperor born in North Africa, who spent three years campaigning against the Caledonians and died here in AD 211. One of his squabbling sons, Geta, was given the status of co-Emperor while here, but he was killed by his brother Caracalla, who then made York the capital of Britannia Secunda when the province was divided in two. Constantius I also died here in 306, also whilst campaigning with his son, who was then proclaimed Emperor Constantine I (later 'the Great') by the army.

The impressive city walls now visible only partly follow the lines of their Roman predecessors. During the town's evolution through the medieval period they enclosed a large area on both sides of the Ouse, incorporating two Norman motte and bailey castles. There was substantial rebuilding in the Victorian period, including a widening of the wall walk.

The Yorkshire Museum (Museum Gardens, YO1 7FR) is undoubtedly the best place to start. A fine purpose-built Greek Revival-style building, it opened its doors in 1830 and lies in the gardens beside the ruins of St Mary's Abbey.

The nationally important collection includes Roman finds from York and the rest of the county. These are a fantastic array of high-quality mosaics and wall-paintings, burials, altars and architectural pieces. Of particular interest are a head pot which may depict the face of Julia Domna, the wife of Septimius Severus, and a twice life-sized carved stone head of Constantine, both of whom had stayed in the city.

There is also a soldier's discharge diploma found near Malton and an important tombstone of a standard-bearer of the Ninth Legion in full regalia who came from Vienne near Lyon. His name was Lucius Duccius Rufinus, and he lived twenty-eight years.

A skeleton with injuries that suggest that he may have been a gladiator is shown, with information about another twenty found with similar injuries. Some of the bodies found in York had been encased in gypsum within the coffin, which allowed exceptional preservation. A young woman's auburn bun of hair, with hair pins still in place, is particularly moving. Evidence for a variety of religious cults has been found, including a statue of Arimanius, the lion-headed deity of Mithraism, though his head is missing.

Two important coins hoards are on show, the Overton hoard of silver denarii and the Wold Newton hoard of over 1,800 copper coins. The coins of the latter were deposited in a jar in date order, suggesting that the pot was for savings rather than being hidden in an emergency.

Whilst in the museum, two non-Roman must-sees are the Middleham Jewel and the Anglo-Saxon Yorkshire Helmet.

The Multangular Tower stands outside in the Museum Gardens, and is the most substantial surviving part of the fortress defences. It once stood at the west corner and there would have been another at the south corner, with six great interval towers between them facing the river along the fortress wall. The towers may have been added to the existing fortress wall by Septimius Severus, or as part of a rebuilding programme in the early fourth century under Constantius or Constantine. The tower has ten sides and the band of red tiles, still clearly visible, would have helped to bind the structure together. Roman layers are easily identifiable from the higher, later, larger stones. A length of the wall is visible behind the tower.

Bootham Bar is a medieval gate, but it stands on the site of one of the main gates into the fortress, the *Porta Principalis Dextra*. Nearby, just on the other side of St Leonard's Place, is a short stretch of the Roman wall in the car park next to the council offices, revealed in the nineteenth century. On the other side of the fortress, at **Monk Bar**, the remains of the east corner tower of the fortress can be seen from the wall walk. Between Monk and Bootham Bar the current wall walk follows the line of the Roman fortress wall.

The Multangular Tower at the west corner of the fortress defences at York (Eboracum).

York Minster lies above the headquarters building of the fortress, and outside in Minster Yard a monumental column from this building has been re-erected. It was found collapsed, with the column drums still resting next to each other, during excavations under the Minster in the late 1960s. Nearby is a modern but rather grand statue of Constantine I, who was declared Emperor in York.

The Minster Undercroft Museum has been recently upgraded to a state-of-the-art display explaining and exhibiting all the many layers of history lying underneath the cathedral. The first excavations took place in 1965–72, when emergency work was needed to stabilise the existing structure, especially the collapsing central tower. In 2012 there were more excavations to enhance knowledge of what lay beneath and to create the new museum. It is a masterpiece of engineering, and all is vividly explained. You can see a large section of wall of the fortress *principia*, as well as a large section of elaborately painted wall plaster from an anteroom added to the main hall in the late fourth century, used by the commander and senior officers.

Gravestones associated with the first, wooden Saxon minster are also displayed, and the development of the building from the Norman rebuilding in stone is explained. Computer graphics show how this was built right in the centre of the fortress site, at about 45 degrees to the grid of the barracks and other fortress structures. This would also have been the street pattern at the time of the Norman Conquest, so it was a bold statement of domination to ignore this orientation.

The Roman Bath Pub in St Sampson's Square is a little treasure. Beneath it is a cornucopia of a museum run by knowledgeable and enthusiastic volunteers. Descending to the cellar by a side door one is greeted by a hypocaust rather than beer barrels, found during excavations in the 1930s. The remains are part of the *caldarium* of the third and fourth-century legionary bath-house, the whole of which covered a much larger area. Finds include tiles with the prints of sandaled feet, and an extensive display of replica equipment, some of it available for dressing up should you feel inclined.

The streets of York have handsome plaques that often reveal their Roman origins. Stonegate gets its name from 'gate', Viking for street, and 'stone', showing that it was laid with stone slabs. It was first paved by the Romans of course and was the *Via Praetoria* of the fortress.

York has a Roman Festival which is usually scheduled in June.

8

The Hadrian's Wall Frontier
Running through Cumbria and Northumberland

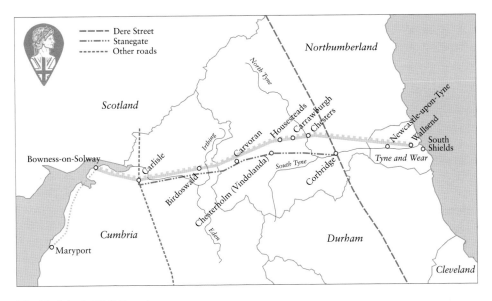

The Hadrian's Wall Frontier.

'Hadrian was the first to build a wall 80 miles long to separate the Romans from the Barbarians' – thus wrote Hadrian's unknown biographer, and it is as good a starting point as any to consider this immense monument. It is indeed 80 Roman miles long from sea to sea, across the relatively narrow line from the Solway to the Tyne estuaries. A Roman mile was 1,000 paces (*mille passum*); in the sixteenth century miles were fixed at a slightly greater length than this, so the distance is now measured at 73 miles (117.5 km). The system continued, without the joining wall, for at least 25 Roman miles along the Cumbrian coast south of Bowness-on-Solway.

Apart from the wall itself, it has the greatest concentration of forts, milecastles, turrets and other Roman buildings to be seen anywhere in Britain, and the associated museums are also high in both quantity and quality. It is, without a doubt, the best Roman frontier in the world, in a spectacular landscape – no other province has one quite like it. It has been a UNESCO World Heritage Site since 1987.

Since the opening of the Hadrian's Wall footpath in 2003 it is possible to walk the whole length, in either direction, starting along the edge of the Solway estuary or walking through Newcastle suburbs. If time is limited, the most spectacular stretch of wall and rugged scenery is the 10 miles (16 km) between **Housesteads** and **Carvoran**. All the Wall forts named in our section headings, below, should be a priority. Diversions should be made from the footpath to **Vindolanda** and **Corbridge**, neither of which is actually on the Wall, but part of an earlier frontier system, the forts of which became an integral part of the Wall infrastructure. Best of all, you should keep going back until you have seen every bit of it.

As this is all one huge monument, we have abandoned the alphabetical order of the other chapters and organised the sites into ten target sections, following the numbering system of milecastles from east to west. Each of these has easily accessible highlights, with an opportunity to explore further features for a distance in both directions.

The entire structure is in England – it doesn't form the border with Scotland, as many people think. The frontier wasn't conceived as a single plan: it moved several times, and the construction of the wall itself changed. It's worth getting the basic sequence straight in order to make some sense of the abundance of monuments.

Gnaeus Julius Agricola is the Governor of Britain about whom we know the most, mainly because his son-in-law was the historian Tacitus, whose account of the conquest of Britain is a rousing read. After finishing the conquest of Wales and northern England, Agricola took his troops north in AD 79, penetrating Scotland way north of the Forth–Clyde line, building a string of forts as they went. His army inflicted a defeat on the Caledonians at the Battle of Mons Graupius in AD 84, but he was recalled to Rome from Britain the following year. It was during his governorship that the **Stanegate Road** was constructed across northern England as a strategic supply route between forts at **Corbridge** and **Carlisle**, both of which also stood on major routes to the north. The Stanegate followed the valleys of the Tyne and Irthing rivers, to the south of the line of Hadrian's Wall, which came later. The forts of **Vindolanda**, **Carvoran** and **Nether Denton**, amongst others, were built on this line at this time.

Agricola's ambitious occupation of Scotland did not last for long, and the Stanegate became the northern frontier of Roman Britain in the early years of the second century, when the territory north of it was abandoned. The garrisons at forts including Vindolanda and Corbridge were changed, the forts were rebuilt and others were added at one-day marching intervals along it, that is 14 Roman miles (13 miles, 21 km). The Stanegate was never a continuous fortification like the later Wall, and there is nothing much to be seen of it today. Parts were still used as a road until the Military Road was built by General George Wade in 1746 after the Jacobite risings (using much material from Hadrian's Wall), which is part of the modern B6318. The best place to see a short stretch of the Stanegate is where it runs through the site at **Corbridge**.

Then in AD 122, after an uprising in the north, the Emperor Hadrian came to Britain to see for himself the state of affairs and to secure the frontier. This may be the year that the wall-building began, and the number of the modern bus that ferries people backwards and forwards along the B6318 commemorates this. However, some think the building started before Hadrian's visit.

The initial plan was for a continuous ditch and a wall running from Newcastle to Bowness-on-Solway, a few miles north of the Stanegate, following the high ground with commanding views. From Newcastle to the River Irthing this was to be of stone, while west of the river the paucity of building stone led to the decision to make it of turf. At intervals of 1 Roman mile there was a milecastle (stone-built east of the Irthing, timber to the west), each with two stone turrets between them. At this stage the existing Stanegate forts were considered sufficient to house the auxiliary soldiers who were to hold the wall. Labour was supplied by the three British legions, and inscriptions and different building styles have allowed many of the different allocations to be identified.

It is clear that milecastles and turrets were built ahead of the curtain wall, because there were then at least two changes of plan. Around AD 124 the decision was made to add twelve forts to the wall itself (later the number rose to sixteen), and at the same time or soon after to narrow the width of the wall from 10 feet to 8 feet, to extend the stone-built wall for 5 miles (8 km) west of the Irthing, and to extend the Wall itself from Newcastle to Wallsend. It seems to have been at this time, too, that the system of milefortlets and towers was added down the west coast for at least 25 Roman miles.

The numbering system for the milecastles on the Wall is modern rather than Roman, firmly established in 1930. It starts in the east with Milecastle 1 near the fort at Wallsend and ends in the west with Milecastle 80 at Bowness-on-Solway. The two turrets between them have the same number with the suffixes a and b. The full extent and number of structures down the Cumbrian coast is still not certain, because of the changing coastline, but it starts with Milefortlet 1, situated 1 Roman mile from Milecastle 80 at Bowness-on-Solway, and the last numbered Milefortlet is 25, not far south of **Maryport**.

When the change of wall width was implemented, building had reached all sorts of stages in different parts of the Wall. This means that in some parts there is a narrow wall on narrow foundations, sometimes a narrow wall on broad foundations, and sometimes a broad wall on a broad foundation. Many of the turrets and milecastles had been constructed with wing walls anticipating a broad curtain wall. Where these met the narrow wall, offsets were left on the south side of the wall, so a consistent front was maintained to the north. These 'points of reduction' can be seen on many milecastles and turrets. After the forts had been built the huge earthwork known as the Vallum, a deep, wide ditch flanked with earthen mounds, was constructed to the south of them. This lay parallel with the wall, presumably to delineate a military zone into which no unauthorised person should stray; it is perhaps the most visible continuous feature along the line of the Wall. The remaining turf parts of the wall were then rebuilt in stone *c.* AD 200.

It has all made for a fascinating field of study, with much opportunity for relative dating. There are reconstructions of the wall showing its various stages, and with various hypothetical plastered and painted finishes at **Wallsend** and at **Vindolanda,** a wonderful scale model of the whole thing at the **Great North Museum in Newcastle** and a reconstruction of the turf wall in the **Tullie House Museum in Carlisle.**

As well as all the military structures described above, there were bridges built over the River Irthing at **Willowford,** and over the North Tyne at **Chesters.** There are also temples, such as the mithraeum at **Carrawburgh,** and the civilian settlements which grew around the forts, sometimes becoming towns in their own right, especially at **Corbridge.** Inscriptions on dedicatory stones and altars tell us stories of the soldiers and their families who came from all over the Empire to serve here, and the museums have a rich collection of these. Stories less official than those carved in stone come from the incredible **Vindolanda tablets,** wooden postcards from the past, some displayed at the site museum, others in the BM. The **Roman Army Museum at Carvoran,** recently refurbished, will tell you everything you need to know about how this incredible diverse yet united force functioned. W. H. Auden's poem 'Roman Wall Blues' captures the isolation auxiliary units may have felt on this distant frontier:

> The mist creeps over the hard grey stone.
> My girl's in Tungria; I sleep alone ...

Dere Street was the main terrestrial supply route for the eastern part of Hadrian's Wall, running between York and Corbridge, where it crossed the Stanegate, and continuing north through Port Gate on the Wall. The forts from Piercebridge to High Rochester, south and north of the Wall, are often regarded as outliers of the frontier system, though we have described them with the other Dere Street forts in Chapter 7. Similar outliers lie along the north–south road west of the Pennines, from Old Penrith to Birrens.

The later history of the Wall is equally interesting. Not long after Hadrian died in AD 138 there was an advance of the frontier to a line along the Forth–Clyde isthmus, where the **Antonine Wall** was constructed of turf in AD 142 (Chapter 9). The Hadrian's Wall forts were evacuated, but not for long, as the garrisons returned somewhere between AD 158 and 162 (opinions differ), and Scotland was abandoned once more. There are suggestions of withdrawal of some troops from Hadrian's Wall during the bid by Clodius Albinus to become Emperor in AD 196–7, and there may have been a brief reoccupation of some of the forts of the Antonine Wall when Septimius Severus was campaigning in Scotland in AD 209–11, but this too was brief.

During the early years of the third century there were general repairs and improvements made to the frontier system, including rebuilding the western turf section in stone. Times were changing, though, and the defences built in the third century along the Saxon Shore and the west coast were against new sea-borne raiders from outside the province. By the late third and early fourth centuries the army had been reorganised into frontier and field troops (*limitanei* and *comitatenses*) rather than legionaries and auxiliaries. The wall continued to be maintained, repaired and garrisoned, at least in part, to about AD 400, and some forts were occupied well into the fifth century, providing ready-made defences in uncertain times. It then became a quarry for building stone. However much survives, and in its twenty-first-century resurgent state it should not be missed, under any circumstances.

Starting from the East end, where many modern travellers will arrive first, and counting 'Wall-miles', the accepted terminology for Roman miles here:

1. Newcastle upon Tyne and around, Wall-miles 0–20

South Shields supply fort; Wallsend wall fort; Great North Museum; Benwell Roman temple (EH) and vallum crossing (EH); first glimpse of Wall at Turret 7b (Denton); long stretch of Wall at Heddon-on-the-Wall (EH); Rudchester wall fort.

South Shields (Arbeia) ****

Supply fort beyond the east end of the Wall; impressive granaries; reconstructed gate, barracks and commander's house; museum. Seasonal opening.

The site of Arbeia fort lies surrounded by Victorian terraced houses in the Tyneside town of South Shields (Baring Street NE33 2BB). Roman remains were discovered during housing construction in the 1870s, attracting so much interest that they were kept open as part of a public 'People's Park'. The excavated area was extended after the First World War, and during the 1970s nearly all the modern buildings were cleared from the site, with the exception of a school on the southern section, which forms part of the current museum and 'Timequest' activity centre.

Reconstructed West Gate of South Shields (Arbeia) auxiliary and supply fort.

This was the most easterly of the garrison forts of the wall system, lying on a spur at the mouth of the River Tyne, to the south of the river itself. The wall never reached this far, finishing at Wallsend, north of the river. The first fort was constructed *c*. AD 129, and this later became a key supply fort for the frontier, with a changing, typically cosmopolitan garrison of troops. Two tombstones in the museum illustrate this wonderfully well, both in memory of former slaves. One was a Catuvellauni girl, Regina, who married her former master, a merchant from Palmyra, and died aged thirty. She is depicted finely dressed and seated in Roman style, the archetypal Roman matron. The other, Victor, was Moorish in origin, who died aged twenty to be remembered by his former master, a Spanish cavalryman, 'with all devotion'. His image reclines languidly on a dining couch, being served by his own slave.

Inscriptions and excavation have revealed the changing nature of the fort. It was built by the Sixth Legion Victrix, and first garrisoned by a cavalry regiment from Pannonia (modern Hungary). Around AD 208 it was converted to a supply base for the northern campaigns of Septimius Severus. Barracks were demolished to make way for granaries, and the garrison changed to the Fifth Cohort of Gauls. Another seven granaries were built in the AD 220s, a vital part of the supply chain for Hadrian's Wall. Goods could be offloaded from larger sea-going vessels nearby and carried along the Tyne by river barge. During the late third and fourth centuries a company of Mesopotamian boatmen from the Tigris were garrisoned here and it is possible that the name Arbeia derives from 'fort of the Arab troops'.

Today you can explore substantial Roman foundations, which are dominated by the only permanent stone-built Roman granaries yet found in Britain, as well as the impressive reconstructed West Gate, barracks block and commander's house. These were all built on the foundations of the originals between 1987 and the early 2000s, giving a splendid idea of the original appearance of the fort, based on evidence from this and other sites.

Wallsend (Segedunum) ****

Most easterly Wall fort at the start of the Wall; Wall reconstruction; museum.

The clue is in the name – this is the fort at the eastern end of Hadrian's Wall, on the banks of the River Tyne (Buddle Street NE28 6HR). Its Roman name was Segedunum, which means 'strong place', and it represents an eastward extension to the Wall built perhaps five years after the initial project was started, to protect the river crossing at Pons Aelius (Newcastle) from attack via the Tyne estuary.

It is therefore either the starting point or the finish for those walking the wall, depending on which direction you have chosen. As you approach the site from the car park you are first greeted by a huge sculpture made of weathered steel girders which give a nod to the Swan Hunter shipyard which once lay adjacent to the site. Erected in 2017, it marked the 1,900th anniversary of the beginning of Hadrian's imperial rule, and the thirtieth anniversary of his Wall becoming a World Heritage Site. A centurion's upper body rises out of a four-storey Roman building, and the first part of his name, Sentius Tectonicus, is that of the centurion who oversaw the building of the wall section closest to Segedunum. As you continue into the site you will see an inscription listing all those whose names have been recorded on building inscriptions – 'the men who built the Wall'. This is a fitting way of injecting humanity into this massive stone monument.

This is also one of the places where you can see a reconstruction of the various elements of the Wall, built to the minimum conjectured height of 12 Roman feet (just over 3.5 metres). It could actually have been higher than this but there is no proof. This has been built just behind the excavated remains of the Wall itself where it ran in a westerly direction from the west gate of the fort, so you have to exit the site and cross the road to find it. Look out for the modern wooden posts inserted where there was once a tangle of sharpened branches to hinder progress between the wall-ditch and the Wall. There are also several possible finishes for the Wall demonstrated. Was it whitewashed? Rusticated? Or smooth with red-painted pointing?

Just close by there are features of a much later date – a shaft of the Wallsend colliery, which opened in 1780. The fort site was once occupied by a coal pit village, replaced by terraced houses lived in by those who worked in the pit or in the late nineteenth and twentieth-century shipyard.

The observation tower beside the remains of the fort gives a splendid bird's-eye view of the layout, with a wonderfully evocative animated timeline of your view. The rest of the museum is housed in former Swan Hunter shipyard buildings, and the sections explaining the history of the fort, with the finds from the excavations, are invaluable.

The main area of excavations took place in the 1970s when the terraced houses covering the site were demolished. This then became the first almost complete fort plan from the Wall excavated under modern conditions, and the best-preserved parts were laid out to view. Excavations on the Wall showed that the extension to Segedunum was of the 'narrow wall' form, and therefore an afterthought, and that the fort was an integral part of this. The wall close to the fort was constructed over unstable ground and had to be repaired a number of times. Evidence for a *vicus* has been found between the fort and the river, as well as another wall running down from the south-east corner of the fort to the river sealing the 'military zone', and a wharf next to the river within this.

The walls of the fort, laid out in stone and gravel at ground level, present a very flat view, and show the buildings as they stood in about AD 200, when 400 infantry and 120 cavalry were stationed there. The barracks, HQ building, commander's house, hospital, granary and other storerooms can all be seen in outline.

A reconstructed military bath-house was based on a structure found at Chesters fort. It looks very striking from the outside, but sadly the interior has been closed for essential maintenance for several years. Nearby you can see the remains of the fort's own baths.

Newcastle upon Tyne*****

The Great North Museum: Hancock.

Named after a Northumberland-born ornithologist and taxidermist, John Hancock, the Great North Museum was the result of a £26 million redevelopment which merged several collections. It now has galleries covering everything from dinosaurs to outer space (it includes a planetarium), specialising in Northumberland's archaeology and natural history (Newcastle University, Barras Bridge NE2 4PT).

It is to the central gallery on the ground floor dedicated to Hadrian's Wall that all those interested in Roman Britain should proceed. This is dominated by a scale model of the entire wall, with all its forts, milecastles and turrets, a must for those about to embark on an exploration. Walk along it, and also view it from the first-floor gallery to appreciate the immense undertaking of this building project.

All around it are the many building inscriptions, altars, funerary and religious reliefs found at sites along the wall, displayed with life-size Perspex figures taking on the characters of people mentioned in the inscriptions, making the stones really speak to us in the twenty-first century. Highlights are the reliefs from the Mithraeum at Carrawburgh; the inscription from a milecastle naming the Emperor Hadrian, the men of the Second Legion Augusta and the Governor A. Platorius Nepos; the relief showing a very British Venus bathing from a water tank at High Rochester and the head of a local god, Antenociticus, found in a temple beside Benwell fort.

There are also wonderful artefacts in themed cases: arms and armour, including pieces from the Corbridge Hoard, pottery, bathing and religion.

These are all the most important finds from the sites along the eastern half of the wall. Finds from the western half are in Carlisle Museum, and Corbridge, Chesters, Vindolanda, and Carvoran also have stupendous site museums.

There was a fort, Pons Aelius, in Newcastle itself, which lay north of the river and was named for the Roman bridge nearby, itself given Hadrian's family name. Much of it lies beneath the medieval castle still visible to the north-west of the Tyne Bridge.

Benwell Temple and Vallum crossing ***

Beside a residential street west of the city centre of Newcastle lie the remains of a second-century temple to the local god Antenociticus (Broomridge Avenue, NE15 6QP). It had a residential setting in Roman times too, within the *vicus* outside the eastern edge of the wall fort of Benwell (Condercum), now buried and invisible. The temple wall foundations are now neatly concreted in the centre of a lawn, with replicas of two of the three altars to the god found during excavations in the nineteenth century. These flank an original statue base, which may have held the image of which the head survives, a striking fusion of Celtic and Classical style. This is displayed in the Great North Museum, along with the original altars. Their different dedications, by a centurion of the Twentieth Legion, the prefect of the First Cohort of Vangiones, originally from the Rhineland, and the prefect of an Asturian cavalry unit from northern Spain, give an indication of the changing garrison of the nearby fort.

The temple may have been destroyed during the late second century and the area used as a cemetery, as two skeletons were found beneath the apse, but the early date of the excavations makes the reading of the evidence uncertain.

Nearby to the west, in Denhill Park road, is the only permanent causeway across the Vallum earthwork to be seen on the line of the Wall, beautifully laid out so that successive resurfacings of the road can be appreciated. Halfway across the causeway was a stone arch with a gate; the western base of the arch survives and can still be seen.

Heddon-on-the-Wall **

Good stretch of Broad Wall, Rudchester fort (Vindobala).

The first sighting of the Wall travelling west from Newcastle is just before **Turret 7b** (**Denton**), beside the road in the aptly named Turret Road (NE15 7TH). The first really significant section, though, is at **Heddon-on-the-Wall** (Hexham Road, NE15 0ED). The local residents are justly proud of their 'little stretch of Hadrian's Wall' and will tell you so. It is a fine example of the Broad Wall, initially planned for the whole part of the stone-built section, and is 330 feet (100 metres) long and more than 6 feet (2 metres) thick in places.

Heddon is also the site of Milecastle 12, no longer visible but lying under a farm in the village. High above the Tyne, it stood at an excellent vantage point with good views to all points of the compass.

The charming Anglo-Saxon church of St Andrew was built in the seventh century with Roman stone quarried from the Wall.

After Heddon, the eighteenth-century Military Road follows the Wall, and for much of its course actually lies on top of it. The Wall provided a good solid foundation for General Wade's road, needed to move troops quickly between Newcastle and Carlisle. Only a couple of hundred years ago the Wall was still fulfilling a military frontier role.

The fort of **Rudchester** (Vindobala) (NE15 0JA) lies next to Rudchester Farm, a couple of miles west of Heddon, and was pretty much flattened by the Military Road. Garrisoned by 500 auxiliaries of the First Cohort of Frisiavones from Lower Germany, who built a temple here to Mithras, the fort was probably destroyed by fire in the late second or early third century. The rampart ditches on the south and west sides are clearly visible from the Hadrian's Wall footpath.

2. Corbridge and around (Wall-miles 20–26)

Corbridge military supply base and town, site museum with Corbridge Hoard, replica Lanx and Corbridge Lion (EH); Arch in Corbridge church; Halton Chesters fort.

Corbridge (Coria/Corstopitum) ****

The next major site in the wall system is **Corbridge**, not on the Wall but 3 miles to the south on the Stanegate (Corchester Lane, NE45 5NT). The town today is picture-perfect, with history at every corner, including an early Saxon church, an ancient market cross or two, water pumps and troughs aplenty and probably the best vicar's pele tower in Britain.

The Roman remains lie a little to the west in an EH site. The central excavated area on display is impressive, even at about one-tenth of the total settlement at its height.

Segmented armour and other finds in the museum at Corbridge (Coria). *Photo: English Heritage.*

The fort was originally established *c*. AD 85 at the east end of the Stanegate road to Carlisle, where Dere Street crossed the River Tyne. It later developed into one of the most important Roman towns in Britain and was indeed the most northerly town in the Roman Empire.

By AD 160 the fort had expanded into a massive military supply base both for the Wall and for periodic campaigns launched to the north. At times it must have felt similar to the British Army's Camp Bastion in Afghanistan, buzzing with men, equipment and all the paraphernalia needed to keep a permanent army in the field. We know from the Vindolanda tablets that it was also the place where soldiers went for R&R when off-duty from their garrison duties along the wall. The town developed around the two military compounds of this base and was occupied until the end of the Roman period.

Written messages on some of the Vindolanda tablets have also confirmed that the Roman name for Corbridge, used locally at least, was Coria, although there does seem to be some link to the name Corstopitum, previously thought to be its Roman identity.

Much of what is exposed on the site inevitably relates to the later military compounds and town, but there are occasional glimpses of the stratigraphy of the four successive earlier forts beneath.

The main street cutting the site in half from east to west is the Stanegate itself, still very impressive. Immediately to the north are two enormous granaries which are the best-preserved of their type anywhere in the Roman world, with vaulted floors of massive paving slabs with supporting buttresses. One of the ventilators that would have helped keep the stores fresh can still be seen in the east granary.

Next to the granaries is a fountain house with a large stone tank marking the end of an aqueduct bringing fresh water to the town. Such a feature is rare in Britain and indicates the high status of the town.

Next to this, the intriguingly named Site XI was a truly monumental courtyard building, the surviving blocks of which are huge. The walls of the headquarters building and commanding officer's house of the earlier fort have been exposed within the courtyard; compare the much smaller size of the blocks used for these with the huge rusticated stones of the later surrounding building. The function of the huge late building is still uncertain.

South of the Stanegate lie the foundations of many barracks, workshops and associated compound buildings.

The museum at Corbridge, beautifully redisplayed by English Heritage in 2018, contains some real delights, not least a Victorian electrotype copy of the Corbridge silver lanx by Elkingtons. The original is in the British Museum, described in Chapter 1, but the replica is now an antique work of art in its own right.

The museum also holds the Corbridge Lion, a fabulous stone carving of a lion attacking a deer, originally meant for a sepulchral monument. At a later date it was transformed into a fountainhead with, alas, some major dental intervention necessary for the lion.

But perhaps the greatest treasure is the Corbridge Hoard of military equipment and armour. Like the Ribchester Hoard in the BM, this was found in the remains of a wooden chest and was presumably buried by the owner for safe keeping. It was found in 1964, deep down in Site XI, dating from the time of the earlier forts. The contents included the most complete sections found to date of the segmented armour of Roman legionaries, the *lorica segmentata* illustrated in the reliefs on Trajan's Column in Rome. These have enabled us to understand how each piece fitted together and how the connecting pieces worked.

The Saxon Church in the modern town is wonderful in its own right, but also contains a magnificent Roman arch salvaged from the ruins. This was probably a gate to Coria which has been re-erected in the tower.

Halton Chesters (Onnum) is the fifth fort built into the Wall from the east, and it lies 3 miles north of Corbridge (NE46 4EU). The Port Gate was once just to the west of here, where Dere Street ran through the Wall, just about where the roundabout taking the A68 runs through the Wall today. The Hadrian's Wall footpath passes through the fort so you can join it here if you wish. The remains of the fort are mainly humps and bumps with the outer rampart ditches being the most visible. Like Rudchester it is bisected east/west by the Military Road. The south section is also cut by the grand drive to Halton Castle, with a picturesque fourteenth-century pele tower.

The footpath can be rejoined here, after diverting to Corbridge, or you can drive straight to **Chesters Roman fort and bridge abutment,** just over 26 Roman miles from Wallsend.

3. Chesters and around (Wall-miles 26–30)

Chesters wall fort with well-preserved bath-house and Clayton Museum; Chollerford bridge abutment (EH). To the east: Turret 26b (Brunton), Church of St Oswald in the Lee and stretch of Wall at Planetrees. To the west: Turret 29a (Blackcarts) and Limestone Corner.

Chesters Wall Fort (Cilurnum) ****

Housesteads and Vindolanda might be today's rock stars of the Wall system, but Chesters is its heart and soul. It was also the home of its salvation.

Nestling on an estate by the banks of the North Tyne, the fort site feels idyllic compared to the rugged central section of the Wall a few miles away to the west (Chollerford, Hexham NE46 4EU).

The Claytons, past owners of this estate, have had a significant effect on the fort and the Wall. Whilst the first owner, Nathaniel Clayton, had the ruins levelled in the late eighteenth century to improve the view, thankfully his son John was fascinated by the Romans. Not only did he excavate and consolidate here but he bought many of the surviving stretches of the Wall and had large sections restored to how we see them today. His son, Nathaniel George, carried on the good works and opened the museum in 1896.

The present access to the fort is via the North Gate which, like the East and West Gates, lies to the barbarian side of the wall. An extra pair of East and West Gates below the Wall allowed access to the south. The fort had a standard playing card plan, but today the separate exposed sections, each surrounded by metal railings, make it feel like a jigsaw with half its pieces missing. This is the legacy of the archaeological digs

The bath-house by the River North Tyne at Chesters (Cilurnum). *Photo: English Heritage.*

of the Victorian period. The fort gates, some of the barracks, the commanding officer's house and headquarters building are displayed, with large areas of undisturbed lawn in between. There has been little modern excavation, so much still lies buried.

The most impressive ruins are those of the **baths** outside the fort to the east, down towards the River North Tyne. There is a good view of them from the remains of **Chollerford bridge abutment** (NE46 4EN) on the other side of the river, accessible from the east side of the modern bridge. A viewing platform shows the line of the bridge and wall over the river, and submerged stones of the bridge piers can be seen when the water is low. There were two successive bridges here, one built in the Hadrianic period, the other in the later second century. Many carved stones from the superstructure can still be seen on site, and a water channel may have led from here to a mill downstream.

The Clayton Museum at Chesters is a wonderful antiquarian collection, painstakingly labelled and displayed with pride. It houses a fabulous array of tombstones, altars, milestones and sculptured stones of all shapes and sizes.

A mile to the east of Chesters, is **Brunton Turret 26b** which, as one of the best-preserved on the Wall, is well worth the visit. A little further east is a fine stretch of Wall at **Planetrees** which shows the broad to narrow wall transition well. Milecastle 26 lies here, but little can now be seen of it. The **Church of St Oswald in the Lee** nearby contains some fine Roman stones including a 5-foot-tall altar.

A walk to the west towards the high country will take you to a good section of Wall, **Blackcarts Turret 29a** and **Limestone Corner**, which can also be accessed from Carrawburgh fort (see below).

The wall and bridge abutment at Chollerford.

4. Carrawburgh and around (Wall-miles 30–36)

Carrawburgh wall fort with Mithraeum (EH). To the east: spectacular stretch of Wall including Limestone Corner. To the west: Turret 33b and Milecastle 35 (Sewingshields).

Carrawburgh (Brocolitia)***

The playing card shape of the fort platform at **Carrawburgh** (pronounced Currabruff) is immediately apparent adjacent to the car park (Humshaugh, Hexham NE46 4DB). The fort was a late addition to the frontier works, being built after the Wall and Vallum had been completed. It lies completely south of the line of the Wall and the Vallum has been flattened to accommodate it.

The site is notable for its **Mithraeum**, a temple to the god Mithras, lying beyond the south-west corner of the fort down a slope. It was excavated in 1950, revealing the temple and its three altars, the originals of which are in the Great North Museum in Newcastle, with replicas here on site. The building dates to *c.* AD 200, and the three altars were dedicated in the late third century by soldiers from the fort's garrison of Batavian auxiliaries, originating in the Rhineland.

The mystery religion of Mithraism was popular with soldiers and similar temples have been discovered at Rudchester and Housesteads. The damage done to the monument here, including the smashing of the Mithras statue, is likely to have been inflicted by later Christians, who regarded the religion with suspicion, rather than

The *Mithraeum* at Carrawburgh (Brocolitia) with three altars dedicated to Mithras.

by attacking barbarians. Another sanctuary, often interpreted as a shrine to the water nymphs, was found outside the entrance to the temple-cave.

A third religious site close by is **Coventina's Well**, where thousands of coins and other votive offerings were made to the local deity of the sacred spring. Many of the 13,000 coins, sculptures and altars found here in the late nineteenth century are in the museum at Chesters. All that is visible at the site is a pool on the site of the spring.

A short distance to the east of Carrawburgh lies **Limestone Corner**. This is the most northerly point on the wall and therefore, apart from the brief expansions into Scotland, the most northerly point of the Empire for nearly 300 years. As the name suggests, there is a break in direction of the wall here as it veers south-easterly towards Chesters. However, limestone is a real misnomer as the rock is actually the extremely hard igneous quartz-dolerite whinstone. Perhaps because of this, the wall ditch was not finished at this point, but left full of large chunks of stone, with areas where quarrying started but was then abandoned. This has left clues to the methods used by the soldiers, including drill- and wedge-holes. In defence of the work ethic of the legionaries, the Vallum was successfully quarried out of the same stone yards to the south.

A walk to the west of Carrawburgh takes you to Turret 33b and Milecastle 35 (Sewingshields), with exposed masonry and superb views.

5. Housesteads and around (Wall-miles 36–42)

Housesteads wall fort with well-preserved latrines, Murder House, museum (EH & NT). Great central section of Hadrian's Wall with tough walking and fabulous views. To the east: Knag Burn Gate, Milecastle 35 (Sewingshields). To the west: Milecastle 37 (Housesteads), Milecastle 38 (Hotbank), Milecastle 39 (Castle Nick), Turret 41a (Caw Gap), Milecastle 42 (Cawfields).

Housesteads (Vercovicium)*****

Housesteads is the superstar amongst the Wall forts. Here, high up on the Whin Sill more or less in the centre of the Wall line, the sense of the remote frontier is intense, with spectacular views all around. Its isolation has meant that much of its stonework has been spared later quarrying. The hike up to the ridge across the vallum and through the site of the *vicus* is well worth the investment of energy. There is a good small **museum** to the south-west of the fort, en route to and from the car park, containing some wonderful finds from the site, including some splendid window arches (Haydon Bridge, Hexham NE47 6NN).

The fort makes the most of the local topography and sits south of the Wall with its long axis parallel to it, rather than straddling it with short axis parallel like most of the other Wall forts. The change of plan by the authorities in adding the forts to the Wall line is graphically demonstrated here on the north wall of the fort, where the foundations of Turret 36b and the original line of the Wall can be seen, both demolished to make way for the new fort.

The communal latrine at Housesteads (Vercovicium) with water channel for cleaning sponges, or perhaps moss.

Many of the internal buildings can be seen in detail, including the commanding officer's house, the headquarters building, the hospital, barrack blocks, granaries, and storerooms. Perhaps the best-known of all the facilities here is the extremely well-preserved latrine block. The water channels and drains are in amazingly good order. The reconstruction illustration showing the soldiers sitting in companionable relief, sharing their sponges on sticks, provides endless fascination for visitors of all ages. Archaeological evidence seems to suggest, though, that clumps of moss were the major mode of personal hygiene rather than sponges in this part of the world.

The South Gate is a little confusing as the structure is complicated by the walls of a sixteenth-century bastle house. Nearby are the remains of the stone buildings of the *vicus*. One of these is now known as the 'Murder House' after two skeletons were discovered in the 1930s, buried under the clay floor. One was identified as a male, the other female, and the tip of a knife was found between the ribs of the former. It was illegal to bury bodies within a settlement, so there seems little doubt that this was indeed a murder.

The East Gate has some intriguing modern folklore attached to it. The threshold stones have pronounced wheel ruts, formed from years of wear by carts passing through. It is said that George Stephenson, who at one time lived close by, measured the distance between the two and used this as his gauge for the first railways.

However, since wagons in use in his time had changed little since the Roman period it may just be that this shows continuity rather than a deliberate throw-back.

The North Gate of the fort appears to open onto terrain that would negate its use but remember the ramp that would have made it viable is now lost. Nevertheless, an extra opening, the **Knag Burn Gate**, was added beyond the north-east corner probably in the fourth century. This might have been to allow a more efficient traffic flow north–south, but gates at each end of the passage may have been for stopping and searching travellers, or certainly controlling who passed through. Continue walking east and you will eventually come to Milecastle 35 (Sewingshields), also accessible from Carrawburgh (above).

The 3-mile walk west of Housesteads to Steel Rigg car park is one of the most exciting stretches of all, rising over crags and dropping into gaps. Shortly to the west of the fort is **Milecastle 37 (Housesteads)**, one of the best-preserved, its North Gate boasting the highest remains of an arch on the wall. The springer stones plus three voussoirs on each side provide valuable evidence of the minimum possible height of the wall and perhaps a wall walk. Recently there has been much academic debate on whether the Wall did indeed have a wall walk and parapet or not. This will remain a mystery as nowhere does the wall exist to its original height and there is a dearth of contemporary depictions to enlighten us. Continue past this to **Milecastle 38 (Hotbank)** down to Sycamore Gap with its famous tree, then on to **Milecastle 39 (Castle Nick)**, all through fabulous swooping scenery. The 10-mile walk from Housesteads to Carvoran is a must if you can do it.

Knag Burn Gate through the wall, just east of Housesteads Wall Fort.

6. Chesterholm (Vindolanda) *****

Fort and vicus on the Stanegate; site museum with Vindolanda tablets; reconstructed Hadrian's Wall section; reconstructed temple.

Vindolanda is outstanding, its isolated location in a bleakly dramatic landscape having been transformed by excavations directed by three generations of one family, the Birleys (Bardon Mill, Hexham NE47 7JN). These have uncovered treasures beyond any wildest dreams – not gleaming gold or jewels, but the words and artefacts of ordinary people in their everyday activities, shining a bright light on what it was like to live in Roman Britain.

The remains of the fort buildings have been exposed over a large area, untangling at least nine phases of rebuilding, the earliest of timber, the later ones of stone. It is these later third and fourth-century remains that are visible today. The first forts predate Hadrian's Wall, which lies about 1 mile (1.6 km) to the north of the site, the military base having been established here in about AD 85 after the northern campaigns of Agricola. It therefore began life as a part of the late first-century Stanegate frontier, then became an important military base as part of Hadrian's frontier, and in the third and fourth centuries became the base for the Fourth Cohort of Gauls.

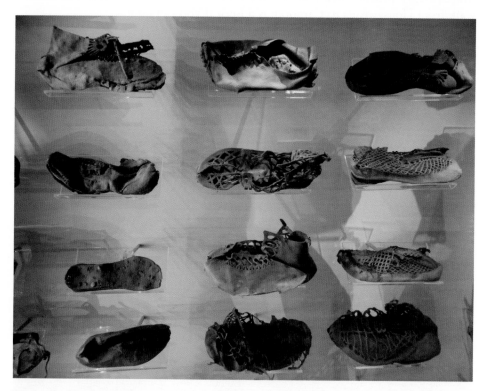

The wall of leather shoes in Vindolanda Museum. *Photo: The Vindolanda Trust.*

Activity continued on the site for several centuries after the end of any Roman army presence in Britain, and it was not abandoned until the ninth century. Recent excavations have concentrated on tracking how these changes in use manifested themselves. The site is well signposted, and if you visit during the summer months you will probably see ongoing excavations.

Beside the excavated area there is a reconstruction of a section of Hadrian's Wall in turf, timber and stone. It is close to here that the findspot of the remarkable Vindolanda tablets is signposted – thin, postcard-sized sheets of wood with inked hand-written messages from the period AD 92–103, written and received by those who lived here and subsequently thrown onto rubbish heaps. They survived because of the waterlogged conditions beneath the piles of rubbish and subsequent buildings. About 500 were discovered in the 1970s and 80s, and more have been found since. The majority now reside at the British Museum but the fabulous site museum contains a fair number, with translations of the messages. They include an invitation to a birthday party, movements of troops, descriptions of the locals, letters home and all sorts of incredible everyday details which usually disappear in a matter of years, let alone millennia. There is a website with transcripts on-line: http://vindolanda.csad.ox.ac.uk/tablets/. Their place in history as the earliest surviving hand-written documents from Britain has been supplanted by those found at the site of the London Mithraeum on the Bloomberg site but they remain the most abundant and the first recognised examples of their kind, revealing unprecedented details about life on the northern frontier.

The museum is housed in what was originally a private house, called Chesterholm, built in 1831. It is a world class treasure-house of remarkable objects, much enhanced by the organic items preserved, like the famous tablets, by the soggy conditions on the site.

The wall of leather shoes of all sizes is a revelation, with a particularly fine ladies pair sporting the maker's impressed label. No attempt has been made to repair them, so the owner must have been wealthy, probably the commander's wife.

Other highlights include a lady's wig made of moss, which might have offered some protection against midge bites, and a leather chamfron from a cavalryman's mount. A marvellous reconstruction shows how splendid this would have appeared when new. More rare surviving leather artefacts include the recent find of an extraordinary pair of boxing gloves, showing that pugilistic training was carried out at the fort.

All sorts of wooden tools and everyday artefacts such as baskets and rope are exhibited in the new 'Wooden Underworld' gallery. There are also the more durable materials, including part of a bronze calendar, a beautiful glass cup with enamel-painted gladiators (found in three pieces over different excavation seasons in disparate locations) and an altar which names the site, Vindolanda, one of the only two sites on the Wall system with an inscription set up by the inhabitants with the full name, the other being at Birdoswald, below.

Outside, the garden has some delightful monumental Roman facsimiles, including a temple to the water nymphs, a house and shop and a pottery kiln.

7. Carvoran and around (Wall-miles 42–47)

Carvoran fort on the Stanegate and Roman Army Museum. To the east: Great Chesters wall fort (Aesica); Turret 44b (Walltown) and Turret 45a (Mucklebank). To the west: Milecastle 48 (Poltross Burn).

Carvoran (Magnis)****

Situated 250 yards (230 metres) south of the Wall, the fort at Carvoran was one of the original Stanegate forts that was corralled into later duty as part of the Hadrianic frontier. The vallum passes to the north of it, and recent geological survey has indicated that it faced south, all unusual features. It has been very little excavated, and there is only the fort platform to see, immediately behind the Roman Army Museum. A few stones of the north-west tower are visible, as well as the playing card outline of the ramparts.

The **Roman Army Museum** (Greenhead, Brampton CA8 7JB) is a sister establishment to Vindolanda and is a great aid to understanding the Wall. The displays and films explain the history of the Roman frontiers, the make-up of the army and what life was like on these outposts of empire.

The film *The Edge of Empire: The Eagle's View* is the highlight, using live action and 3D reconstruction to show what life and death were like in the second century. Don't miss the video graphic *The Structure of the Roman Army* where Legions, Cohorts, Centuries, Signifers and Centurions are all brilliantly and succinctly explained.

Hadrian's Wall at Walltown Crags.

The full-scale models of artillery, chariots, and soldiers are endlessly fascinating, and there are also genuine artefacts. One of the garrison units here comprised Hamian archers from Syria and the model of one of these mounted cavalrymen shows the importance of wearing a shield on your back. Presumably these auxiliaries were experts at turning in the saddle and firing a Parthian shot to the rear. An inscribed altar shows their worship of the Syrian mother goddess.

Other fascinating exhibits include a bovine skull that was used for archery practice, the only find of a helmet crest in Britain and a set of Roman horseshoes or hippo-sandals. The museum has been so expertly put together that even the toilets are fit for an emperor.

To the east of Carvoran is one of the finest stretches of wall over Walltown Crags where the Wall clings to the crags of Whin Sill, including the well-preserved **Turrets 45a and 44b**, to the fort of **Great Chesters (Aesica)**, 3 miles (4 km) from Carvoran. This, too, has not been excavated and it is probable that many wall walkers pass straight through it without noticing. It is a great place to see a fort in the wild, and its isolated position up on the crags means it has suffered less from stone-robbing than elsewhere. The walls, although overgrown, are relatively high and the gates well-preserved, with mounds and bumps covering the internal structures.

To the west, more fine walking will take you to Milecastle 48 (Poltross Burn), one of the best-preserved, and the River Irthing crossing, which can also be accessed from Birdoswald, below.

8. Birdoswald and around (Wall-miles 48–53)

Birdoswald wall fort and museum (EH). To the east: Willowford Bridge abutment; Milecastles 48 and 49; Turrets 48a, 48b. To the west: Turrets 51a, 51b, 52a; Hare Hill highest piece of Wall; Pike Hill signal station; the longest stretch of the Wall.

Birdoswald (Banna), Cumbria *****

Not so long ago Birdoswald was a working farm and one could only peer over the wall and dream of how wonderful it would be to live within the confines of a Roman fort (Gilsland, Brampton CA8 7DD). The farm buildings now comprise a visitor centre and museum and the farmhouse, a romanticised idea of a border fortified house and tower built in 1858, largely from Roman stone. The latter is a hostel for budding archaeologists and walkers.

The fort is built high on the escarpment above the River Irthing, with a stunning view over the river gorge. The vallum here doglegs to squeeze itself between the fort and the cliff edge, which has suffered from extensive erosion as the river changed its course over the last 1,800 years.

The gates and outer walls of the fort are well laid out and sign-posted, as are the granaries and drill hall. Excavations here in the 1980s furnished the first

South wall of Birdoswald (Banna) Wall Fort, with the farmhouse beyond. *Photo: English Heritage.*

The beginning of the bridge over the River Irthing at Willowford. *Photo: English Heritage.*

evidence for the immediate post-Roman story of Hadrian's Wall, with timber halls constructed over the granaries in the fifth century. These are marked out by modern timbers on the site.

East of the fort is a very fine stretch of wall heading towards Willowford Bridge, where the wall crossed the River Irthing. There are some entertaining carvings here, comprising two *phalluses* and two centurial stones. **Milecastle 49 (Harrow Scar)** lies at the end of this stretch, as the Wall disappears at the river gorge to reappear on the other side as the **Willowford bridge abutment** for another long fine stretch towards Gilsland. A centurial stone can be seen as part of a barn wall and there are two turrets, **48b and 48a**, before **Milecastle 48 (Poltross Burn)**. This is the only place on the whole Wall where it is possible to see two milecastles and both intermediate turrets and is thus the best place to get a feel for the system.

West of Birdoswald is one of the most interesting stretches of the Wall, as the 30 Roman miles west of the River Irthing was originally turf-built, later replaced in stone. Beyond the fort to the west there is evidence of two walls, the original Hadrianic turf wall which bisected the fort and the later Severan stone wall following the line of the fort's north wall. Beside the road are the remains of two turrets, **51a (Piper Sike) and 51b (Lea Hill)**.

Further west is **Pike Hill signal station**, a pre-wall Stanegate communication tower which was then incorporated into the wall. Close by is **Turret 52a (Banks)**, which has parking for both monuments. Further west still is the tallest stretch of the Wall at **Hare Hill**, its towering state being helped by some judicious rebuilding in Victorian times.

West of here there is little to be seen of the Wall to Carlisle, Wall-miles 53–65, and indeed all the way to Bowness-on-Solway, although there are glimpses of the ditch and Vallum.

9. Carlisle and the Solway Firth (Roman Miles 65–80)

Tullie House Museum with Ilam Pan and Caurausius Milestone; Stanwix wall fort (Uxelodunum / Petriana); to the west: Burgh on Sands, Drumburgh, Bowness-on-Solway.

Carlisle (Lugovalium & Uxelodunum/Petriana), Cumbria *****

Carlisle owes its name to the anglicisation of the Welsh Caer meaning fort or fortress, its post-Roman name being Caerluel. It is the home of two Roman forts. Lugovalium was first built as part of the Stanegate frontier and lies completely hidden under the medieval castle and the Tullie House Museum, high above the south side of the River Eden. The other, just north of the river, was on the line of the Wall, now in the suburb of Stanwix, and itself has two names, Uxelodunum and Petriana.

The Tullie House Museum (Castle St, CA3 8TP) is a delight to visit even without its Roman galleries. It has fine collections of early twentieth-century art, beautiful early musical instruments and a great array of items that tell the history of Carlisle. Our focus, though, is the three magnificent Roman galleries.

The Roman Frontier Gallery, downstairs to the left of reception, has superb displays of artefacts from sites along the western end of the Wall. It is also sometimes the home of the Ilam Pan, aka the Staffordshire Moorlands Pan, a small enamelled bronze bowl found in 2005. It moves between the British Museum, Tullie House Museum and the Potteries Museum in Stoke-on-Trent, which jointly purchased it. Like the Rudge Cup, it is a souvenir celebrating Hadrian's Wall, engraved with the names of a number of wall forts on the western side of the wall, including Uxulodunum (below). The only other vessels of this type are the Amiens Patera and a recently discovered fragment in Essex.

Don't miss the milestone of the rebellious military commander Carausius, the self-proclaimed Emperor of Britain and northern France who ruled here until he was assassinated. After this the milestone was inverted and reused with the Carausius inscription consigned underground.

A macabre display immortalises a crime scene, as if awaiting the attentions of Marcus Didius Falco, of a man's skeleton found at the bottom of a well, with evidence of injuries inflicted by a third party.

On the first floor is a fabulous reconstruction of a section of the turf Wall, with legionary paraphernalia on top, including the opportunity to fire a reconstruction of a *ballista*. From the top one can read a superb Tube-style map of Hadrian's Wall and its associated sites from Ravenglass through to South Shields.

Below and behind this is a gallery full of sculpted stones, figural pottery and bronzes from Carlisle itself, one of the finest collections in the country.

At **Stanwix**, north of the river, only a line of the fort platform can be seen, with a little masonry near the north-west corner of the fort, in the grounds of the Cumbria Park Hotel (18–32 Scotland Road, CA3 9DG). The name Uxelodunum is taken from the *Ravenna Cosmography*, and appears on the Hadrian's Wall souvenir vessels described above; the name Petriana is used in the *Antonine Itinerary* and seems to refer to its garrison, a 1,000-strong cavalry unit, the Ala Petrionis. Maybe a scribe confused the name of the cohort with that of the fort? A recent discovery was the fort bath-house in the grounds of Carlisle cricket club, but nothing is visible of this.

Stanwix was the largest fort on the Wall, and it is thought that the commander-in-chief of the whole wall garrison may have been stationed here. If the whole line of the frontier is taken to include the Cumbrian coast forts as well as the Wall, this fort is in a central position.

There is nothing much left of the Wall or its buildings west of Carlisle to Bowness-on-Solway. However, Roman stones aplenty can be seen recycled in Drumburgh Castle (Wigton CA7 5DP), a fortified farmhouse, and the parish churches of Beaumont and Burgh by Sands. The Hadrian's Wall footpath continues along the Firth to Bowness-on-Solway, with far-reaching views across to Scotland.

10. Cumbrian coast defences

Maryport and the nearby Milefortlet 21 are the most rewarding sites to visit on this stretch of the frontier system. Some believe that the system may have extended as far south as Ravenglass, which is described in Chapter 7, but there are ongoing arguments for and against.

Maryport (Aluana) and around ****

Senhouse Museum: Jupiter altars, the Serpent Stone; reconstructed watchtower, auxiliary fort platform. To the north: Milefortlet 21 (Swarthy Hill); Church of St John the Evangelist, Crosscanonby.

The fort of Aluana can be seen on the northern fringe of Maryport, high on the cliffs above the old port. The views from here over the Solway to the hills of Dumfries and Galloway are stunning and the strategic military advantages of the site are obvious, utilised not only by the Romans but in later eras too.

The **Senhouse Museum** (CA15 6JD) occupies a battery built as a naval training school in the 1870s. The collection is based on that of the Senhouse family, who amassed a truly impressive number of inscribed stones from the area over nearly 500 years; more inscribed stones and altars have been found at Maryport than any other single Roman site in Britain. William Camden, the great Cumbrian antiquary,

The Senhouse Museum and reconstructed fort watchtower at Maryport (Aluana).

described some of these in his magnus opus, *Britannia*, published in 1695. A copy of this seminal book is on display.

They include an amazing sequence of altars dedicated annually, mostly to Jupiter Greatest and Best (IOM), which provide a unique record of the regiments and their commanding officers stationed at Aluana. There are at least twenty-three, erected by three different regiments: Cohorts I Hispanorum, I Delmatarum and I Baetasiorum, originally from modern-day Spain, Croatia and Germany respectively. These list ten different commanding officers. Seventeen of the altars had been found in pits in the nineteenth century, originally thought to be a ritual burying of the dedications, but more recently identified as post-holes of a massive late Roman building, with the altars reused as convenient packing stones around the posts.

Inscriptions indicate that both the Second and the Twentieth Legions were involved in construction work here. A most unusual piece, found in the cemetery and therefore probably a grave marker, is known as the Serpent Stone. This 4-foot-high phallic-shaped monument, reshaped from a large standard altar, has a human head on one side and a snake writhing its way to the top of the stone on the other.

Behind the museum the impressive remains of the unusually square **fort platform** are clearly visible, with prominent ramparts and ditches. The best view of this is from the top of a reconstructed fort watchtower, which also gives magnificent views of the Solway. Excavations and survey work have shown that this fort partly overlay an earlier, larger one, and also that there was an extensive *vicus* and at least two temples, one of which claims to be the most north-westerly Classical-style temple known. There was a port here and an important supply depot.

Milefortlet 21 (Swarthy Hill) is the most visually rewarding of all the structures of this type along the coast, 3 miles from Maryport along the A5130 coast road north. The best place to park, avoiding a steep climb, is at the Beech car park at the turn-off to Crosscanonby, from which a footpath leads to the site. The turf walls which once faced a sand core have been reconstructed and are therefore very clearly demarcated. Extensive excavations have revealed two gates and a central passage with barracks on each side of this. There is good on-site information.

After your visit continue along this road towards Crosscanonby and visit the **Church of St John the Evangelist**, built of red sandstone blocks taken and reused from the fort at Maryport. An arch inside is sometimes said to have been taken from the West Gate of the fort.

9

Scotland

Scotland was never really subject to Rome in the same way as the rest of mainland Britain. A military presence was established several times, but it was always short-lived, following waves of campaigning and fort building. This started in the later first century and was finally abandoned soon after AD 200, although intermittent campaigns took place until the very end of Roman Britain. All the remains are of a military nature, and although civic settlements inevitably attached themselves to the forts, these never lasted for long enough to evolve into independent towns. The attempts to establish a permanent presence in potentially hostile territory have produced wonderfully complex defensive systems, and much material for those interested in the Roman army.

The routes into Scotland were extensions of Dere Street, via Corbridge and with a major hub at **Newstead**, and the western main road north via Carlisle. The eastern route of Dere Street was extended much further north through Perthshire and towards Angus, with forts and temporary camps identified all the way to Aberdeenshire and Moray, possibly almost as far as Inverness, but nothing in the far north or western regions.

The local people most mentioned by the Roman historians were those of Caledonia, whose territory extended over much of the central Highlands, although names of a number of other tribes are also known. The man who has traditionally been recognised as the scourge of the Caledonians, and the leader of the campaigns against them in the late first century, is Gnaeus Julius Agricola, Governor of Britain from AD 75 to 85. He was the father-in-law of the historian Tacitus, whose *Agricola* recorded these achievements in glowing terms, and expressed resentment at his final recall to Rome by a jealous Emperor Domitian. It was Tacitus who put the famous anti-Roman words into the mouth of the Caledonian chief, Calgacus, after a final battle at an unidentified location called Mons Graupius: 'To ravage, to slaughter, to usurp under false titles, they call empire; and where they make a desert, they call it peace.' (*Agricola*, 34).

Since Tacitus also tells us that Agricola first subdued the tribes of Wales and northern England before turning his attention to Scotland, this would date the first campaigns here, with accompanying fort-building, between AD 79 and 85. However, archaeological investigations at these forts, particularly along the **Gask Ridge System**

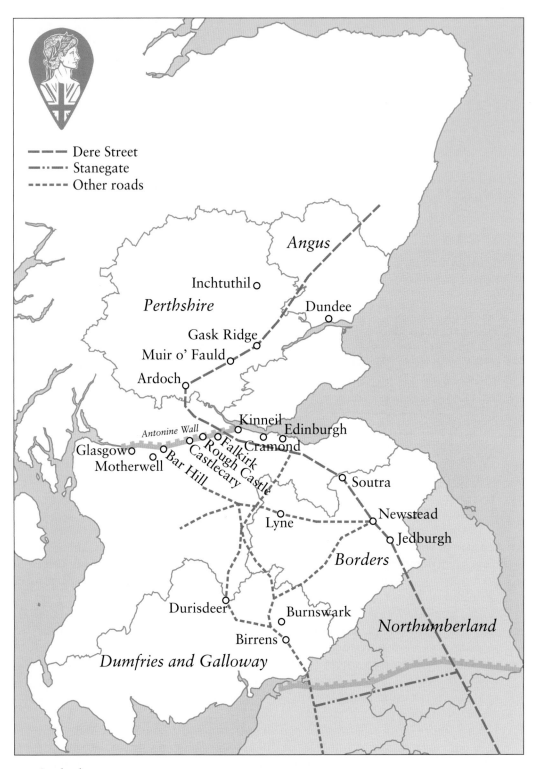

Scotland.

on the northern extension of Dere Street, shows that activity may have started earlier than this. Tree-ring dating at the fort of Carlisle demonstrates that it was founded in AD 72, under Petillius Cerialis, Governor of Britain AD 71–74. Tacitus tells us that Agricola sent the prefect of the fleet around the north of Scotland, confirming that Albion was an island, and received the submission of the Orcadians of Orkney. This may also have taken place earlier than Agricola's command. The Battle of Mons Graupius is believed to have taken place in AD 83, somewhere in the outlying hills of the Grampians (the name later derived from Graupius) within sight of the North Sea, but there are many candidates for the exact location. Whoever was responsible, the Gask Ridge System, now believed to be the first frontier in Britain, was abandoned and systematically dismantled by AD 86, after Agricola was recalled from Britain. The most visible parts of this today are the fort at **Ardoch**, the legionary fortress at **Inchtuthil** and some of the watch-towers, including **Muir O' Fald** and **Kirkhill**.

The next period of intense military activity in Scotland was shortly after the death of Hadrian in AD 138, when the historians describe further campaigns against the Caledonians (see below). Following these, the new Emperor Antoninus Pius, who never came to Britain, ordered the building of a new frontier wall 99 miles north of Hadrian's. **The Antonine Wall**, built of turf rather than stone, and just over half the length of its predecessor, was constructed from AD 142 across the shortest distance coast to coast, between the Firth of Forth and the Firth of Clyde. The successful campaign against the Caledonians was perhaps commemorated in a remarkable domed victory temple that stood at Stenhousemuir until 1743, when it was demolished for its stone. Known as Arthur's O'on, a glimpse of its splendour can be seen in a replica built as a dovecote at Penicuik House in 1767. Was keeping the upper hand in Caledonian territory now a priority or was it a prestige project for the new Emperor? In any case, this, too, was relatively short-lived, and by the early 160s AD the Wall and its forts were abandoned for a return to Hadrian's Wall. The process may have taken some time, as dating evidence suggests that the two frontier systems overlapped.

The Caledonians were again the focus of campaigns in the early third century, when the Emperor Septimius Severus and his family established a base at York before leading a large army in AD 208 up Dere Street to the Forth. The provocation was probably an increase in raiding parties to the south, perhaps because Clodius Albinus had withdrawn legions from Britain into Gaul during his revolt against Severus in 197. Severus was also employing the time-honoured method of consolidating his position as Emperor with a victory against barbarians. Reaching the Antonine Wall was relatively easy, but further north the guerrilla tactics of the Caledonians took a heavy toll. Many of the first-century forts were also re-garrisoned and plans were made for a ruthless punitive expedition led by Caracalla, the son of Severus, with the Emperor himself following on behind, but all was thwarted by the illness and subsequent death of Severus at York in February AD 211. Caracalla had ambitions of his own to pursue elsewhere, including the murder of his brother Geta, and Scotland was left to its own devices once more. We are left with another feisty quote from a Scottish local in Cassius Dio's account of the campaign. The unnamed wife of the Caledonian chief Argentocoxos answered a criticism by Severus' wife Julia Domna of the morals of the Caledonian women with the retort: '… we consort openly with the best men, whereas you let yourselves be debauched in secret by the vilest'.

In the late third century there is the first written reference to the Picts, 'the painted ones', a tribal confederation north of the Forth and Clyde, perhaps partially descended from the Caledonians. They were the focus of the next Roman campaign launched by the Emperor Constantius in AD 305. He claimed a great victory and the title Britannicus Maximus, but then became ill and returned to York, where he died in July 306. His son Constantine was declared Emperor, continued the campaign for a while, claimed to have restored order but then left for Gaul. This, and other campaigns through the fourth century, are archaeologically invisible but described by the historians. In AD 367 they describe the Great Barbarian Conspiracy, when the Hadrian's Wall garrison rebelled, allowing Picts and Attacotti from Scotland and Scotti from Ireland (who settled and ultimately gave Scotland its name) to take over large areas of western and northern Britain. A relief force under Flavius Theodosius landed at Richborough in 368, eventually overcame the invaders and a new province Valentia was established somewhere in the north. In another forty years, all of Britain was left to its own defences.

Thus Scotland, never Romanised as such, played an important role in defining Roman Britain. The most visible sites are described below, but many others can be seen just as slight earthworks or occasional cropmarks. As with the sites along Hadrian's Wall, those on the Antonine Wall are grouped from east to west rather than alphabetically, for ease of exploration, highlighting the best examples of forts, distance markers, fortlets and lengths of the wall itself.

Antonine Wall (East to West)

'Antoninus waged a large number of wars through his governors. Through the governor Lollius Urbicus he defeated the Britons, and having driven back the barbarians, he built another wall, this time of turf.' This much we know from the biographer of Antoninus Pius, and in AD 142 the construction began of a new frontier fortification, 99 miles (160 km) north of Hadrian's Wall. This ran across the shortest distance between the east and west coasts, from Carriden, near Bo'ness, on the Firth of Forth to Old Kilpatrick on the Firth of Clyde, 39 miles (63 km) in all.

It is possible that the new wall may have been planned first as a stone construction, because a stone foundation, 13 feet (4 metres) wide, has been found along its length, and some forts built along it also had stone foundations and wing walls, the latter presumably to link them into the curtain wall as it rose. However, as on Hadrian's Wall, building plans were fluid, and a change to turf construction was soon implemented, the stone foundation providing a firm base for this. Turfs were laid front and back, forming sloping cheeks, and soil from a deep ditch dug to the north was used to fill the gap between these, as well as forming a northern counterscarp bank. The resulting height of the wall was 13 feet (4 metres) and a wooden palisade may have been constructed on top. There was no equivalent to the southern Vallum on Hadrian's Wall, but there was a Military Way running along the wall on this side, facilitating communication and movement.

It is possible that initially forts were planned at intervals of 6 miles (10 km), but this was quickly revised to every 2 miles (3.3 km), resulting in nineteen forts in total. In addition, there were at least nine fortlets, a Roman mile apart. Other features are known as 'expansions', not fully understood but possibly thought to be platforms for signal fires. There were also a number of coastal installations both east and west which were outposts and supply bases for the frontier.

A feature unique to the Antonine Wall was a series of spectacular carved stone distance markers, inscribed and decorated with scenes of military victory and religious iconography, inserted at intervals along the wall. Bright painted colours on these have been revealed by surface-enhanced Raman spectroscopy and portable X-ray fluorescence, though nothing can be seen by the naked eye. The inscriptions tell us which of the three British legions completed each length of Wall. It has been estimated that it might have taken up to twelve years to complete, and was then only used for another eight years, before abandonment and a retreat back to Hadrian's Wall in the early AD 160s. It seems that the fearsome Caledonians were never really subdued.

After a particularly unsettled period at the end of the second and early third century, Septimius Severus arrived in York in AD 208 with his family and troops to campaign and secure this northern frontier once more, repaired and re-occupied, but only for a few years, before a permanent move south to Hadrian's Wall.

The Antonine Wall became a World Heritage Site in 2008, and whilst its turf-built structure has not survived as well as the stone-built Hadrianic frontier, there is still much to see. The interactive map on www.antoninewall.org is highly recommended and a downloadable interactive app (Antonine Wall) is available for iPhone and Android.

1. Bo'ness, Bridgeness and Kinneil, West Lothian *

Bridgeness Distance Stone replica; Kinneil fortlet. HS.

The eastern end of the wall is largely obscured now by motorways and the refineries of Grangemouth. However, the ridge on which it was built can clearly be seen between Falkirk and the terminus at Bo'ness.

The main thoroughfare through Bo'ness is called Graham's Dyke Road, suggesting that the rampart and ditch were very prominent here not so long ago. The giant or superhuman Graham, or Grim in other parts of Britain, is often credited with the monumental earthworks of the Roman engineers.

Just off this road, down Harbour Road is an exact stone replica of the **Bridgeness Distance Stone** (EH51 9LD), based on laser scanning of the original, and standing close to where this was found. It is a monumental chunk of stone propaganda, declaring that the Second Legion had constructed 4,652 feet of wall, and picturing Roman cavalry running down and decapitating the barbarians. The original stone is in the Royal Museum of Scotland in Edinburgh.

Just west of Bo'ness, there are some interesting vestiges of the Wall in the grounds of **Kinneil House** (EH51 0PR). In the care of Historic Environment Scotland, the now mainly seventeenth-century house is charming and has a real feel of a Robert Louis Stevenson adventure novel. At present the house is a shell. In the grounds you will also find the former workshop of James Watt, the eighteenth-century engineer, where he developed his prototype steam engine.

To one side of the house is a small but well laid out museum displaying a number of Roman finds from the vicinity. The staff will direct visitors to the best-preserved **fortlet** on the Antonine Wall, which lies some way beyond the main house. The ground falls steeply into a ravine behind the house, showing the topography has been utilised as defence for both Kinneil House and the line of the Wall.

Pass through the dell, over a footbridge and up into an open field where the fortlet lies about 500 yards straight ahead. The turf defences are eroded but it is marked out with the original stone kerbing of its ramparts, the north wall of which is the Antonine Wall itself. Timber posts mark the post-holes of the original gate and internal buildings.

2. Falkirk ***
Watling Lodge (HS), Callendar Park.

Situated just to the west of Falkirk is perhaps the most dramatic and finest stretch of the Antonine Wall, certainly the most iconic view of it today. **Watling Lodge** (FK1 4RE), in the Falkirk suburb of Tamfourhill, is now a beautiful wooded linear park with the Wall running through it, the bank and ditch standing to almost the same height as they would have been in the 150s AD. They present a colossal barrier even without the timber rampart on top. The Wall stretches down the side of the B186 for a couple of miles and is clearly visible on either side of Watling Lodge House. The remains of a fortlet stand in the grounds of the house, but this is not open to the public and nothing is visible on the ground.

The bank and ditch of the Antonine Wall at Watling Lodge.

The Forth–Clyde Canal, which follows the course of the wall for many miles, is close here and the Falkirk Wheel is just a small distance west.

In **Callendar Park** (Falkirk FK1 1YR), the line of the Wall can be traced for a good distance, albeit tidied up as part of the garden layout for the house. Callendar House, a grand baronial hall in the Scottish French-chateau style, contains a good small museum with local Roman finds and a detailed explanation of the Wall.

3. Bonnybridge, Falkirk ***

Rough Castle wall fort and annexe; Seabegs Wood (HS).

Bonnybridge is a pleasant but unremarkable small town about 13 miles west of Bo'ness on the Forth–Clyde Canal. This is where the most visible and interesting stretches of the Antonine frontier can be seen.

Less than 2 miles (2 km) to the south-east is the fort of **Rough Castle**, the best-preserved on the Antonine Wall, albeit the second smallest. It is signposted along a side road from the B816 between Bonnybridge and High Bonnybridge, or park at the top car park for the Falkirk Wheel and follow the signs through the woods.

A good stretch of well-defined rampart and ditch section of the Wall is clearly visible, and the turf ramparts and associated ditches of the fort and its annexe are also very clear. The remains of several stone-built buildings within the fort have been discovered, although these have not survived above the ground. The bath-house was built in an annexe. Perhaps the most interesting remains are the pits laid out in a regular quincunx pattern, lying to the north of the fort. Caesar described such features as lilia, Latin for lilies, in his *Gallic Wars*, and the examples here are now

The lilia pits at Rough Castle, once about 3 ft deep and possibly concealing sharpened stakes.

visible as oval depressions but they would once have been about 3 feet (0.9 metres) deep and may have had sharpened stakes concealed within them. Negotiating a way through them would have slowed down anyone attacking the vulnerable North Gate. The Military Way to the south of the fort is still visible, and there is a good length of rampart and ditch to be seen to the west, with an expansion, possibly a base for signal fires, some 430 yards (400 metres) from the fort.

We know from inscriptions found here that the fort was garrisoned at one point by auxiliary troops recruited from the Nervii tribe from north-eastern Gaul, where Belgium is today.

A mile to the west of Bonnybridge there is another picturesque and impressive tree-lined section of the Wall, just where the B816 runs beside the canal, at **Seabegs Wood.**

The wall bank and ditch are very well defined for a good distance, as are the parallel remains of the Military Way. There was also a small fortlet here at the end of the stretch open to visitors, where the fortlet platform can be seen in the contours of the landscape.

4. Castlecary, North Lanarkshire **

Castlecary wall fort platform; Garnall and Croy Hill stretches of Wall.

Follow the B816 further west to the scant remains of **Castlecary fort**, now sadly dissected by the railway line and with the M80 motorway as an all-too-close new neighbour. On the other side of the motorway there is one of the longest continuous stretches of well-preserved Wall at **Garnall**. This starts behind the Castlecary House Hotel (G68 0HD). If driving west, take Eastfield Road right off the B816, and another good stretch of wall can be seen at Dullatur. Turn right again onto

The line of the Antonine Wall imaginatively demarcated at Garnall.

the B802 and seek out the long, high section of wall over **Croy Hill**, which has wonderful views to the Firth of Forth and the surrounding hills. There was a fort, a fortlet and a temporary camp here, no longer visible, but you can spot two expansions attached to the south face of the Wall.

5. Bar Hill and Kirkintilloch, Dunbartonshire ✳✳✳

Bar Hill wall fort (HS); Kirkintilloch Museum; Peel Park.

Two miles west of Croy Hill as the crow flies, but nearer 3 miles via the B802, the B8023 and Main Street, above the village of Twechar, lies a real gem of the Wall, the Roman fort at **Bar Hill**. Follow signs for the John Muir Way for a short but brisk walk uphill. The fort occupies the copse on the high ground to the west. The fort platform is clearly evident and the remains of the central buildings and baths of the fort are in good order. Also very prominent here for a good distance is the ditch and rampart of the Wall.

Unusually the fort was set back from the wall itself, making use of the high ground of Bar Hill, a vantage point with clear views towards the Kilsyth Hills to the north. The Military Way runs between the fort and the Wall.

The bath-house at Bar Hill Fort.

Bar Hill fort was first garrisoned by the First Cohort of Hamian Bowmen, a regiment from Syria, who had previously been garrisoned on Hadrian's Wall. In the late 150s AD they returned to Carvoran and were replaced by the First Cohort of Baetasians from Germany.

A great variety of finds from excavations here are now housed in the Hunterian Museum in Glasgow. These include objects, some of them organic, thrown down a well, probably when the fort was abandoned, such as shoes from men, women and children, wooden beams, a pulley and building columns.

Kirkintilloch lies in the centre of the Wall, west of Bar Hill, and this small market town is home to the delightful **Auld Kirk Museum** (Cowgate, G66 1HN) with a display on the history and construction of the Wall. The name Kirkintilloch derives from the ancient British name Caerpentalloch.

Architectural pieces include some fine columns and there is a reproduction of a legionary uniform. Many of the distance stones now in the Hunterian Museum in Glasgow were found in the vicinity and their story is told here.

Next door to the museum lies **Peel Park**, where markers show the line of the Wall. The view from this high ridge over the valley towards the Campsie Fells and Kilsyth Hills shows the strategic advantage of the siting of the Wall. A wall fort once stood here, but the earthworks are confused with, or obliterated by, those of the medieval castle which later shared the site.

6. Glasgow *****

Hunterian Museum; Bearsden Roman fort baths (HS); Bearsden Cemetery stone base of the Antonine Wall.

The Hunterian Museum and Art Gallery is the oldest museum in Scotland, part of the University of Glasgow, and is now situated in the west end of the city (82 Hillhead Street, G12 8QQ). The Roman gallery is stunning.

The Antonine Wall: Rome's Final Frontier provides the overture to the museum, made special by the collection of decorated distance stones from the Antonine Wall. These masterpieces of sculptural corporate art displayed within the structure of the Wall made up for the lack of panache of the turf construction.

All but three of the nineteen known stones are in the collection here. The Bridgeness stone is in the National Museum of Scotland in Edinburgh, one is owned by Glasgow Life and housed at the Glasgow Museums Resource Centre, and one more was, alas, destroyed in a fire in the USA. Reproduction casts of these missing stones are displayed to complete the set.

Far more elaborate than the centurial stones on Hadrian's Wall, but having the same function, the distance stones record which sections were completed by whom. Many display the boar or the capricorn, the emblems of the Twentieth and Second Legions respectively. The stones were removed from the wall and buried when the retreat back to the Hadrianic frontier was ordered, so that on many the relief is extremely crisp. It is estimated that the sixteen stones here represent half of the total number, some of the rest having been destroyed or reused. Perhaps there are a few yet to be discovered.

The Antonine Wall Gallery – Rome's Final Frontier – in the Hunterian Museum, Glasgow. *Photo: Hunterian Museum.*

Other great items include the stone columns from the *principia* of the fort at Bar Hill and an oak barrel found in the well there. The window glass and grille from this site are a wonder to behold, as are a fine bronze jug from Sadlerhead and an ornate drain cover from Bothwellhaugh in Strathclyde Country Park.

Bearsden, Dumbartonshire, is an upmarket suburb to the north-west of Glasgow city centre, and here we are once again back on the course of the Antonine Wall with the fine remains of a **wall fort bath-house**. The baths are the most complete in Scotland, and this is the best-preserved stone structure from the Wall. The furnace arch is particularly well preserved. It now lies in a housing estate, signposted from Bearsden Cross on the A810 (8 Roman Court, G61 2HS). Most Roman forts placed their bath-houses, a potential fire hazard, outside the ramparts but here on the Antonine Wall they were often inside the annexes. Presumably it was felt too dangerous territory to be caught unawares.

New Kilpatrick Cemetery (Boclair Road, Hillfoot, Bearsden G61 2AF) is the best place to see the stone foundation of the Wall, including kerbstones, cobbled surface and drains. There are two exposed sections exposed between the gravestones, looking to all intents and purposes like a Roman road.

Roman Park, on the west side of Bearsden, also has a short section of the Wall base, and a well-preserved section of the ditch. A footpath runs to it between Westbourne Crescent and Milverton Avenue.

The last glimpse of the Wall travelling west (or the first, travelling east) is in Golden Hill Park, **Duntocher**, south of the A810. A short length of stone base, surrounded by railings, can be seen. A fort once stood at the top of the hill, the bath-house of which was excavated. The sites of the fort, fortlet and annexe are marked out through differential grass cutting. Although the western parts of the Wall are now elusive, several distance stones have come from sites in this area.

Ardoch (Aluana?), Perthshire ***

Auxiliary fort with multiple rampart defences; Gask Ridge watch towers.

The defences at Ardoch are extraordinary both for their complexity and for their degree of preservation, thanks to the late eighteenth-century landowner who enclosed them as a protection against ploughing. They still give a sense of the threat that an auxiliary detachment may have felt in this wildest of frontier posts.

The fort lies just to the north of the village of Braco, on high ground above the bridge over the River Knaick, to the east of the A822. It is part of the privately owned Ardoch Estate, but there is public access: park in the village and follow the signposts.

It was part of a chain of forts a day's march apart, running from Camelon, just north of the Antonine Wall, in the south to Strathcathro to the north-east. A parallel chain of forts guarding the entrances to the valleys was also built at this time. Between the forts at Strageath and Bertha a line of signal towers, or watch towers, has been identified. The whole military complex of sites is known as the **Gask Ridge System** (below). Some sites had a very brief period of occupation, but others, including Ardoch, were reoccupied several times during various campaigns and the use of the Antonine Wall frontier, before final abandonment by the early AD 160s.

The multiple banks of ramparts at Ardoch are truly remarkable, and indeed are some of the best-preserved Roman military earthworks in the Roman Empire.

The remarkably well-preserved multiple ramparts at Ardoch Fort.

The site was first noted in the late seventeenth century, visited by Victoria and Albert in 1842, and subject to intermittent excavations from the late nineteenth century on. What you see on the ground is the defences of two intersecting forts, one of the first century, covering 8.6 acres (3.5 ha), the other from the middle years of the second century when the Antonine Wall was occupied, covering 5.7 acres (2.3 hectares). The north and east sides were protected by five or six ditches with ramparts between them. Attempting to scale them today is exhausting so what a deterrent the full defences must have been when the fort was built.

Within the fort the outline of a small compound can be seen. This was a medieval chapel that once stood on the site.

There is evidence of a fort annexe and other enclosures to the north, and many temporary marching camps have been identified in close proximity to the fort. It was a veritable hive of activity over different periods, but although we know a lot about the sequencing between the sites, their dates remain elusive.

Birrens (Blatobulgium), Dumfries and Galloway *

Auxiliary fort platform, temporary camps, altar stones, Dumfries Museum.

Birrens lies at the northern end of the route through Britain that starts as Watling Street (sometimes, though not universally, the same name is used for the northern part of the route). The Roman name has been identified as Blatobulgium from the *Antonine Itinerary*, perhaps deriving from 'flowery hill' or even 'flour sacks' due to the granaries there.

The fort lies about 2 miles (3 km) south of the siege site at Burnswark (below), on the banks of the River Mein Water and its confluence with the Middlebie Burn. It is not easy to find: take the A74M north of Gretna Green, turn right onto the B722, cross the railway bridge then turn left towards Middlebie. The fort is on the left just after you have crossed the river, with the fort platform clearly visible, although much of the south rampart has been eroded by the river. On the other side of the river there are the remains of three temporary camps.

The first turf and wood fort was built during Agricola's campaigns *c*. AD 80 and rebuilt in stone with the push north of Hadrian's Wall around AD 140. More rebuilding took place *c*. AD 160 with the withdrawal back to the Hadrianic frontier and an annexe was added to the west. The annexe and the north side of the fort are defended by multiple ditches and embankments suggesting that there was a real threat of attack, realized at least once, as there is evidence of destruction by enemy action.

The early garrison of the fort has been identified as the First Cohort of Nervians from present-day Germany; after AD 160 the Second Cohort of Tungrians from Belgium appear to have been in residence.

Finds, including many altar stones from Birrens, can be seen in the Sacred Stones gallery at **Dumfries Museum** (The Observatory, Rotchell Road, DG2 7SW). The museum also has a wonderful eighteenth-century camera obscura, making a visit even more worthwhile.

Burnswark, Dumfries and Galloway **

Hillfort, Roman camps (siege-works or artillery platforms).

The dark brooding outline of the hill of Burnswark dominates the landscape of south-west Scotland. It rises about 1,000 feet (305 metres) above the village of Ecclefechan and the Solway plain, clearly visible for many miles around. Little wonder that it was chosen as the site for a hillfort by the local Selgovae tribe.

The archaeological remains around the fort paint a tough picture of life here in the second century AD. Two Roman camps, one to the north and one to the south, are evidence of military interest in the hillfort. For many years they were interpreted as siege camps, then in the 1960s a theory arose that they represent a military practice area, perhaps an artillery range. However, recently the pendulum has swung back as evidence has been interpreted to suggest a bloody siege, perhaps resulting in the population inside the hillfort being all but wiped out.

The action may have been retaliation for some Hadrianic conflict, but it is perhaps more likely that the Siege of Burnswark was one of the first major skirmishes in the advance north by Quintus Lollius Urbicus around AD 140. Ultimately this led to the establishment of the Antonine Wall.

Large numbers of Roman lead slingshot bullets have been found, in a pattern suggesting this was a battle in earnest or repeated training exercises in the early Antonine period. Many of these missiles have been found with a hole or indentation, which experiments have shown to produce an eerie noise when the shot is in flight. The noise, coupled with the fact that these missiles had similar kinetic energy to a modern handgun bullet, must have terrified the defenders of the hillfort.

Stone *ballista* balls and bolts have also been found, suggesting that both legionaries and auxiliaries were deployed in the siege.

The two camps can be clearly seen today on either side of the hill, the south camp being particular interesting. It best approached from the east of Ecclefechan, on a small road off the B725. Some gate-climbing is required to see the remains up close and to walk up to the summit of the ill-fated hillfort.

The fort at Birrens (above) is just a couple of miles further along the B725, and there was another fort between Birrens and Carlisle, at Netherby, but nothing is visible here.

Dundee, Angus *

McManus Museum with finds from the fortress; possible naval base at Carpow.

The port city of Dundee, famous for jam, jute and journalism, is now home to a spectacular new museum, the eye-catching V&A Dundee, on the waterfront. However, it has another quality museum at least its equal, the McManus Museum and Art Gallery (Albert Square, Meadowside DD1 1DA), housing a great collection of Roman finds from the important fortress at Carpow, on the southern side of the River Tay estuary. There is also more general information about the Roman presence in Tayside.

The large fortress at Carpow, covering nearly 30 acres (11 hectares), is thought to have been a major naval supply base used for a short time in the early 200s AD during the campaigns of Septimius Severus and his son Caracalla. There is evidence of occupation by units of both the Second Legion Augusta and the Sixth Legion Victrix. Some fine fragments of gate inscriptions include one with the Sagittarius sign of the Second Legion.

Amongst other items on display there are some sections of scale armour from around AD 210, some of the best-preserved examples in the Western Empire.

Durisdeer, Dumfries and Galloway **

Fortlet, earthworks, beside route of Roman road.

Take the A702 as it branches off the A76 off Carronbridge; turn right at Durisdeer Mill to Durisdeer Church. A walking track heads north-east from here up the river valley. Just under a mile up the track you will see the well-defined fortlet earthworks on the slope overlooking the river to your left.

The fortlet was partially excavated in 1938, showing that occupation dated to the Antonine period, contemporary with the Antonine Wall, perhaps in two separate phases. The earthwork ramparts are impressively well-preserved. It would have guarded this route through the Lowther Hills, and two temporary camps have been identified from air photos to the south, closer to the village.

Durisdeer Church and the adjoining Queensbury Aisle contain some impressive funerary marble monuments to the Dukes of Queensbury, whose seat was at the nearby Drumlagrid Castle.

Edinburgh, Midlothian ****

National Museum of Scotland with the Newstead cavalry helmets, Bridgeness Distance Stone and Traprain Treasure; Cramond fort and naval base.

The **National Museum of Scotland** (Chambers Street, EH1 1JF) opened in its current form in 2011, amalgamating the collections of the National Museum of Antiquities and the Royal Scottish Museum. The superb collection of Roman artefacts from Scotland is displayed with those from prehistory and later periods in the Early Peoples galleries on the lower floor of the modernist extension.

Objects are often displayed according to theme and usage rather than date, so you have to look at the timelines in the cases to determine their age. There are many wonderful objects from the eastern end of the Antonine Wall and a veritable treasure trove from Newstead near Melrose.

As at Vindolanda, waterlogged conditions at Newstead preserved many wooden items including wheels and sections of carts and wagons. A late first-century pit here produced parts of three cavalry parade helmets, one of which, of beaten iron, is substantially complete and is known as the Newstead helmet. Traces of silver plating and a woollen lining still adhere to the iron. A bronze visor-mask also came

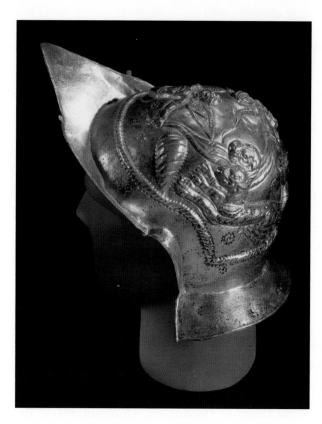

Helmet from Newstead
in the National
Museum in Edinburgh.
*Photo: National Museum
of Scotland.*

from a pit in the bath-house. Only a small number of these flamboyant helmets have been found in Britain: one at Ribchester in Lancashire, now in the British Museum, and one at Crosby Garrett in Cumbria, now in private ownership, as well as these examples from Newstead. Used in the display and competition of horsemanship skills called the Hippika Gymnasia, these full-face helmets would have inspired awe, and would have been treasured items of bling for the cavalry soldier.

The collection of altars, grave markers, milestones and other inscribed stones is outstanding. One exceptional piece is the Bridgeness Distance Stone from the eastern terminus of the Antonine Wall (see above), the only one not held in the Hunterian Collection in Glasgow and perhaps the most impressive. Crisp and detailed carvings show, to the right of the inscription, officers and soldiers of the Second Legion Augusta involved in a sacrificial ritual with sheep, calves and a pig. On the left-hand side is a piece of unambiguous propaganda: a triumphal cavalry man riding down naked warriors, one of whom has been decapitated. The carving is similar to that seen on cavalry soldiers' gravestones.

The Traprain Treasure is another highlight, discovered in 1919 within the hillfort of Traprain Law in East Lothian, consisting of over 50 lb (24 kg) of Roman silver, the largest hoard from outside the Empire. Many of the items were of the highest quality, a mix of pagan and Christian artefacts, mostly cut up into small pieces, called hack silver. Why such a large amount of Roman silver should have found its way to Traprain Law is a question of some conjecture. Perhaps it was booty from a raiding party further south, or maybe the Roman equivalent of Danegeld to buy peace for the area. The latest coins in the treasure date to the earlier fifth century, clipped around the edge to preserve the face-value, so it is tempting to believe the latter is more likely.

One of the most important pieces of sculpture in the museum is the Cramond Lioness, depicted in the act of killing a male bound prisoner. It was probably once part of an officer's tomb associated with the fort, below, but was found at the mouth of the River Almond by a ferryman.

The remains of the **Roman fort of Cramond** (Rumabo?) (EH4 6NS) lie on the west side of Edinburgh, in a well-to-do suburb reminiscent of *The Prime of Miss Jean Brodie* territory. Lying on the Firth of Forth, where the River Almond flows into the Forth, this was the fort and port supporting and supplying the Antonine Wall, first built around AD 142. Like the Wall it fell out of use when the frontier was re-established on Hadrian's Wall. However, it was recommissioned during the campaigns of Septimus Severus around AD 210. It has tentatively been identified as the Rumabo named on the seventh-century *Ravenna Cosmography*. There is a small museum here with finds and information.

The fort's restored ground plan is laid out in parkland to the east of Cramond Glebe Road, just beyond Cramond Kirk, the medieval tower of which looks very much like Historic Scotland's earlier logo. It no doubt took much of its building stone from the fort, which is one of five stone-built forts in Scotland, with walls only 3.6 feet (1.1 metres) thick, backed by a clay rampart. The barrack blocks and granaries are easily spotted to the north of the church. The bath-house is more difficult to find, lying closer to the Firth, much of it buried amongst a morass of later overgrown buildings. Many finds from the site, including the stone lioness, can be seen in the National Museum.

Gask Ridge, Perthshire **

Kirkhill, Muir O'Fauld and Midgate watch-towers; Midgate fortlet.

The Gask Ridge is a 10-mile (16 km) ridge running roughly east–west north of the River Earn through beautiful countryside. The name comes from the Scottish Gaelic word gaesg, meaning a projecting tail or strip of land. It has long been recognised that a number of Roman structures once stood along the ridge, and that the military system of fortifications extended a long way beyond the ridge in both directions. Over more than twenty years the sites have been intensively studied through the Roman Gask Project, looking at activity north of the Antonine Wall. There is an excellent website with excavation, survey and research results: www.theromangaskproject.org.

They have concluded that this system of forts, watch towers and fortlets was the earliest land frontier in Britain, built in the 70s or 80s AD, predating Hadrian's Wall. Forts such as Ardoch (above) may have been a part of the wider system.

Remains of some of the watch-towers can still be seen, notably at **Kirkhill** and **Muir O'Fauld**, even though their use might have been very short-lived, perhaps as little as ten years.

Muir O'Fauld lies 1 mile (1.6 km) north of Trinity Gask off the B8062 Crieff to Auchterarder road. This is the route of a Roman road, which turns into a woodland path at a sharp corner; follow the Old Roman Road signpost. The site is surrounded by pine forest which would not have been there when the signal stations were in use, but it gives a bit of an eerie Teutoburg Forest feel to the walk. A circular bank and ditch can be clearly made out, and on-site information has reconstructions of the central wooden watch-tower.

Kirkhill lies beside the same Roman road, nearly 1 mile west of Muir O'Fauld. This, too, is visible as a circular bank and ditch. At **Midgate**, about 3 miles to the east, a tower and a fortlet were situated right next to each other, the earthworks being visible beside the road.

Inchtuthil (Pinnata Castra), Perthshire *

Legionary fortress site.

There is not much to see of this most northerly and short-lived of legionary fortresses, but those who wish for a sense of having completed their exploration of Roman Britain might persevere. Turn south off the A984 east of Spittalfields, continue along minor farm roads, south of the hamlet of Delvine, and it lies in an open field north of the River Tay.

There is no signage or information, just a low spread bank and ditch marking the perimeter, particularly visible on the east and south sides. This is the only legionary fortress in Scotland, and the only one in Europe completely uncluttered by later building, so that you can stand on one side of it and see right across to the other, giving a sense of the vast scale. It was established by Agricola *c*. AD 83/4 as the lynchpin of his campaigns in the region and abandoned about three years later, its existence linked to the career of just one man.

Excavations took place here in 1901, then again in 1952–65, showing that whilst the barracks and a small headquarters building had been built, there was no commander's house by the time it was abandoned and dismantled. During the excavations a pit in a workshop was found to contain nearly 10 tons of iron nails, more than a million, presumably too heavy to carry south with the other salvaged building material. Many of these were sold to finance further digging, so a lot of people ended up with a few of these nails.

Jedburgh, Scottish Borders *

Inscribed stone in Jedburgh Abbey. HS.

The ruined Augustinian Jedburgh Abbey (Abbey Bridge End, TD8 6JQ) is one of the most spectacular visitor attractions in Scotland. Founded in the twelfth century on the site of an earlier Anglo-Saxon church, it is outside the remit of this book, but following the time-honoured tradition of reusing stone, it is a bonus for those seeking Roman remains.

In the nave are two narrow staircases to first floor level, which allow a wonderful view over the ruins. At the foot of the north turret stair (used by visitors to descend) look up to see an inscribed Roman altar, reused in the ceiling above you. The inscription is a dedication to Jupiter, Greatest and Best (IOM), by the tribune of a *vexillation* of Raetian spearmen, originally from the Alps.

Lyne, Scottish Borders *

Auxiliary fort platform.

The fort of Lyne lies about 4.5 miles (7 km) to the west of Peebles, north of Lyne Water and just north of the A72. Continue past the hamlet of Lyne and take a small road north towards Kirk Lyne. Just to the west of the church is a small knoll called Abbey Lowe, providing a great vantage point over the fort platform. The ground below is quite boggy so closer inspection might require wellington boots.

The turf ramparts and gates can be seen very clearly but nothing remains above ground of the local red sandstone central buildings. It was large enough to accommodate a garrison of a 1,000-strong mixed infantry and cavalry unit. The archaeological evidence suggests that it was occupied through the Antonine period but not later. It would have been built to protect the route between Trimontium fort (Newstead, Melrose, below) and Castledykes, near Lanark. Evidence has also been found for an Agricolan period fort to the south side of Lyne Water and two marching camps a short way down the valley to the east.

Interestingly, the hillock is also home to three early cist burials, dating somewhere between the sixth and eighth centuries AD, when this part of Upper Tweedsdale was part of the Christian kingdom of Northumbria.

The picturesque kirk is rightly proud of its very rare early eighteenth-century Adam and Eve gravestone, which has recently been expertly restored.

Melrose, Scottish Borders **

Newstead auxiliary fort site; Trimontium Museum; Abbotsford with inscribed and sculpted stones.

Situated in a loop of the River Tweed in the shadow of the three Eildon Hills, the three mounts of Trimontium, the fort guarded the river crossing on the route north to the Antonine Wall.

Newstead (Trimontium) was one of the largest forts north of Hadrian's Wall and its situation at a hub on the network of roads through the Lowlands meant that it played an important part in all the successive campaigns into Scotland, starting with those of Agricola in the 80s AD. At one time it was garrisoned by an auxiliary cavalry unit, the Ala Augustae Vocontiorum from southern Gaul, but there were also sometimes legionary units here. There is little to be seen above ground but aerial photographs of crop marks have revealed a complex series of forts, fort annexes, ancillary buildings and, most extraordinarily, a small amphitheatre comparable, perhaps, to the one at Tomen y Mur in North Wales (Chapter 6 above).

The best way to see and understand the fort is in the capable hands of a guide from the **Trimontium Museum of Roman Scotland** in the centre of Melrose (The Ormiston, Market Square, TD6 9PN). The museum is currently undergoing redevelopment to provide even more exciting displays. The guided route includes Melrose Abbey and the Roman fort. In the village of Newstead there is rather splendid granite milestone erected to celebrate the millennium, and another splendid memorial in the form of a giant Roman altar, the Trimontium Stone, lies by the site of the fort.

The Trimontium Museum itself is charming and has a wonderful collection of artefacts from the site brought together by the enthusiasts of the Trimontium Trust. There is a replica of one of the Newstead helmets, the originals being in the National Museum in Edinburgh (above). In addition, it has a fabulous hoard of silver denarii from Synter, a purchase made possible by a well-thought legacy. Other treasures include an intaglio gemstone depicting the Emperor Caracalla.

Trimontium figures highly in literature about Roman Britain and features in Rosemary Sutcliff's *The Eagle of the Ninth* and in a very short story by Sir Arthur Conan Doyle, *Through the Veil*.

Next door to Melrose is Abbotsford, the beautiful former home of Walter Scott, inventor and master of the historical adventure novel. Scott was an avid collector of antiquities and curiosities, or gambions as he referred to them. His collection includes altars and many inscribed stones from Roman Britain set into the walls of the garden in front of the house, including a fine example from the Antonine Wall near Falkirk.

Motherwell, North Lanarkshire *

Bothwellhaugh auxiliary fort & bath-house, non-Roman bridge.

The site chosen for Bothwellhaugh auxiliary fort was on high ground close to the confluence of South Calder Water and the River Clyde. The terrain has changed enormously in recent times, as the old mining village of Bothwellhaugh was flooded in the 1980s to create Strathclyde Loch. The line of the Roman road, known here as Watling Street, now lies under the lake, and the site lies in Strathclyde Country Park, overlooking the loch, to the west of Motherwell city centre.

The fort was a large one and is thought to have been garrisoned by a mixed infantry and cavalry regiment. Dating to the Antonine period, *c.* AD 140, it was part of a chain of forts linking the Antonine Wall to the south. Little can be seen of the remains of the fort itself which today lies under trees and undergrowth.

The remains of the bath-house, however, are splendid. Now lying on the edge of the loch, they are not quite in their original situation as they were moved to higher ground when the village was flooded. They were large, and the remains clearly show the *caldarium*, *tepidarium*, *frigidarium* and, unusually, the *praefurnium* or furnace room. A superbly ornate geometric drain cover, along with other finds, is on display at the Hunterian Museum in Glasgow.

Bothwellhaugh bath-house at Motherwell.

Close by the baths is a very handsome fifteenth-century bridge erroneously known as the Roman Bridge. However, it is always possible that it could have replaced an earlier Roman one.

Soutra, Scottish Borders *

Dere Street, well preserved length of road running through fields.

Take the B6368 south off the A68 (between Carfraemill and Fala), and about 100 yards past a ruined building, Soutra Aisle, there is a layby parking area, on the other side of the road from the Aisle. There is an information board here to help with orientation.

This is the northern point of a well-preserved 2.5 mile (4km) length of Dere Street, now rather grassed over but still visible, running between the Lammermuir and Moorfoot Hills. Soutra Aisle was an important medieval hospital, the House of the Holy Trinity, founded by Malcom IV in the twelfth century, reworked into a burial vault for the Pringle family in the seventeenth century. The hospital was built beside Dere Street as it was still an important routeway in the medieval period.

Glossary

Numbers in italics are page references.

Amphitheatre: Literally 'double theatre', an elliptical building with a central arena ('sand') and banked seating, used for games including gladiatorial combat, wild beast hunts and public capital punishment for criminals. *20, 29, 41, 42–3, 49–50, 54, 81, 101, 124–5, 136, 145–6, 149, 152, 160, 166, 240.*

Antonine Itinerary: A document giving details of the road network and stopping places around Europe, with fifteen itineraries for Britain. The date of the original survey is uncertain, but traditionally ascribed to the reign of Antoninus Pius in the second century. The earliest surviving copy dates to *c.* AD 300. *24, 53, 66, 86, 110, 119, 134, 218, 233.*

Auxiliary fort: Base for an auxiliary unit of between 500 and 1,000 non-Roman citizens, which could be an ala of cavalry, a cohort of infantry or a mixed cohortes equitatae. Smaller version of a legionary fortress. *126, 132, 133, 148, 144, 146, 155, 156, 160, 168, 170–75, 177, 179, 181–87, 189–90, 199–201, 219, 232–3, 239–40.*

Basilica: Public building where law courts were held, usually situated next to the forum. The usual plan was a nave with two aisles with a raised platform at one end and an apse at the other. This plan was adopted for early churches, also called basilicas. *27, 42, 55, 79–81, 101, 113, 115, 124, 128, 130, 138, 148–9.*

Ballista, ballistae: Artillery weapon using torsion springs to shoot bolts or stone balls at a distant target. *19, 36, 54, 57, 99, 175, 218, 234.*

Caldarium: The hot room of a bath-house, with hot air circulating under the floor and up the walls via a hypocaust system. *32, 178, 194, 240.*

Canabae: Civilian settlement next to a legionary fortress. *125, 145.*

Cantharus: Two-handled wine cup. *61, 66.*

Cella: The central sanctum of a temple, usually housing a cult statue of the deity. *88, 107.*

Century: Unit of men within a legion, originally 100 but by the first century it had been reduced to eighty. Led by a **centurion**. *105, 131, 200, 214.*

Client king: A local chief allowed to continue to rule his people as long as he was loyal to Rome. None lasted for more than one generation after an invasion. *8, 20, 24, 43, 94, 114.*

Colonia: A high-ranking chartered town established with retired legionaries, who were Roman citizens, and were allotted land. British *coloniae* were Colchester, Gloucester, Lincoln and York, possibly London. *72, 82, 104, 106, 118, 129, 130, 165, 192.*

Civitas capital: Towns that were administrative centres for local government, often based on a pre-Roman tribal capital. British civitas capitals include Aldborough, Caerwent, Caistor St Edmund, Chichester, Carlisle, Cirencester, Exeter, Ilchester, Silchester, Winchester, Wroxeter. *18, 42, 44, 46, 80, 101, 127, 128, 138, 142, 148, 151, 165, 166.*

Contubernium: Group of eight men who shared a tent and messed together. Also used for a barrack room.

Duplicarius: Pay grade in army receiving double basic pay, sometimes awarded for bravery or exceptional service. *105.*

Fogou: Cornish for 'cave' – underground dry stone passages of the Iron Age and Romano-British periods, unique to Cornwall. *49, 52.*

Forum: Central meeting point in a town; religious, administrative and religious centre. *18, 27, 29, 42, 55, 76, 80–81, 101, 113, 115, 131–1, 139, 149, 151, 166.*

Frigidarium: Cold room in a bath-house, usually with a plunge pool. *64, 68, 85, 240.*

Genius cucullatus: Local deity depicted wearing a hooded cloak, popular in Britain.

Gyrus: Circular cavalry training area. *120.*

Hypocaust: 'Heated from below' – hot air from a furnace running through flues under the floor and behind the walls. *18–19, 32, 35, 47, 53, 62–4, 75, 77, 88, 100, 114, 124, 125, 136, 139, 146, 171, 178, 194, 242.*

In situ: Still in its original position.

Insula: Island of buildings between the grid of streets in a town. *39, 42–3.*

Laconicum: Sweating room in a bath-house. *174.*

Legionary fortress: Base of a legion of 5,000–6,000 men. Standard form is rectangular with rounded corners ('playing card') with a gate and road in the middle of each side, meeting in the centre. The *praetorium* and *principium* lie here. *45, 55, 72, 83, 101, 104, 118, 122–5, 129, 138, 140, 144–7, 163, 165, 191–4, 238.*

Macellum: Market, usually for food. *129, 139.*

Mansio: Inn or official stopping place for use by officials whilst travelling. *22, 41, 102, 134, 136–7, 161.*

Municipium: Town with a charter, though not quite as high-ranking as a *colonia*, incorporating both local and Roman laws and practices. British municipia were Canterbury, Dorchester, Leicester and Verulamium. *113.*

Notitia Dignitatum: Administrative document of the late Roman Empire, probably *c.* AD 420 in the west, listing military commands and administrative posts. *14, 37, 38, 96, 98.*

Nymphaeum: Shrine to the water nymphs, usually at a spring or a fountain. *78.*

Oppidum: Pre-Roman defended settlement. *42, 58, 103, 107.*

Optio: A centurion's deputy, second-in-command of a century. *149.*

Phallus: A penis, usually depicted erect as an apotropaic charm, to ward off evil and bring good luck. *217, 220.*

Pilae: The pillars supporting the raised floor in a hypocaust, made of stacked tiles or stone. *77, 88, 159.*

Praetorium: Commanding officer's quarters in the centre of a fort or fortress. *57, 145, 168, 170–2.*

Principium: Headquarters building in the centre of a fort or fortress, with regimental shrine, strong room and armouries.

Quadriga: Chariot pulled by four horses. *41, 102, 176.*

Ravenna Cosmography: A seventh-century list of place-names compiled by a monk in Ravenna, covering the world from India to Ireland. *121, 126, 170, 218, 237.*

Reiter stone: German term for a stone depicting a cavalryman riding down a barbarian. *177–9, 185-6.*

Saxon Shore Forts: Eleven forts built on strategic estuaries along the east and south coasts of England to protect trade routes and ward off raiders. Nine are recorded in the *Notitia Dignitatum*. Three were built in the early third century to a traditional 'playing card' plan; eight have more irregular plans, and external rounded bastions, and date to the late third century. *14–15, 18, 21–2, 34–40, 96–9, 142, 165.*

Tepidarium: Warm room in a bath-house. *240.*

Vexillation fort or fortress: A base for a detachment of between 2,500 and 4,000 troops operating away from the main unit. *82, 110.*

Vicus: Civilian settlement attached to a fort. *76, 80, 98, 99, 126, 133, 143–4, 151, 161, 168, 178, 181–2, 184–5, 190, 202–2, 209–10, 212, 220.*

Villa: Country house on an agricultural estate. British villas are most often of the descriptive types known as Corridor villas, more elaborate Winged corridor villas, or the most lavish Courtyard villas. *8, 10, 14–18, 24–5, 33–5, 44, 46–8, 52, 54, 56, 59, 61–6, 68–70, 72–3, 76–80, 82, 84–7, 89–95, 109, 111, 115–6, 118, 142, 165, 168–9, 176–7, 180–1.*

Roman Road names

The names now used for the Roman roads crisscrossing Britain are not Roman in origin: Watling Street, Ermine Street, the Fosse Way, Dere Street, the Stanegate… Most are derived from post-Roman place names on the routes, which continue to be used for main roads even today, like Waeclingacaster for Verulamium (Watling Street); the Anglian kingdom of Deira between the Humber and Tees (Dere Street); Earningas in Cambridgeshire (Ermine Street) and so on. We don't know the Roman names for these routes.

Roman Legions in Britain

Four legions came with the initial invasion force; three were permanently based here:
Second Legion Augusta; fortress at Exeter, then Gloucester, then Caerleon.
Ninth Legion Hispana; fortress at York, then left Britain.
Fourteenth Legion Gemina; fortress at Mancetter, then Wroxeter, then left Britain AD 67.
Twentieth Legion Valeria Victrix; fortress at Chester.
Sixth Legion Victrix replaced the Ninth at York after AD 119.

The People of Roman Britain

Numbers in italics are page references.

Britons

Argentocoxos: Caledonian chief in early third century, best known for his unnamed wife's retort to Julia Domna, wife of Septimius Severus. *223.*

Boudica: Queen of the Iceni tribe of East Anglia, led a rebellion against the Romans in AD 60/61 following their rapacious behaviour when her husband Prasutagus died. Defeated at Battle of Watling Street. *27, 43, 72, 92, 94, 101, 104, 105, 109, 110, 111, 114–5, 120.*

Calgacus: Chief of Caledonians during Agricola's campaigns in Scotland, defeated at Battle of Mons Graupius AD 83. *221.*

Caratacus: Chief of the Catuvellauni tribe with stronghold at Camulodunum (Colchester). Led resistance to Rome in AD 43 with his brother Togodumnus, defeated, fled to Wales to continue fighting, defeated, sought sanctuary from Cartimandua, handed over to the Romans. Taken to Rome as booty, after impressive speech to Claudius allowed to live freely in Rome (possibly). *248.*

Cartimandua: Queen of the Brigantes tribe of northern England. Loyal to Rome (see Caratacus), supported by Rome during clashes with anti-Roman ex-husband Venutius but disappeared AD 69. Northern tribes caused trouble into the third century. *163, 192.*

Cogidubnus: See Togidubnus.

Cunobelin: King of the Catuvellauni tribe, Shakespeare's Cymbeline, legendary Old King Cole. Father of Adminius, Togodumnus and Caratacus. Ambitious, apparently pro-Roman, political manoeuvres contributed to invasion. Died *c.* AD 40. *103–4.*

Prasutagus: Husband of Boudica, client king *c.* AD 45–60. His bequest, sharing his kingdom between his widow and Rome, and the rapacious reaction of Rome, led to Boudican rebellion. *94, 114.*

Togidubnus: Chief of the Regnenses (or Regni) tribe in the first century AD, possibly heir of the Atrebates tribe prior to the invasion. Loyal to Rome, made a client king after the invasion; the palace at Fishbourne may have been his. He died sometime in the AD 70s. *20, 24, 43.*

Venutius: Husband and then ex of Cartimandua. *163, 192.*

Romans

Agricola, Gnaius Julius: Campaigned in Britain under Paulinus and Cerialis; Governor of Britain AD 77–85. Campaigned in Wales, northern England and Scotland, father-in-law of historian Tacitus, who wrote his biography. *115, 133, 137, 140, 147, 161, 163, 171, 196, 212, 221, 223, 233, 238, 239.*

Allectus: Finance minister of Carausius, murdered him AD 293, ruled for three years until killed by army under Constantius Chlorus.

Antoninus Pius: Emperor AD 138–161, ordered an advance into Scotland and construction of Antonine Wall (142). Completed *c.* 154, it was abandoned *c.* 162. He never visited Britain. *179, 223, 224.*

Caesar, Julius: General, politician and dictator of the Roman Republic, led the first Roman troops into Britain in 55 and 54 BC. Assassinated March 44 BC. *6, 12, 248.*

Caligula: Roman Emperor AD 37–41, known for erratic and violent behaviour. Planned but aborted an invasion of Britain. *13.*

Claudius: Roman Emperor AD 41–54, ordered invasion of Britain AD 43, with army of *c.* 40,000. He came to Britain for sixteen days after the initial victories had been won. *8, 13, 22, 103–5, 109.*

Caracalla: Son of Septimius Severus, declared joint Emperor with brother Geta at York in AD 211. Killed Geta and ruled alone until 217. Re-established Hadrianic frontier; extended Roman citizenship to all free men within the Empire. *8, 192, 223, 235, 240.*

Carausius: Commander of the British Fleet, accused of corruption and sentenced to death. Declared himself Emperor of Britain and northern Gaul in AD 286; murdered 293 by his finance minister Allectus. *14, 69, 218.*

Cerialis, Petillius: Campaigned in Britain under Paulinus, was defeated at Camulodunum (Colchester) by Boudica's forces; Governor of Britain AD 71–74, campaigned in northern England and Scotland. *223.*

Classicianus, Julius: procurator of Britain in AD 60s, after Boudican revolt; advocated reconciliation rather than revenge. *28.*

Clodius Albinus: African by birth, commander of British troops, declared himself Emperor in 196, supported by legions in Britain and Spain. Defeated and killed by forces of Septimius Severus. *198, 223.*

Constans I: Emperor AD 337–350, youngest son of Constantine the Great, campaigned in Scotland 343. *249.*

Constantine I ('the Great'): Proclaimed Emperor at York 306. Restored order, toleration for Christians in the Edict of Milan, founded Constantinople, campaigned against barbarians, died 337. *56, 66, 69, 191–4.*

Constantius I ('Chlorus'): Emperor 293–306, campaigned in Britain, defeating Allectus' forces in 296, and in Scotland in 306, died at York. Father of Constantine the Great. *191–93, 224.*

Constantine III: Roman general, usurper, declared himself Western Roman Emperor in Britain AD 407–9, co-emperor with Honorius 409–11. Took troops from Britain to campaign in Gaul, leaving it defenceless against Saxon raiders; Britain withdrew support for him in 409. Heralded the end of 'Roman' Britain. *250.*

Diocletian: Roman Emperor AD 284–305, introduced many reforms to achieve new stability, divided Britain into four provinces. *130, 146.*

Geta: Brother of Caracalla, killed by him. *192, 223.*

Hadrian: Emperor AD 117–138, traveller and builder, visited Britain 122 and ordered a wall to be built. This was the northern frontier except when it briefly advanced into Scotland. *27, 122, 139, 144, 174, 191, 195, 202, 223.*

Honorius: Western Roman Emperor 395–423, youngest son (aged eight at accession) of Theodosius the Great. In 410 he appears to have sent a reply (a rescript) to a request for support, perhaps in Britain, stating that Britons should look to their own defences. This is traditional end to 'Roman' Britain, but facts open to doubt. *250.*

Magnus Maximus: Commander of Britain, usurper, proclaimed Western Roman Emperor by his troops 383–88, defeated and killed by Theodosius I. Contributed to withdrawal of troops from Britain. Continued in Welsh legend as Macsen Wledig. *142, 188.*

Paulinus, Suetonius: Governor of Britain AD 58–61, led campaign in Wales, assault on druids on Anglesey and won final Battle of Watling Street against Boudica's army. *72, 92, 94, 140, 153.*

Plautius, Aulus: Roman general in command of AD 43 invasion force; first Governor of Britain AD 43–46. *248.*

Postumus: Roman military commander and Governor of Germany, declared himself Emperor of the breakaway Gallic Empire in AD 260. Britain declared allegiance in AD 261. Killed by his own troops in AD 268; Gallic Empire came to an end in AD 274. *48.*

Septimius Severus: Emperor AD 193–211, after a period of turmoil. Born at Leptis Magna, died at York after military campaigns in Scotland. Split Britain into two provinces, Inferior (north) and Superior (south); reoccupied the Antonine Wall. *191–3, 198, 200, 223, 225, 235.*

Theodosius, Count: Senior military officer, made Comes Britanniarum (Count of the Britons) for quelling the Great Barbarian Conspiracy AD 368; accompanied by his son Theodosius the Great. *188.*

Theodosius I (the Great): Emperor AD 347–395, the last to rule over both western and eastern empires. Made Christianity the state religion, outlawed paganism. *59–60, 224.*

Vespasian: Commander of Second Legion Augusta in AD 43 invasion of Britain, later Emperor AD 69–79. *20, 45, 50, 69, 91, 115.*

Timeline for Roman Britain

First century BC: first contact, campaigns of Julius Caesar

55	Julius Caesar's first British campaign
54	Julius Caesar's second British campaign
34, 27 and 25	Invasions planned by Octavian/Augustus but called off

First century: Claudius' invasion, client kingships, campaigns west and north, Boudican revolt, frontier along the Stanegate, campaigns in Scotland.

40	Caligula's abortive invasion
43	Claudian invasion: four legions commanded by Aulus Plautius landed in the south-east; Claudius' triumphal entrance into Camulodunum (Colchester), capital of the new province.
44–60	Legions advanced west and north; campaigns in Wales, opposition led by Caratacus. Civil war led by the Brigantes of northern England.
60/61	Anglesey attacked, druid stronghold destroyed; Boudican Revolt: Colchester, London and St Albans burnt; final Battle of Watling Street against Boudica's forces, 80,000 Britons killed; Recovery and rebuilding; London made the new provincial capital by the end of the first century.
69	Year of Four Emperors – turmoil in Rome.
71–84	Conquest of Wales and northern England completed; permanent Legionary Fortresses at Caerleon, Chester and York; Stanegate forts established. Advances into Scotland, Gask Ridge frontier.
c. 100	Scottish territory abandoned.

Second century: Hadrian's Wall frontier, prosperity in towns, northern revolts, Antonine Wall frontier built and abandoned, Imperial turmoil late in century.

118	Revolt in northern Britain.
122	Hadrian visited Britain, wall begun across Tyne–Solway isthmus.
139–42	Frontier advanced to Forth-Clyde isthmus, new wall built on orders of Antoninus Pius.

162	Antonine Wall abandoned, Hadrian's Wall restored.
193–97	More imperial turmoil: Clodius Albinus, Governor of Britain, claimed imperial throne, defeated by Septimius Severus; unrest in Britain, forts in northern Britain burnt, towns given earthen defences.

Third century: Two British provinces, campaigns in Scotland, citizenship extended, Empire in crisis, breakaway Gallic Empire, Saxon Shore forts built.

197–208	Britain divided into two provinces (Superior and Inferior, south and north, capitals London and York); Hadrian's Wall and Pennine forts restored and reconstructed.
208–11	Septimius Severus and his sons Caracalla and Geta campaigned in Scotland; Severus died at York, Caracalla had Geta murdered.
212	Caracalla issued an edict declaring that all free men throughout the Empire were granted Roman citizenship, and all free women had the same rights as Roman women (to increase tax revenue?).
235–85	Empire in crisis due to inflation, plague, invasion and civil war; stone walls built around towns in Britain.
260–74	Britain became part of a breakaway Gallic Empire (one of three competing states) under Postumus, Governor of Germany.
275–94	Saxon Shore forts built around south and east coast; Carausius, commander of the British fleet, called himself Emperor of Britain and Northern Gaul.
284–305	Diocletian's reforms, Empire divided into east and west, each ruled by a senior Emperor (Augustus) and a junior (Caesar). Britain divided into Britannia Prima (capital at Cirencester) and Maxima Caesariensis (capital London).

Fourth century: Four British provinces, campaigns in Scotland, state toleration of Christianity, prosperous British villas, barbarian raids, British usurpers, five British provinces, gradual abandonment of military stations, pagan cults outlawed.

296–305	Constantius I (Chlorus) regained control of the western Empire, Britain divided into four provinces (Britannia Prima and Secunda; Flavia and Maxima Caesariensis), capitals probably Cirencester, York, Lincoln and London respectively.
306	Constantius I campaigned in Scotland, died at York, Constantine the Great proclaimed Emperor there.
313	Edict of Milan gave Christianity legal status within the Empire; tolerated along with other religions.
306–42	Period of great prosperity for Britain; some villas enlarged and enhanced into huge wealthy estates.
342–67	Unrest and harassment by barbarians continued; outpost forts north of Hadrian's Wall abandoned; Emperor Constans campaigned in Scotland; Saxon Shore forts strengthened under a Count of the Saxon Shore.

367/8	Great Barbarian Conspiracy: simultaneous attacks by Picts, Scots and Attacotti; Franks and Saxons attacked Gaul. Count of the Saxon Shore killed, some villas abandoned.
369	Count Theodosius came to Britain to restore order; fifth province of Valentia established, location uncertain, perhaps in north-west. Hadrian's Wall restored, as were some northern forts. Some villas and towns continued to be prosperous beyond AD 400.
379–80	Theodosius the Great proclaimed Emperor in the East; Christianity the official religion, pagan cults outlawed.
383–88	Magnus Maximus claimed imperial throne in Britain. Took British troops to campaign further in Gaul, but defeated by Theodosius the Great. End of Roman presence in the west and northern England.

Fifth century: Withdrawal of troops continued, Britain rejected officialdom of usurper Constantine III, no further troops available for defence, no further hierarchical central government, villas downgraded, a few towns continued. Anglo Saxon settlement in the south and east, sub-Roman culture in the west.

395–407	More expeditions against marauding Picts, Scots and Saxons; more troops removed from Britain to campaign in Europe; more Imperial usurpers and general unrest; end of military presence on Hadrian's Wall.
409	Britain withdrew support for usurper Constantine III; effective end of Roman rule in Britain.
410	Western Emperor Honorius tells Britons (possibly, unless it was Bruttium in Italy) to look after their own defences. Traditional date for the end of Roman Britain.

Further Reading

Many of the sites in this book have their own guidebooks, written by those who have excavated there and know them best. The English Heritage guidebooks are particularly good. These overviews of Roman Britain are particularly recommended:

Breeze, David, *The Antonine Wall* (Birlinn 2006); Forty, Simon, *Hadrian's Wall Operations Manual* (Haynes 2018); Higgins, Charlotte, *Under Another Sky: Journeys in Roman Britain* (Vintage 2014); Hobbs, Richard and Ralph Jackson, *Roman Britain* (The British Museum Press 2010); Manning, William, *A Pocket Guide to Roman Wales* (Cardiff University of Wales Press 2001); Moorhead, Sam and David Stuttard, *The Romans Who Shaped Britain* (Thames and Hudson 2012); Salway, Peter, *Roman Britain: A very short introduction* (Oxford University Press 2015).

Ancient sources on Roman Britain include:

Cassius Dio, *Roman History* (written early third century); Julius Caesar, *Gallic Wars* (written mid-first century BC); Tacitus, *Agricola* (written c. AD 98).
Many others can be found in Ireland, Stanley, *Roman Britain: A Sourcebook* (Routledge 2006).

Amberley books:
Birley, Robin, *Vindolanda: A Roman Frontier Fort on Hadrian's Wall*; Ford, Simon, *The Romans in Scotland and the Battle of Mons Graupius*; Jones, Rebecca, *Roman Camps in Britain*; Poulter, John, *Roman Roads and Walls in Northern Britain*; Rotherham, Ian D., *Roman Baths in Britain*; Southern, Patricia, *Roman Britain: A New History*.

Novels set in Roman Britain:

Davis, Lindsey, *The Silver Pigs*; *The Body in the Bath-house*; *The Jupiter Myth*
Downie, Ruth, *Medicus* (Chester); *Terra Incognita* (Corbridge); *Momento Mori* (Bath); *Tabula Rasa* (Hadrian's Wall); *Caveat Emptor* (Verulamium); *Semper Fidelis* (York).
Sutcliff, Rosemary, *The Eagle of the Ninth*.

Acknowledgements

Denise and Mike met on an Andante Travels tour to Pompeii and the Bay of Naples. Mike had been looking for this book in vain, so we decided to write it.

Denise's career in archaeology has including digging, specialist work on Roman glass and organising and leading tours around the world. The pleasure of revisiting and discovering new sites for this book has been increased enormously by those who went with her from time to time, good friends and three generations of her family, already hooked on archaeology: Tom Allen and Gwen Turner, Betty, George and Teddy Paton, Dot Smith, Chris Gill, Karen Mills, Christine Burls and Mary Reynolds.

Mike has spent most of his life visiting and enjoying Roman sites in Britain and abroad. Heather, his wife, has shared this passion for these 'Roman Holidays' and ancient sites, in particular the excitement of discovering the little-known places, the odd stranded milestone or fabulous volunteer-run museum. Without her, the idea for this book would never have been made real.

Other great supporters deserving of much gratitude for helping hunt out Roman remains are Norman and Sue Haddock, Steve and Kate Hull, Simon and Liz Plumb and in particular Mike's late, great, father-in-law Rob Adams who, at the age of eighty-eight, gamely climbed the heights of the Antonine Wall and found himself in cul-de-sacs in Prestatyn.

Many great archaeologists have been extremely helpful in fact-checking, editing chapters and site descriptions for the places they know so well. These include David Allen, Paul Bennett, Peter Berridge, Philip Crummy, Rebecca Jones, Bill Manning, David Rudling, John Shepherd, Tony Wilmott and Roger White. Any remaining mistakes are our fault. Inspiration and support have also come from Roger Goodburn, Sally Stow and Frances McIntosh. Heather Adams read through the whole manuscript with her expert editor's eye. Thanks also to John Button for turning rough sketches into smart maps, and Johnny Paton for enhancing them with our Roman Britain pin logo. Johnny Paton also did the artwork for the cover.

Many thanks, too, to all the staff at the sites and museums the length and breadth of the country who have been very generous in their support and enthusiasm for the project, sometimes opening their doors on days when they were closed so that the long journeys worked logically. Several have provided us with professional photos or given permission for us to use our own. These are acknowledged in the captions; all the rest were taken by us.

We have met many wonderful volunteers along the way, and the great new friends made on the Hadrian's Wall Pilgrimage also deserve a mention for their excitement and enthusiasm for the book.

Ours is not the first guidebook to Roman Britain, and we owe a debt to those who travelled before us, especially Roger Wilson (*A Guide to the Roman Remains in Britain*) and David Johnston (*Discovering Roman Britain*), both now out of print. We were influenced in our approach by Simon Jenkins' *England's Thousand Best Churches*. Other good reads on Roman Britain are listed in 'Further Reading'.

We are also flattered by the great encouragement of bestselling authors Lindsey Davis, Conn Iggulden and Ben Kane.

And lastly thanks to you, the reader, for buying the book. We envy the expeditions and new discoveries it might inspire.

These organisations provide information about sites, sometimes free or reduced entry fees, conferences and fieldtrips, and publications to keep you up-to-date with discoveries and research.

English Heritage: www.english-heritage.org.uk
Association for Roman Archaeology: www.associationromanarchaeology.org
Cadw: www.cadw.gov.wales
Historic Scotland (Historic Environment Scotland):
www.members.historic-scotland.gov.uk
National Trust: www.nationaltrust.org.uk
Roman Finds Group: www.romanfindsgroup.org.uk
Society for the Promotion of Roman Studies: www.romansociety.org
Vindolanda Trust: www.vindolanda.com

Index of Sites